The Industrial Market
Research Handbook

THE INDUSTRIAL MARKET RESEARCH HANDBOOK

PAUL N. HAGUE

FRANKLIN WATTS
NEW YORK 1988

658.83
H14i

Library of Congress Catalog Card Number 87-51314
ISBN 0-531-15530-7

Copyright © 1985 by Paul N. Hague
First published in 1985 by Kogan Page, Great Britain
First published in the United States in
1988 by Franklin Watts, New York
6 5 4 3 2 1

Contents

List of diagrams

List of tables

Preface

Marketing is concerned with the satisfaction of consumers' needs. It has, however, a broad role. A sale at a silly low price can be achieved by anyone, with a disastrous effect on profits. Production lines can be filled temporarily by a quick push on exports but long-term damage will occur unless distribution and service give the necessary support, so marketing should also pay regard to long-term profitability. This requires planning which in turn needs facts.

Businesses succeed through understanding their customers' needs and responding to them. As companies grow, investment decisions get larger and the customer becomes separated from the directors by tiers of managers, salesmen and distributors. In order to plan for long-term profitability, boards of directors need objective facts which market research can supply. Market research may not give a categorical red or green light to the decision makers but it will further their understanding of the subject and enable action to be taken with a lower level of risk.

Industrial market research is as much an art as it is a science. As in all crafts, practice is important to develop skills, and yet the subtleties which accumulate to provide that experience are difficult to teach formally. It is easier for marketing students to study the scientific techniques of consumer market research than it is to struggle with the nuances of industrial market research.

This book is one small step to rectify the situation by passing on the hints and wrinkles collected during the management of a busy industrial market research consultancy.

There are five major parts to the book. The first deals with information that can be made available by market research. In this section I discuss the assessment of market size, market structure, market shares and market trends — all the classic components of a market research report. My aim is to describe what these components are, why they are useful and briefly, how such data is obtained.

Part Two describes the uses of market research, positioning it in the context of the marketing plan, improving the competitive position, influencing the buying decision, evaluating new products and services – all the manipulations of marketing strategies which are made so much easier with the data market research can provide.

The third part shows how to organize a market research project from defining the problem through to the administration of the study. The fourth part describes all the methods which are available to researchers in the collection of data. Part Five shows how to process and present market research information in the most effective manner.

Finally, there are two appendices. One is an introduction to the important statistical methods with which market researchers need to be familiar and the other provides a listing of key sources of information which I have found valuable in my own work.

Inevitably, the layout of the book in five major sections has resulted in a certain amount of repetition. The marketing student will forgive me, for the presentation of subjects in the different context of each part will deepen his understanding of industrial market research in the complex jigsaw of the business environment.

The market research practitioner can be selective in his reading of the book and will probably gain most from Part Four on methods.

Senior management will benefit especially from Parts One and Two which describe the information that can be made available by market research and which show how this can be used to reduce business risk and increase profitability.

In the same way that some other jobs and professions change their titles to raise their status or more aptly describe their work, we agonize over whether we should be called marketing or market researchers. I am sure that the title marketing researcher more accurately describes the wider responsibilities to which we aspire and no doubt one day this will be broadened still further to become business researcher or even decision consultant. With no more justification than my view that the term *market* researcher scans well and has a long tradition of use, I have opted for this term throughout the book.

In the text it was necessary to refer to market researchers by a single gender; the constant use of 'he/she' would have become tedious. Again, influenced by what I thought sounded right, I elected for a masculine market researcher. I hope my female colleagues will not consider this chauvinistic, as ours is a profession where women play a very strong role and can excel without the prejudices they sometimes face in other occupations.

Acknowledgements

A number of people have helped to make this book possible and I would like to express my thanks to them.

Over the last eight years my good friend Frederick Polhill has encouraged me to write for his quarterly journal *Industrial Marketing Digest*. Much of the material obtained and research which was carried out in the preparation of these articles have been used to write this book and I am grateful to Frederick for his permission to draw upon it.

I am indebted to my business partner Peter Jackson who has stoically tolerated my whim to write a book. I have learned much from working alongside him for over 17 years, and our many discussions on the problems of our job have inspired me to show how most industrial market research is based on common sense rather than sophisticated techniques with remote relevance to real life.

I must pay homage to a small band of people who have played very specific roles in the preparation of the book. Ann Kemp and Mike Allen, researchers in my company, dug out or checked many of the facts which are quoted. Bill Davis read and constructively suggested ways of improving the appendix on statistical methods. Anne Kennerley, Lesley Kerney, Gill Lawrence and Megan Stephens patiently put up with my alterations to the text as they typed and re-typed the manuscript. I received considerable help in confirming sources of information on the USA from Kevin McMahon of Ducker Research Company, Inc., in Birmingham, Michigan.

Notwithstanding the help I have received, there will be errors and omissions which are due to me alone as it was I who made the final decision in all cases.

Finally, I would like to thank my wife Christine and two children, Nicky and Chrissie, who have provided every encouragement and never once grumbled, even though they were deprived of a husband and father for most evenings and weekends during the nine months it took to write the book.

Paul Hague
January 1987

Introduction

Throughout this book, reference will be made to the special status of industrial marketing compared with its consumer counterpart.

Characteristics of industrial markets

The characteristics of industrial markets pose particular problems to the market researcher. They influence the approach to sampling, interviewing and other methods of data collection, and demand skills quite different from those of the consumer researcher. It is important, therefore, that the characteristics of industrial markets are fully understood.

Derived demand

Industrial products or services are bought on behalf of or for use by companies or organizations. They are usually consumed in the production of other products which ultimately are bought by private consumers.

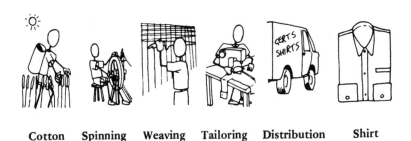

Cotton   Spinning   Weaving   Tailoring   Distribution   Shirt

DIAGRAM 1
The chain of derived demand

17

Every time a householder buys a shirt, a frozen chicken, a car or a house, his action sends waves back down the production chain creating a demand for cotton, animal feedstuffs, steel and bricks, among many other products or services used in their manufacture. This chain, with one product deriving its demand from that for another, is responsible for the interdependent structure of industrial organization.

As with all chains, acceleration or deceleration at the end can become magnified as the reaction moves backwards down the line. Consumers can adjust their buying patterns more rapidly than the industrial units in the chain. Firms require lengthy lead times to commission new plant in response to an increase in demand; on the other hand, they cannot readily shed labour if they suspect a fall in sales is only temporary. Similarly, a rise or fall in consumer sales triggers off a chain reaction of stocking or destocking out of all proportion to final demand.

Product life cycle

The demand for products and services waxes and wanes as fashions and technology change. For centuries the copying of documents was entirely by hand. The invention of carbon paper in 1806 together with the type-writer in 1843 speeded up the copying process, but these have been dwarfed by photocopying made possible by xerography discovered in 1937.

When the demand for industrial products is plotted over time, a curve similar in shape to a sand dune is created. Sections of the curve represent

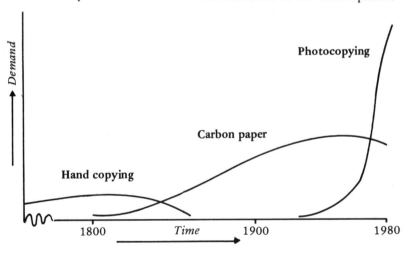

DIAGRAM 2
Life cycles in methods of copying

18

youth, maturity and old age just as they do in the human life cycle. After a period of relatively slow sales the product or service gains acceptance, demand builds, levels off and eventually falls away as it is replaced by a new product or service.

In consumer markets the life cycle of a product is shorter and more easily recognized. Industrial products have a long gestation period before achieving commercial success. Their life expectancy is measured in years rather than days or months and so the ups and downs of business cycles confuse the smooth lines of the theoretical cycle. The constant improvement of products means that after many years there is little resemblance to the initial specification. The life cycle of an industrial product is in fact made up of many smaller cycles.

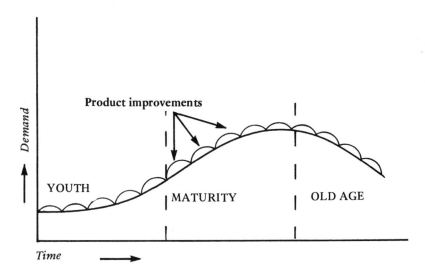

DIAGRAM 3
The construction of a life cycle for an industrial project

Industry structure

A single high street consumer occupies so small a position within the total market that his influence, taken in isolation, is insignificant. Whereas there are 173 million adult consumers and 87 million households in the USA, there are only 2.9 million incorporated establishments and as few as 260,000 of these are manufacturing concerns. It is a maxim that 20 per cent of these establishments account for 80 per cent of industrial production (and consumption). Unlike individual consumers, single firms can

19

have a significant effect on the market. The purchasing power of large companies is so great that their views must be consulted in any survey.

Consumers may differ in class, race and creed but they still wear clothes, eat food and travel by car. There are differences, of course, between consumer groups but not to the extent of industrial establishments. The nature of products manufactured and services offered by companies differs markedly and with it their growth prospects, distribution network and buying motivations. There are few similarities between manufacturers of basic chemicals, electronic component producers, bankers and plumbers' merchants. Each occupies a segment of the market which must be studied separately.

There are strong pulls on industry to locate according to customer demand, the availability of raw materials or nodal points of transport. Concentrations of industry have built up and, despite government incentives, the tendency to remain in an area has proved hard to change. There is, therefore a three-dimensional structure of industry with varying sized firms in different segments of the market located in centres across the world.

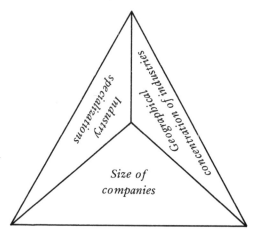

DIAGRAM 4
*The segmentation of industry by company size,
location and specialization*

The effect of the characteristics on industrial marketing

The characteristics of industrial markets which have been described affect all aspects of industrial marketing. They impact on buying, selling, promotion, service and distribution.

Industrial buying behaviour

The buying decision in industry is seldom simple. The larger the company and the more complex the product, the greater the likelihood of more than one department having an influence on it.

The purchase of a simple rivet, for example, may originate with the designer who decides what type of fastening system to use after consulting his production colleagues. Having made the decision to use a rivet rather than a screw, weld or adhesive, the choice of brand is passed across to the buying department who make their selection on commercial factors such as price, quality, delivery and sales service. At each stage in the decision process the buyers and specifiers are acting on behalf of their companies and should be more objective and knowledgeable than the domestic consumer when he goes out to buy. This is not always the case. Many industrial products are so similar the buyer ends up choosing a supplier on emotive grounds — perhaps because he likes the representative or trusts the company more.

Loyalty is a strong influence on industrial buying motivations so it cannot be assumed that a revolutionary new product at a lower price will win quick acceptance. Reciprocal agreements on buying and internal directives within groups confuse the supposedly rational approach. Nor is it possible to generalize about buying motives even within the same industry. The largest companies look for savings of fractions of a penny on every component they buy and may not chance doing business with a new and unproven supplier. The small buyer does not have the purchasing muscle to obtain massive discounts but he can afford to risk trying a new supplier who promises better service and innovative products.

Industrial promotion

Industrial promotion budgets are paltry compared with consumer appropriations. The industrial company is, however, selling to a much smaller number of buyers. In some industrial markets the customers may number less than 100, while 5000 potential customers or more is sizeable. Personal selling is one of the most important methods employed by industry to reach actual and potential customers. The industrial company knows who the top 50 buyers are in their segment of the market and can organize a sales force to hit them directly. The remaining potential cannot be ignored but it does not justify vast sums for promotion. As the potential buyers are all identifiable, if not by name at least by market sector, they can be reached by direct mail, specialized directories and trade journals or exhibitions. Two per cent of sales revenue is a generous advertising budget in industrial marketing and half this figure may be spent on non-media promotions such as brochures, exhibitions or office keepsakes.

Industrial service

The consumer who buys a product from a store has learned to expect a falling standard of sales service. He will be lucky to have his product wrapped and may have to pay for it to be delivered to his home.

The industrial buyer, however, expects and receives service. At the time the buying decision is under consideration, a series of sales visits will be made and the buyer could receive an invitation to the supplier's factory to see the product being produced. Later there may be problems which must be resolved by a delegation of technical, production and sales personnel from the supplier. Meanwhile, contact with the buyer is maintained weekly by a honey-voiced telephone sales girl and every two months by the sales representative. As technology and production techniques make products more difficult to tell apart, suppliers place effort behind service to differentiate themselves, raise their image, and help their products command a premium price.

Industrial distribution

When there is a large user market to serve, suppliers set up their own depots around the country or appoint distributors to stock and resell their products.

As the costs of servicing small customers with directly employed sales representatives rise, industrial distributors grow in importance. They already occupy important positions in the automotive sector, fork-lift trucks, electronic components, building materials and office equipment.

Distributors are an extension of a supplier's company and function as his depot. They provide a stocking and sales point but often cannot offer technical advice or even repair the products they have sold. Suppliers, therefore, back up distributors with promotions to bring custom in and technical service teams to provide advice.

The place of industrial market research in the business environment

What is industrial market research?

Industrial market research is the collection, analysis and interpretation of data on industrial markets. Industrial markets have been described earlier in this chapter as being made up of organizations which acquire goods and services, not for their own sake, but to facilitate the supply of other goods and services which ultimately may be bought by domestic consumers.

Unlike marketing which focuses on the needs of the buyer, and selling

22

which is more concerned with the needs of the supplier, industrial market research has a wide-ranging brief. The industrial market researcher is as interested in why the buyer buys as why the seller sells. He also questions what, where, when and how. The industrial market researcher is a fact finder who seeks the most accurate information possible within imposed constraints of time and money. His *raison d'être* is to reduce risk by taking the guesswork out of business decision.

Industrial market research as a tool

The spearhead of any business is the sales and marketing function. Every company exists by virtue of its sales, and the volume and price which can be achieved for those sales is a principal determinant of profits. Companies also need production of some sort. In a manufacturing plant, production is obvious — it is visible on the assembly line. Distributors, advertising agencies, banks and cleaners are also occupied in production of a kind. They stock, design, advise and produce services which incur costs due to the employment of labour, materials and overheads.

At its simplest, marketing and sales generate revenue; production incurs costs. Other activities such as accounts, personnel and buying are subservient to the marketing and production functions but are still essential ingredients in the operation of a business.

From 1945 to the early 1970s, world economies grew rapidly with occasional hiccups due to political changes or capital investment cycles. The problem faced by businesses in those years was the acquisition of sufficient resources for production rather than a shortfall of sales. Companies had sales departments which allocated production to customers rather than actively sold. If for some reason domestic sales fell back, it was usually a temporary relapse countered by pushing exports to keep production lines running. Businesses were very often successful because they operated in a favorable environment rather than as a result of efficient marketing and production.

In the 1970s and 1980s world economies began to slow down and for some countries they moved into reverse. Many companies that had once worked at full capacity faced meager order books and had to examine more closely their markets and products. Reduced demand created a highly competitive environment.

Inferior products which were acceptable even when the earliest possible delivery dates ran to three months could not compete unless redesigned to give the customer the quality, efficiency and value for money he demanded. The customer had become king.

Pressure fell on the marketing departments to win more sales. Knowledge of markets, customers' needs and new opportunities became essential to survival. Market research grew in stature and has become an accepted tool which can provide this knowledge.

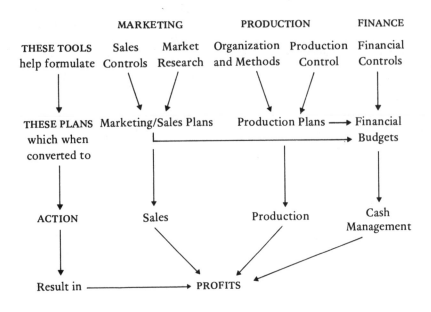

DIAGRAM 5

The place of market research as a business tool

In the future, competitive pressures will intensify. Technology enables companies to produce to common standards so that customers cannot differentiate products on the grounds of design, quality or performance. The use of the same production techniques throughout industry and similar raw materials costs means that prices, too, are being driven towards a standard. Knowledge is becoming increasingly important. Companies with knowledge will make products which meet their customers' needs, they will see gaps into which they can expand, they will be able to adjust quickly in response to changes in the competitive environment. Market researchers who can provide this knowledge will be in great demand.

Summary

Industrial markets are distinguished from consumer markets by purchases which are made on behalf of companies or organizations rather than individuals. Demand in industrial markets is derived from interdependent organizations which ultimately depend on the consumer in the high street.

The life cycles of industrial products are hard to recognize. They are made up of many small cycles created by constant product improvements while the major cycle is spread over many years.

Compared with consumer markets, industrial markets have few customers. However, some of these customers are so large that their actions affect the market segment in which they are positioned. Industrial markets are concentrated in size, specialization and geographical locations.

The purchasing decision in industry is often influenced by a number of departments which are motivated by different requirements. Technicians set specifications, buyers select brands, though consultation occurs between departments when the product or service which is being bought is complex and costly.

Personal selling is an important means of promoting industrial goods and is made feasible by the small number of customers on which firms depend for most of their sales. Modest advertising budgets back up the sales force and are spread across print, media advertising, PR and exhibitions.

Service has become an important means of differentiating companies and their products from one another.

As direct selling costs rise, an increasing use will be made of distributors. Competitive pressures are forcing companies to produce universally acceptable products. Commercial success in the future will be dependent on knowledge of markets which the industrial market researcher can provide.

Part One:
Information that can be made available by market research

Chapter 1
The Assessment of Market Size

What is market size?

Market size is a measure, at a point in time, of the sales (or purchases) of goods or services in a territory. This brief definition embodies a number of words which require further explanation.

Market size is usually expressed either as a monetary value or units. Sometimes one of these measures is unsuitable. For example, the market size for construction fixings in the USA is valued at over $1 billion. This figure is, however, a compilation of many segments from wood screws costing a few cents to cartridge fasteners or wood screws costing a few dollars. Though all are fixings and used in the construction indusry, they are so different that any aggregation of unit sales is meaningless.

When assessing the market size for services, it is nearly always necessary to use monetary value. A market size expressed in number of jobs would be nonsensical if the value of each job differed widely.

Wherever it can be used, unit volume is a preferable measure to value as year-to-year comparisons are possible without the need to adjust for inflation. The measure of unit volume varies from product to product. Components and finished machines are quantified in numbers, textiles in linear or square yards/metres, liquids in gallons or litres, commodities in tonnes or some other measure of weight.

Market size refers to the value or volume of goods and services bought in a specified year. It can be expressed as an equation:

$$\text{Market size} = \text{Total sales} - \text{exports} + \text{imports}$$

That part of production or sales which is exported is, therefore, subtracted while goods entering the territory are added on. The expression of market size in this simple equation serves to explain the relationship between market size, production, exports and imports. There are circumstances in which the figures require qualifying.

Sales made in the USA but subsequently exported are domestic purchases but not domestic consumption. This is frequently the case in spares
markets where, for example, large quantities of machined castings may be
purchased in the USA by the plant designers and subsequently shipped
throughout the world.

It is important to define market size by stating whether it refers to
manufacturers' sales or end-user demand. A manufacturer of engineers'
tools considers his product sold when it has been delivered to a customer,
which to him is an engineers' merchant. However, the sale of tools by the
engineers' merchant to the user (ie, true market demand) may show little
sympathy with manufacturers' sales as inventories are either built up or
run down.

Assessments of market size are usually for a country, but could be for a
county or a sales region. Whatever the size of the territory, it is important
to define it. The UK embraces England, Scotland, Wales and Northern
Ireland. Britain or the British Isles excludes Northern Ireland. North
America comprises the United States *and* Canada. The European Economic
Community is in the throes of change, and adjustment must be made for
the inclusion of Greece, Spain and Portugal.

Market size is sometimes erroneously used as a measure of *market
potential* whose correct definition is those purchases (or that consumption)
which could be realized if the substitution of one product for another
ever took place. The UK market size for timber frame housing was 33,000
units in 1983, not 150,000 units per annum which was the total number
of houses built in that year, most using conventional methods of bricks
and mortar. 150,000 units represent the potential market size which may
never be fully realized even after a period of many years.

Occasionally, market size is used incorrectly to describe the 'parc' of
a product. This is the number of products which are installed or are in use
in a territory. The figure can be used to calculate the market size in a
mature market where there are few first-time purchases. Knowledge of
the commercial vehicle parc by age of truck has long been used by researchers to predict the size of the replacement market. Parc data is
therefore a useful measure for suppliers of equipment in a mature market.

The life span of products constantly changes and impacts on the size
of the parc and market size. Restrictions on capital expenditure delay
the purchase of products and depress market size. The parc size remains
static if products can be maintained and kept going. When the products
become irreparable and purchases are still being deferred, the market
size and parc both fall. Improvements in technology make old products
redundant, shorten the life span and increase both the market size and
parc size.

How useful is market size?

Market size is a benchmark against which company performance can be measured and goals set. Over a period of time, market size establishes a trend and a pointer to the future.

Without knowledge of market size, a company cannot know its share and, therefore, cannot know whether it is worth while or possible to increase it. With a share below 20 per cent it is nearly always possible to win more, and this is especially so if it is as low as just one or two percentage points. In contrast, a share of over 50 per cent can present problems for expansion, as buyers encourage competition and support second and third tier suppliers to prohibit the domination of a market by only one or two. Frequently, companies with shares of between 20 and 50 per cent compete with suppliers of a similar size, experiencing fluctuating gains and losses in percentage points as they fight for supremacy.

A company which contemplates entering what is for it a new market needs to know the market size to decide if its interest is justified. As might be expected, markets which attract managements' attention are new and growing rapidly. All too frequently, media 'noise' leads to a widespread belief that these markets are bigger than they actually prove to be; companies misguidedly enter the market and within a short space of time there are many fall-outs.

Market size is one of the first things asked for by a sponsor commissioning a study. It is important, but only for answering the following questions:

Where are we now?
Where are we going?

Knowledge of market size will not show how to get there. This requires answers to how and why people buy, and how to beat the competition.

The importance of market segmentation

Market size is made up of a number of segments or groups of products. The US market for construction industry plant was valued at over $9 billion in 1982 but within this figure are hidden a number of segments which combine to make the whole — dumpers, concrete mixers, earthmoving plant, etc. Any one of these product groups can in turn be isolated and split into sub-segments. The market for concrete mixers is just one of these segments and accounts for only one per cent of the total market. This in turn can be divided by size of plant to show the demand for products below 3 cubic feet mixing capacity, 3 to 7 cubic feet, batching plant, truck mixers, etc.

Markets can be segmented in many ways, the most usual being by:

- ☐ size/capacity/shape of product ct
- ☐ price of product
- ☐ size of user
- ☐ geographical area
- ☐ industrial classification of user.

The segmentation of market size enables a company to obtain an understanding in depth of what certain groups of customers want. It identifies niches where the company is strong or weak, where the competition is less active or where there is room for expansion.

The methods of assessing market size

Prior to making an assessment of market size the researcher should be clear about the reason the information is required. The cost of assessing market size to a high level of accuracy could be formidable whereas a quick, inexpensive approximation may be sufficient for the purpose of the exercise. Generally, a high level of accuracy is only necessary when a substantial investment is to be made or a company has a large market share, in which case every one or two percentage points it can win becomes critical. A company with a low market share or considering entering a market for the first time may be better advised to carry out a broad assessment and refine it later should other factors also seem promising.

A number of commonly adopted approaches used in the assessment of market size are listed below.

Desk research

There are numerous sources of published data which can be used to obtain an assessment of market size. (A more detailed discussion of this topic can be found in Chapters 17 and 18.)

Government statistics. A guide to US statistics can be obtained from *US Statistics at a Glance* published by the Bureau of Census, Data User Services Division in Washington. In the UK, the source of government statistics is the *Guide to Official Statistics* published by the Central Statistical Office in London.

Trade associations. These can prove extremely valuable sources of data in some markets though they are often restricted to members only. They tend to record production rather than sales and are most comprehensive in some of the older established industries where, prior to the Federal

Trade Commission Act (and its predecessors), there were manufacturers' clubs to protect prices, exchange data and carve up markets.

Trade journals. Occasionally trade magazines and the serious press (especially the *Wall Street Journal*) publish articles on industrial markets.

Consultants' reports. There are many consultancy companies that speculatively publish reports on industrial markets at prices which range from below $100 to over $2000. If a report covers the subject area of interest it can be a quick and inexpensive means of obtaining the data. A comprehensive list of published consultants' reports is available in a British Overseas Trade Board booklet entitled *International Directory of Published Market Research.*

Analogous markets

The size of a market can be assessed by making comparisons with another which bears strong similarities or — where an association is obvious — between two products, one of which has a known market size. The market size for industrial products in the USA is frequently six times that of the UK — a figure which reflects the difference in size between the two economies. A rough and ready approach like this can only be a starting point, as technological differences, custom and practice, and the number of years a product has been on the market, can affect the calculation.

The association between two products can also provide a starting point. Commercial vehicle production statistics, for example, enable reliable estimates to be made of the original equipment demand for truck tyres.

User and distributor interviews

In a market with a limited number of buyers or distributors it is possible to carry out a comprehensive program of interviews to identify their purchases and, by addition, arrive at the market size. In practice some companies may not cooperate, others may simply not know their purchases in the form suited to the survey. Time and cost may prevent contact with everyone. It is necessary, therefore, to group the user companies into strata in which buyers are believed to be of approximately equal size and to make estimates for those whose figures have not been obtained for whatever reason.

This approach can be extended to larger universes. It is impossible to know or even guess in advance the size of each company's purchases in a large and unknown market, and so a telephone screen must be applied to the sample to achieve stratification.

Market size is derived by grossing up in each stratum and summing these sub-totals.

The judgements which are required to fill in the gaps on user purchases, the inadequacies of suitable sample frames and the errors which users often make in providing purchasing data, can make user interviews a dubious method of industrial market size assessment. Wherever possible a cross check should be obtained from one of the alternative approaches.

Competitor/supplier interviews

Suppliers to a market have a precise knowledge of their own sales and, more often than not, a good idea of the size of their competitors. On a *quid pro quo* basis most suppliers are prepared to discuss their knowledge. Even if they are unwilling to talk about their own company, their views on other suppliers may, together with data from other interviews, provide an accurate assessment of what share each supplier holds. In the narrow market niches in which researchers frequently work, these interviews with suppliers are one of the most reliable methods of market size assessment.

The assessment of sales area potential

Knowledge of market size helps set national goals for products but it is less useful to a sales or marketing manager who needs to know the potential for each of his sales areas. The assessment of sales area potential has many similarities with that of assessing market size, but there are differences because of the limited size of territories being studied.

Desk research

Directories. It is a relatively simple procedure to screen directories for companies which fit the class of industry to which the sales force sell. The source can vary from a specialist list supplier to local telephone directories, or suppliers' guides in trade journals. A straight count of the companies within a region may be a guide to the potential for a product. If, for example, it is known from experience that lithographic printers each use a certain number of printers' blankets per year, then a company marketing these products can obtain a rough approximation of the area's sales potential by simple multiplication. This method of assessing sales potential is most suited to industrial products where there are numerous end users generally of small size — like printers, foundries, plumbers, electricians, general engineering workshops and schools.

Employment statistics. The Census Bureau produces comprehensive and up-to-date statistics showing the number of employees by standard region, within broad industrial classifications: agriculture, forestry and fishing; manufacturing industries; and service industries. Using this data it is possible, for example, to calculate by region the number of overalls consumed per employee in woodworking, metal manufacturing or construction industries. The regional breakdown provided by the census enables analyses of potential to be carried out by standard region, including major conurbations. The ratios are all the more valid if they relate to products which are consumed by employees themselves (such as personal safety equipment). Nevertheless, scope exists for using the same economic activity statistics to calculate the regional demand for drive belts in the textile industry or the consumption of cement in the construction industry.

Regional statistics are also available showing the number of companies, by their size, measured in employment terms. Lists of companies within various industry sectors are available from any of the commercial directories (see Chapter 16), classified by size and geographical area. This could be of value to an industrial caterer who defines his target as those companies employing 500 people or more. It may help a supplier of photocopiers to decide how many models of different sizes he can sell in a region based on his knowledge of the popularity of particular models to certain sized businesses.

Population statistics. The more general population statistics published in the census of population are not as useful to the industrial market researcher as employment figures. Nevertheless, they can be of value to certain types of companies. A manufacturer of house bricks (or window frames) may be able to use the statistics to establish the approximate regional potential for his products in the knowledge that most members of the population are housed in dwellings constructed with his materials. Producers of goods purchased by local authorities (from dustbins to wheelbarrows) can obtain a reasonable estimate of demand within an area from the population that the authority serves.

By association. In the same way that market sizes can be assessed by using a known association between two products, so too can a sales area's potential. A salesman selling work rolls to strip rolling mills would not be able to find published figures showing the annual consumption of his products. However, it is relatively easy to establish the number of work rolls used per 1000 tons of strip produced. Statistics are readily available on the output of steel strip, from which a calculation can easily be made to show the sales potential for rolls. Also through association, the output of sand and gravel influences the consumption of screening meshes, sales of industrial bobbins are linked to the output of cloth, and sales of guillotine knives depend on paper production. In some circumstances, estimates of the potential for industrial goods may be calculable from the regionally available rateable values of industrial properties. Even the regional incidence of sunlight and population may be useful to some industrialists if, for example, they produce solar water heaters.

Fieldwork. A sales manager should aim eventually to be able to list every prospect and customer in his sales territories. For each prospect it is helpful to know their total annual purchases broken down by source of supply. Detail of this type is never published — it requires a fieldwork program to find it out. Telephone interviews and/or visits are required and these are best undertaken by a trained and objective researcher rather than the sales force whose preconditioning and vested interests could bias the findings.

Summary

Market size is a measure of the purchases of goods or services in a defined area for a specified year. The assessment of market size plays an important role in most market research studies. Together with the known sales, it shows where a company stands at a point in time and enables goals to be established for future campaigns. Market size is most useful when it is analysed by segment.

Market size can be assessed by a variety of methods, the most important being desk research, analogy, end-user interviews and interviews with competitors.

The assessment of a sales area's potential bears many similarities to that of market size and can be calculated by employment and population statistics, by association with some other product on which statistics exist, or by a special fieldwork program.

Chapter 2
The Analysis of Market Structure

What is market structure?

In the simplest form of industrial markets there are only producers and buyers of goods. Such a structure exists within narrow market segments — manufacturers of power generating and steelwork plant sell direct to power stations and steel companies. Where, however, there are a large number of buyers and the product is widely used, a complex chain of supply develops through which distribution takes place. This arrangement of users, sellers and distributors, whether simple or complex, is termed market structure. It is the organization of and relationship between suppliers, distributors and users of industrial products.

Market structures can be examined over a small part of the vertical chain of production or down its complete length. As the industrial market researcher is usually concerned in any single study with just one product group, the structure of the market some distance up or down the chain is an irrelevance. For example, in a study of powder metal parts used in commercial vehicle fuel pumps, the researcher is principally interested in the number of component suppliers and the number of fuel pump manufacturers who respectively constitute the competition and potential customers. The suppliers of the iron powder raw material may be of passing interest as a source of information but, at the other end of the spectrum, the size and structure of the commercial vehicle industry which uses the pumps is too distant to be of importance (see table 1).

The organization and complexity of a market structure differs according to the characteristics of the industrial product.

Within a classification of undifferentiated products such as basic raw materials it is possible to have a complex market structure. Large engineering works buy steel direct from the mill while smaller companies use a network of steel stockholders. The market structure for industrial components shows similar variability. Simple components such as pressings, castings or injection molded plastic parts are usually sold direct as they

37

TABLE 1
*Market structure in the supply of sintered parts
to fuel pump manufacturers*

Industry groups	No of companies in group	Relevance to the study
Iron powder suppliers	3	Of some relevance
Powder metal component manufacturers	10	Of key relevance
Diesel fuel pump manufacturers	2	
Commercial vehicle manufacturers	6	
Commercial vehicle distributors	100s	Of little relevance
Commercial vehicle operators	50,000+	

are fabricated to the buyer's specification, often with a tool which he owns. This can be compared with the many electrical sub-assemblies which are sold via distributors. In these products buyers can find a ready-made design to meet their needs and, because they use fewer such components, they cannot justify direct supply.

The types of industry structure are illustrated in table 2 which is divided into the four broad classes of industrial goods (and services).

How useful is market structure?

Market structure, like market size, is featured in most market research studies. Together with market size it is one of the important measures which enables a company to see where it stands in relation to its competitors, customers and potential customers. It is a snapshot at a point in time though, of course, all market structures have in-built dynamics and are changing in terms of the numbers of companies which make up the fabric. Market structure, as with market size, is useful to the planner. It is another piece in the jigsaw of information which shows, 'Where are we now?'. It will also help that planner set goals for his marketing strategy over the forthcoming years and will in part tell him how to get there as the strengths and weaknesses of companies' distribution policies are revealed. However, his detailed plans for expansion can only be completed with a full explanation of the motivations of buyers and specifiers which show why they select one supplier in preference to another.

Listed below table 2 are five important uses which the market researcher derives from his understanding of market structures.

TABLE 2

Classification of industrial markets by industry structure

Classification type	Examples of type of product	Type of industry structure
Raw materials	Fuel, chemicals, cement, aggregates, ore, sugar, timber, steel, aluminium	1. *Commodities:* agents arrange sale. Small number of large buyers. 2. *Fuels:* distributors used for small buyers. Direct supply to large ones. 3. *Manufacturing materials:* many buyers with wide range of consumption levels. Distributors are important. Some direct supply to large buyers.
Components	Construction materials, metal and plastic parts, cable, instruments, motors, electrical and mechanical parts, filters	1. *Simple components:* supplied in large volume, usually direct. Replacement items supplied via distributors. 2. *High tech/assembled components:* buyer specification leads to direct supply but distributors important for electronic equipment.
Capital goods	Plant and machinery, vehicles, office machinery	1. *Installed equipment:* small number of buyers requiring tailor-made plant, therefore direct supply. 2. *Standard equipment:* large number of buyers supplied via distributors.
Industrial services	Finance, marketing, plumbing, electrical, transport, local authority services	Large number of buyers and suppliers. High level of personalized service, therefore direct supply.

Clarification of interrelationships

Some markets are a jungle of suppliers, distributors, service companies and end users. The researcher needs to analyse each part of the market structure so that the relationships between the participants are made clear. It is helpful to set these out in diagrammatic form as in diagram 6.

Indication of the size of the marketing task

The analysis of numbers and classification of user companies and distributors shows the difficulties and cost of reaching them with promotions or a sales force. A fragmented end-user market with an established distribution network is likely to persuade a supplier to concentrate on selling into distributors and pulling demand through by means of an advertising campaign directed at the users. Conversely, a small number of end users or a select band of large users may point to the need for personalized selling.

Indication of the size of the competition

Assessing the shares of the market held by competitors is one of the fundamental pieces of information required of a market research exercise. Suppliers' shares are one measure of their strength, though it is necessary to have further data such as trends in share movements and reasons for these to provide a full analysis. On the occasions when suppliers' shares are small, the researcher must determine whether the company is a serious competitor or not. It could, for example, sell a very high-priced product and be content to cream off the top layer, or sell a speciality product appealing to a minority group. On the other hand, a small share may reflect the neglect of a company's management whose main interest is directed elsewhere.

The analysis of market structure

Market structures are analysed using the orthodox techniques available to market researchers — desk research and fieldwork. The paragraphs below summarize how these are applied to the analysis of market structure, while a more detailed discussion can be found in Part Four.

Desk research

The level of information required on companies differs according to the objectives of the survey. It may be essential to identify the strengths and weaknesses of competing suppliers, in which case a detailed dossier must be built up on each company. Similar detail could be provided on prospective customers but such an exercise would be both costly and unnecessary. In most cases, a good sales lead is simply the prospect's name, address and telephone number.

The more specialized the directories, the more likely they will provide a comprehensive listing. Seldom is a single directory sufficient. Researchers are prudent if they assume, when compiling the list, that some companies are missing. The totally accurate and comprehensive directory is a rarity. Also, it can be rightly presumed that some companies are sure to be incorrectly represented — this is usually the case in spite of painstaking efforts to ensure otherwise.

Product literature. Literature or data sheets from a company will confirm if they actually do offer the product for sale and will give a technical insight into its features and benefits. Literature can be obtained by direct request to the sales department of the company, at an exhibition, from a response to an advertisement or from a data file operated by some specialist companies (eg, Barbour Index — a library system for architects).

Trade journals and the press. Advertisements and press releases in specialist trade magazines can be used to add to the lists of companies known to be suppliers, distributors or buyers. The level of advertising of any one company is a crude indication of its size or its aspirations to grow. The *Wall Street Journal* is a fertile source for company information. For quoted companies, the McCarthy Index, held at most major libraries, simplifies the search.

Financial data. Specialized directories, such as those published by Dun & Bradstreet and Moody's or Standard and Poors, provide a summary of key financial information which can be used as the first step in the assessment of a company's turnover in a particular product area.

More detailed financial data can be obtained from the IOK reports and accounts which quoted companies must make available to the public.

Fieldwork

End-user interviews. Interviews with end users can produce information on what and how much each company buys as well as who supplies it. Interviews are, therefore, a widely used source of data on market structure. Depending on the depth of information required they may be undertaken by telephone or visit: the choice depends on the complexity of the subject. Respondents asked over the phone to recall purchase quantities and break these down by size and supplier must be expected to make mistakes if there is little time to think about the question, let alone look up the answer in a file.

Distributor interviews. Interviews are useful for obtaining information on the purchasing requirements of the distributors who may have useful views on the customers they serve. However, distributors react in a similar manner to most companies and treat any request to divulge the identify of their customers with great suspicion.

Supplier interviews. Just as suppliers can be used to obtain data on market size, so too are they an important source of market share information.

Summary

Market structure is the way in which a market is built up in terms of suppliers, end users and any middlemen such as distributors or service companies. The numbers of companies which form each part of the market and the relationship of one group to another is part of the analysis of market structure.

An understanding of market structure helps the researcher in his assessment of market size and market shares. It also shows how the product moves from production through to the user company.

The analysis of market structure may identify opportunities which can become targets for expansion or development.

Market structure is studied by desk research, especially utilizing lists of companies in directories. Interviews with end users and suppliers also play an important role.

Chapter 3
The Analysis of Market Shares

What is market share?

Market shares are a measure of the size and success of a supplier in a market. The analysis of market shares is, therefore, of considerable importance to the industrial market researcher and consumes a good deal of his time. The subject is worthy of a separate discussion beyond the coverage already given in Chapter 2.

A monopolist is a company which dominates and controls an industry. The share which a company needs to hold of a market to be regarded as a monopolist depends on the structure of the industry. The Anti-Trust Division of the Justice Department becomes most concerned when an industry is highly concentrated with only a few players in it. In general, however, a market share over 20 per cent is deemed by the Department of Justice to be 'dangerous'. This said, it is a state to which most firms aspire since with it comes a concentration of industrial power sufficient to give a company control over the market price for their products or services. The recognition of a monopoly position is not always obvious as it depends on the breadth of definition of the market. A company with a 70 per cent share of the air-powered screwdriver market appears at face value to have an overwhelming monopoly. But is this truly a monopoly when users have the choice of manual or electric alternatives? What is more, screws are only one method of fastening, others being welding, rivets, nails and adhesives. Many of the users of the company's products could consider an alternative to air-powered screwdrivers, and this theoretically reduces its monopoly power.

A variation on the monopoly is a duopoly, in which two firms dominate the market, each with a market share in excess of 25 per cent. However, the degree of competition which each company exerts on the other prevents the price manipulation which is a feature of monopolies. This has been the case in the UK coach building market where for many years the shares were equally divided between Plaxtons and Duple.

One step down from a monopoly and duopoly is an oligopoly in which there are three, four or five firms, with no share large enough to influence the price of their product or their marketing strategies without taking into account the likely reaction of the others. In the 1970s the UK steel wire market comprised Johnson & Nephew, Rylands, GKN and Bridon. The four firms were of roughly equal size and fought for share and volume at the expense of price so that all ultimately suffered a declining trend in profits. Eventually, the industry was forced to rationalize, with the result that some of the companies and many of their plants were closed down. Similar stories exist in the manufacture of glass bottles, paper and tyres.

Oligopolies are frequently found at an early stage in the production chain. They are especially common in the markets for raw materials or semi-processed goods where economies of production demand sizeable manufacturing units. The tightening of the Federal Anti-Trust laws in the USA, and in particular those acts which curbed price fixing, have put paid to the very comfortable markets in which gentlemen's agreements maintained prices at artificially high levels. The result has quite often had the effect of lowering prices without lowering costs and forcing companies to the wall.

The third and final classification of market share is the fragmented supply position: the characteristic of emergent industries in which many companies jostle for position. In fragmented markets most suppliers nibble and are lucky to achieve a 5 per cent share. This is exemplified by the early days of the market for personal computers. Fragmented shares may also result from the need to provide local services. Thus accountants, plumbers and waste disposal companies all operate in a national market in which their shares as individual suppliers are very small.

Factors influencing market share

Success in building a high market share is a consequence of achieving the right formula for the marketing mix. Three factors consistently feature as the chief elements in any share building campaign.

High and consistent quality

Even in the depths of a recession, respondents responsible for selecting suppliers consistently identify high quality as the prime factor motivating their choice. Quality frequently overrides price as a factor influencing the selection of a supplier, and buyers are quick to point out that high quality coupled with a high price can still provide better value for money than low quality and low prices. Quality should, however, be matched by reliability. Examples abound in industry where high quality products regularly fail in use due to bad design or over-sophistication. In the commercial vehicle market Volvo provide an illustration of a company which has succeeded in dominating many markets with its policy of producing high quality, reliable products. On the other hand Jaguar struggled for many years in the quality car market until they improved the reliability of their products.

A high level of marketing activity

Companies which produce high quality, reliable products will only be successful in building market share if they are active in telling users what they are offering and how it will meet their needs. In industrial markets the most widely used means of promotion is the sales force who communicate with and persuade the customer as well as provide service when it is required. Sadly, the impact of marketing activity, including sales forces, is invisible, hard to quantify and slow acting. The marketing budget is, therefore, often in the front line of a cost-saving program which saves money in the short term but ultimately results in a fall in market share.

Launching designs which are ahead of the competition

Companies which achieve and maintain a high market share are consistently one step ahead of the competition with new products or improvements in their range. They keep up with customers' changing needs, sometimes are slightly ahead of them, but never lag behind. In this way customers automatically think of their supplier as being a leader in the field. This approach to innovation should, however, never leave the customer behind. Concorde did nothing for Aerospatial's and British Aerospace's market shares!

How useful is market share?

The ultimate proof of a successful marketing strategy is a high market share, the higher the better. Not at the expense of profits, of course, for any fool can give his products away. Once attained, market dominance brings many advantages. Premium prices can be charged, volume production brings economies of scale; a grip can be exerted on distribution. Research carried out in the United States has shown that the average rate of return for businesses with market shares in excess of 40 per cent is more than twice that for those companies with only a 10 per cent share. In fact, for every 10 per cent increase in market share, the return on investment could be expected to rise by 5 per cent. Thus a high market share brings high profitability in its wake.

The aim must be to achieve such widespread recognition for a product that it is asked for and used to the exclusion of all others. Eventually, it is hoped that the product's brand name will become attributed to all competitor products in its genre. Examples are plentiful even in industrial markets: padded postal envelopes are referred to as Jiffy bags; earth-movers as Cats. Such a high level of awareness becomes generic — it is automatically associated with the product so that eventually it almost sells itself.

Market share should not become an obsession. It is often built up at the expense of profits by highly aggressive marketing policies whose main plank is price cutting: this may pay off in the long term when a monopoly position is eventually achieved. But a high market share carries with it the danger of complacency. Greed may push prices up too high, service falls off and quality is compromised. Competitors, whether home-grown or, as is frequently the case, from overseas, are attracted into the market. A high market share has not protected many companies with household names from being trampled on by the Europeans and Japanese. A high market share is certainly worth striving for, but once attained it should be nurtured with vigilance. There is, after all, only one direction to move thereafter.

The assessment of market share

Desk research

Before committing himself to the expense of a fieldwork program the researcher should examine published statistics for data on market size and the turnover of each supplier. Turnover figures are, however, often hard to obtain. Searches through profit and loss accounts in Dun & Bradstreet's or Standard and Poors may provide a clue, but almost always the figures need adjusting to take account of sales derived from products which fall outside the specific field of interest. From time to time a lucky strike is made and a breakdown is provided in the accounts showing how the sales are made up of the various activities. Trade associations, company literature and even advertisements are all sources worth tapping in the quest for sales turnover data.

Fieldwork

User surveys. A study of desk sources leaves gaps which can only be filled by a fieldwork program. This too has its problems in industrial market research. A large sample of buyers, even though they account for half the total purchases of the market, may not provide a picture of market shares as some suppliers could have large sales to a handful of the largest buyers. If those large buyers are in the sample, the result will be weighted in their suppliers' favour; if they are not, the supplier may not even figure in the table of shares. End-user surveys are a valuable technique for assessing industrial market shares but they should be validated by some other method to check upon their accuracy.

Observation. Sometimes market shares can be measured at a low cost using observation alone. A company wishing to build a new factory to make glass bottles for the food industry required a quick and inexpensive assessment of market shares before the survey began. This was possible by sending teams of researchers into supermarkets to pick up jars of food and observe a small mark on the base of each. These 'punt' marks identified all the major suppliers of bottles to each food manufacturer *before* they were interviewed personally. Also, it showed the penetration of imported bottles and this in itself was one indication of the need for another domestic bottle manufacturer. Many industrial products are branded with the manufacturer's 'signature', thus providing a means of checking a market share by observation.

Manufacturers of electric cable distinguish their products with strands of coloured cotton, foundries mark castings with their logo, injection moulders put an identification mark on their products.

Supplier interviews. Possibly the most neglected method of obtaining or substantiating market shares is a direct approach to suppliers of the products themselves. This demands considerable skills on the part of the researcher. He must seek the interview without in any way misrepresenting its purpose and, having obtained it, he must be able to draw out the information and judge whether it is reliable or not. It is always necessary to collect views from more than one supplier, as only in this way is it possible to get more than one fix on a share and so arrive at a best estimate. The researcher must apply discretion to the amount of information he himself releases in the interview, and great delicacy may be required when discussing the respondent's own sales and share. Even on those occasions when a respondent may prefer not to discuss his own sales, he may be prepared to talk about those of competitors and so provide a cross check against other estimates.

Manufacturers are by no means the only source of an overview on market shares. Distributors, agents, trade associations, managers or salesmen who have parted with their company, all can prove useful. The estimates of market shares obtained by this approach will not be precise. They are nevertheless likely to be closer than shares obtained from user surveys and quite sufficient for most industrial marketing decisions.

Summary

Market share is a measure of a company's sales within a market. This can vary from conditions of monopoly in which one company dominates through to a fragmented number of suppliers each with a small share.

Market shares are built by policies of producing quality products, backing them with a high level of marketing activity and keeping ahead of the competition with new product designs.

High market shares bring rewards of profitability as they allow price leadership.

One of the most useful and yet neglected means of determining market share is through discussions with other suppliers to the market.

Chapter 4
The Analysis of Market Trends

What are market trends?

The assessment of market size and analysis of market shares and structure have both been shown to be a representation at a particular time. And yet, market size shares and structures are dynamic; they grow, decline and change shape over a period. Furthermore, the qualitative aspects of marketing seldom remain the same. The packages of products and benefits presented to users are constantly changing as are the needs and attitudes of those users. The analysis of market trends is the study of these qualitative aspects of a market over time in order to identify, understand and ultimately predict directional changes.

Market trends are studied historically before they are projected into the future. Predictions are at best hazardous and they should only be made after a full understanding of past changes has been achieved. The researcher must study both the universal influences which impinge on a market (the macro factors) and those which are localized to the market (the micro factors). Diagram 7 illustrates the pressures of these various factors on a market.

DIAGRAM 7
Macro and micro factors influencing market trends

Macro factors

The economy. The swings in economic trends, measured by gross domestic product (GDP) or, more usefully for industrial markets, index of manufacturing production, are the backcloth against which market trends should be analysed. Few industrial products are impervious to economic booms or recessions though the market trend may lead or lag behind rather than run in sympathy.

Fiscal policy. Interest rates and the availability of money for investment are manipulated by central government. Raising of interest rates or the imposition of taxes affects capital spending and demand is cut back. Fiscal policy has an effect on investment programmes either through encouraging or dissuading management by the costs of borrowing money, or causing a deferment in capital spending through uncertain economic conditions.

Legislation. Government can introduce legislation and thereby open opportunities or close markets. Legislation can boost demand as was the case when the International Convention for Safety of Life at Sea required all seagoing oil carriers to have tank washing facilities, thus raising the demand for automatic tank cleaning heads during the years up until the deadline given to operators to equip their fleet. In contrast, a government's legislation can wipe out demand for a product at a stroke, as when the US government banned cyclamates in 1970.

Legislation may be introduced to affect employment practices or company operating procedures, in which case it becomes a tool for encouraging or discouraging investment in the same way as fiscal policy. The environmental and safety controls brought in to protect welders have resulted in some companies switching to riveting or screws rather than face the expense of complying with the new procedures.

Publicity. The dangers of asbestosis, only when raised by the media, led quickly to a collapse in sales of asbestos products. The sensational nature of media reporting is such that products are more likely to attract adverse than beneficial publicity.

Politics. Changes in government policy could affect market trends. Governments, through their central offices, nationalized companies and local authorities, are the largest buyers of goods and services in most countries and any change in spending patterns by them can influence industrial demand. Further, their fiscal and legislative policies affect the economy in general and industrial markets to differing degrees.

Micro factors

Product innovations. The introduction of a new or revolutionary product into an established market can affect trends. In their time, plastic injection molding hit demand for steel pressings and fabrications, adhesives eroded the mechanical fastenings market, and plastic laminates reduced the demand for decorative natural wood. In most industrial markets, the effect of a product innovation is gradual and over a long time.

Table 3 illustrates the time that it has taken for some now well-accepted products to achieve commercial recognition. Significantly, the time period between invention and commercial development is today only five to six years compared with 30 to 40 years at the beginning of this century.

TABLE 3

*Length of time taken between invention and commercial launch
of selected industrial products*

Product	Discovery	Production	Lag (years)
Acrylic plastics	1901	1933	32
Helicopters	1907	1945	38
Penicillin	1928	1943	15
Xerox	1935	1950	15
Acrylic fibers	1938	1948	10
Cumene-phenol process	1945	1955	10
Microchip	1948	1959	11
Isothalic (paint additive)	1951	1958	7
High-strength carbon fibers	1965	1973	8
Sintered high-speed steel	1972	1979	7

Patterns of use. Over time, users develop new approaches to solving old problems. Sometimes these approaches are aided by a product innovation, sometimes they are the result of natural evolution. The construction industry today makes widespread use of ready mixed concrete, whereas 20 years ago it was the normal practice to mix on site. Machine tools made earlier this century were heavy, cumbersome and made to last 50 years. Today they are built lighter, more suitable for female operation, and have a 15-year life in recognition that anything longer would be surpassed by innovations.

Pricing. A market can be expanded (or contracted) by a price change. The price change may be caused by external influences, such as a raw material cost increase or decrease, or it could be the manufacturer's attempt to widen the appeal of the product by reducing its market price. Oil price rises throughout the 1970s increased the price of plastics and delayed the penetration they will ultimately achieve. On the other hand, price cutting by manufacturers of word processors has increased the market size by widening their appeal to even the smallest companies.

Education. Suppliers of goods and services to a market can choose to develop it by educating potential users through promotional campaigns. The demand for environmental conditioning systems would undoubtedly have been smaller without Colt International's heavy and widespread advertising program which educated managers of factories, shops and offices to its benefits.

How useful are market trends?

The analysis of market trends tells the market researcher which way the demand for a product is moving and so enables him to react to it. This can be in any one of the following ways:

Goal setting
Through an historical analysis of market size coupled with the known sales of a company, the researcher can plot trends in the overall growth or decline of the market and his market share. The projection of market size into the future enables goals to be set for marketing campaigns. Plotting prices over time, perhaps in relation to the hours of service a product gives, may show if there is scope for reducing or increasing price or product performance. Measures of awareness of a company as a supplier and its image over time could provide data for tracking the success of a promotional campaign and setting targets for the future.

Identifying new marketing channels
By plotting the annual sales of a product by type of distribution outlet, a supplier can identify a trend which his own sales should be following. Similarly, a study of the trend in size of the segments using products may show where sales effort should be placed.

Designing new products
A study of how products are used and satisfaction with them could indicate to the researcher if there is an opportunity for modifications or new designs. Examples of the changes taking place across industry are:

At around 90°F, workers evaporate.

| 65°F He's okay. | 72°F He's feeling warm. | 78°F He's hot and bothered. |

| 80°F He can't concentrate. | 85°F He's fading fast. | 90°F He's disappeared. |

It's a sad fact of life that the 'disappearing workers' actually exist in large numbers throughout industry.

If you're in any doubt, try spending an hour or two on the factory floor one sunny afternoon.

Chances are, you'll find that a number of employees aren't to be seen. Of those who are, many will be present in body, but not in spirit.

The reason will hit you full blast the moment you step in the door. It is, quite simply, the hot, sweltering atmosphere caused by bad ventilation.

Overheating and bad ventilation cause productivity to drop like a stone, accident figures to soar, labour relations to sour, and quality control to go out of the window.

What can be done about it? Do what many, many companies are glad they did – give us a ring at Colt.

Not only can we advise you on the best form of ventilation to give your employees healthier, safer and more productive conditions to work in. We can also make sure that any equipment you install won't strain your energy bills.

For example, we can show you how to recycle and cleanse contaminated air instead of expensively replacing it.

We can supply you with fresh air that cools an individual worker rather than a whole factory.

Negative ions to revitalise the atmosphere.

Efficient ventilation to control hazardous fumes from individual operations.

And special low loss ventilators that minimise heat loss when winter comes around.

In fact, all our ventilation schemes will not only do good for your productivity and your employees' morale, but your energy consumption as well.

Write or phone us soon.

Colt ventilation is the one sure way of making a very real problem disappear.

If working conditions are healthy, business is healthy too.

Colt International Ltd (Health and Safety at Work) Havant, Hants.PO9 2LY
Tel: (0705) 451111. Telex: 86219.

A classic advertising campaign by Colt International which does not show the product — it gets to the specifier by illustrating the problems which occur if there is no environmental conditioning system.

AT 80°F, EVEN SHIRLEY WILLIAMS WOULDN'T CARE WHAT POLONIUS SAID TO HAMLET IN ACT III.

The Great Debate rumbles on.

Should we have a core curriculum? Have we, by our emphasis on creativity rather than grammar and spelling, done a disservice to literacy?

The question of what and how we teach our children must obviously be a subject for continuing deliberation. The conditions in which we teach them should never be.

A child sitting in a stuffy, over-heated classroom cannot maintain a proper level of concentration. His mind will wander, and he will either start day-dreaming, or cause trouble.

Research in America and in the UK proves that the productivity of industrial workers is severely affected by rises in temperature.

While a man works best at around 65°F, at 75°F his productivity has fallen by 10%, at 85°F by 20%.

At temperatures above 75°F his accuracy is also impaired, and he is 23% more likely to have an accident.

For a sedentary worker, like a schoolboy, the ideal temperature is probably slightly higher – from 67°F to 73°F.

But increases in that temperature bring about similar decreases in concentration and productivity.

Like the industrial worker, too, overheating will also affect him psychologically.

The industrial worker is more likely to become an absentee, or go on strike.

The schoolboy is more likely to become difficult to control, or even, through boredom, play truant.

Add to that the germ trap a stuffy classroom becomes – teachers catch colds with greater speed and regularity than the average member of the population.

And extend the problem beyond the classroom, to changing rooms, science laboratories and kitchens. And proper ventilation becomes as essential to a school as enough chairs and desks.

Colt have been solving ventilation problems for over 45 years.

The Colt system of ventilation is appropriate to a wide range of buildings – schools, factories, warehouses, shopping precincts, hospitals and prisons.

And it can be operated to provide a safeguard against the effect of fire.

If you are involved in planning ventilation for a new or existing building, or replacing obsolete ventilation, phone or write to Colt now for our free technical advice and comprehensive survey.

After all, we want our schools to make our children "nobler in mind". Not "to sleep, perchance to dream".

Colt International Limited, (Health and Safety at Work), Havant, Hants, PO9 2LY, Havant (0705) 451111. Telex: 86219.

People work better in Colt conditions.

IF THE GOVERNMENT DOESN'T INTERVENE IN BRITISH INDUSTRY, WHO WILL?

Whether you agree with the government's policy or not, one thing is unarguable: industry is being left alone this year.

Where does this leave the man who's trying to run a successful business?

On his own, with a lot of tough decisions to take.

Energy costs will certainly rise.

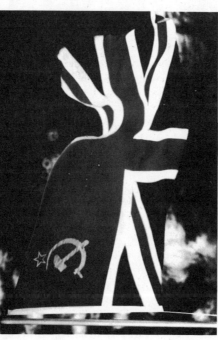

Labour will be even more demanding. Higher productivity will be harder to achieve. Foreign competition isn't going to diminish.

Colt would like to intervene at this time, and offer such men some practical advice.

Have you considered the effect better working conditions can have on both better productivity and profit? On higher wages, too, for both employer and employee?

Colt strongly believe that better ventilation is one excellent way to help industry produce more (and save it a lot of money in the process).

There is an optimum temperature for a man or woman to work in. It's around 65 degrees F.

At 85 degrees F, they will be 20% less productive. At 90 degrees, over 25% less productive.

In addition, too much moisture, or noise, hazardous fumes and gases will cause irritation, aggression, and unnecessary disruption.

We at Colt have been installing ventilation systems in factories and warehouses for about 50 years now, creating healthier, safer and more productive conditions.

The same systems can double to protect your premises in the event of a fire.

Our ventilation equipment, you'll be pleased to know, will also help you breathe more easily over your energy bills.

For example, we can advise you on the efficiency of your heating system and show you how to cleanse and recirculate contaminated warm air without expensively replacing it.

We can remove hazardous fumes from individual working operations.

And install special low-loss ventilators to minimise heat loss in winter time.

If you'd like us to carry out a full, free survey of your premises, why not call on Colt now?

We'll then supply you with a comprehensive report, a quotation, and a 10 years guarantee.

We can even help you with finance – through leasing, advice on taxation advantages and other ways.

There's never been a more critical year for British industry.

If you'd like us to intervene on your behalf, please give us a ring.

Colt International Limited (Health and Safety at Work), Havant, Hampshire, PO9 2LY. Telephone: (0705) 451111. Telex: 86219.

- ☐ an increase in the use of female operatives
- ☐ an increase in the use of robotics
- ☐ an increase in the use of manual aids
- ☐ an increase in the use of safety products
- ☐ an improvement in working conditions (quieter, cleaner, tidier environments)
- ☐ a decrease in the number of hours worked
- ☐ a decrease in the number of staff and operatives required
- ☐ a decrease in the average age of employee (due to earlier retirement)
- ☐ a decrease in planning horizons (due to the problems of looking three years ahead let alone five or ten).

The results of these changes have differing effects depending on the product in question. In general, the pressures will shape the design of new products by making them:

- ☐ lighter
- ☐ faster
- ☐ simpler to use
- ☐ safer
- ☐ quieter
- ☐ cleaner
- ☐ more reliable
- ☐ more aesthetically pleasing.

In addition, there are fewer expectations today (except perhaps in developing countries) for products to last an excessive length of time. Servicing, which once was possible by the user, has become more specialized and it is now growing more acceptable to trade in a broken machine or have it repaired by an appointed agent.

How to carry out trend analysis

Both desk research and fieldwork are widely used in trend analysis.

Desk research

Published data from trade associations or government departments provides the industrial market researcher with sources for an historical picture of demand or production. Care must be taken to ensure the compatibility of data from year to year. A change in methods of classification or the loss or gain of a member to a trade association can affect the comparability of data. Exceptional years can be created by strikes or 53 weeks of trading.

Adjustments should be made to the raw data using judgement or statistical methods to achieve a set of historical data which can be compared from a like base.

Plotting the data on a graph will give an immediate visual impression of the historical trend which itself may be sufficient for the purpose of the study. However, since historical series are nearly always studied as a forerunner to a prediction, some suitable approach must be decided for the forecast — whether this be subjective or objective techniques (see Chapter 26).

Combining historical market size data with company sales gives a picture of market share over time. Projecting market share is of questionable value since share is a synthesis of internal pressures from promotional and sales campaigns and external pressures from the campaigns and sales tactics of competitors. A projection of market share would only have value in illustrating the theoretical eventuality if historical pressures, both internal and external, remained the same, and this is seldom the case.

Fieldwork

Trade associations and government departments cannot always be relied upon for a historical trend of all products and markets. Market researchers often are employed in circumstances where information is not obvious and the marketing prospects for a product or service are uncertain. Although there may be no official published data on the product in question, the researcher may be fortunate in finding two or three companies who are heavily dependent on the product and whose turnovers, extracted from their financial accounts, are reflective of their position in the market as a whole. A strong association between the product under study and one on which there is published data available may also neatly circumvent the absence of market size data on the subject itself, since trends in the associated product will be indicative of those of the subject.

Comparing market size data from past fieldwork surveys is of dubious value as the accuracy of the assessments can seldom be measured and may well have an error of ± 20 per cent. The possibility of such large errors in market sizes which have been assessed at different times makes trend analysis spurious unless the changes have been of a colossal order of magnitude.

Measurements of awareness or image obtained from surveys can be more accurate than market size data as they are responses by individuals on their own knowledge and views. Using large sample sizes (a minimum of 100 responses and preferably 200) repeated studies yield suitable bases for tracking changes.

Depth interviews can be employed to see how respondents use products, what problems they face in that use and how these could be resolved. Answers cannot always be taken at face value. Changes take place over a long period. Employees who move to new positions or even companies after two or three years cannot be expected to identify a long-term structural trend in their use of a product. Trends are often subtle and slow, masked by temporary hiccups which confuse the long-term view.

Only through questioning in depth can the researcher unearth long-term trends.

A prime requirement of industrial market research surveys is to show how companies' consumption of a product has changed historically and how it is expected to change in the future. As well as measuring the past growth or decline in consumption, and asking the respondent for a prediction of his future use, the researcher must study the factors which affect the company's demand. These could vary from changes in output levels of the product which incorporate the subject of study through to substitution by alternative materials or new methods of assembly.

Summary

The analysis of market trends enables the researcher to explain past levels of market size, shares and distribution channels. It helps him to understand what changes are occurring in the use of products and places him in a better position to predict the future.

Market trends are the manifestation of macro factors such as economic and political influences, and micro factors such as technological change, pricing or promotional campaigns.

Market trends are useful to the researcher in setting quantitative goals for market shares or awareness levels. They may point to opportunities within the distribution network or to the need for new product development.

Chapter 5
Information on Customers and Prospects

The importance of knowing the customer/prospect

Marketing is concerned with the profitable satisfaction of consumers' needs. To the industrial market researcher, consumers are any company or person who buys a product or service, not for its own sake, but rather to assist in the ultimate sale of the products or services which he himself sells. In order to sell to an industrial consumer and keep the business long term, a supplier must understand both his needs and his wants — the two are not necessarily the same. A buyer may *want* to buy a small inexpensive photocopier but may *need* a more costly, larger version to cope with his demands.

A depth understanding of the customer plays a role in setting prices as it is what he is prepared to pay, balanced against competitive prices charged by other suppliers, which determine the optimum level. Information from the customer similarly helps determine other parts of the marketing mix — the delivery period, levels of quality, promotional stories, product improvement and new product ideas. It provides an insight into competitors' strengths and weaknesses which, when set against one's own debits and credits, enables tactical plans to be devised.

Information on a consumer only helps understand his needs — but does not in itself get the order. Knowledge of the buying procedures within the consumer company, the roles of the persons involved, their prejudices and bias, becomes a tool which the salesman can use to manipulate the decision to his advantage. With his knowledge the salesman can develop an empathy with his customer or prospect, and so present his product in the most appealing manner. Knowledge or information on customers is, therefore, a means to an end; its value is an aid to winning sales.

Information which can be acquired on customers/prospects

The information which can be obtained on customers or prospects is voluminous and central to most market research studies. It can be classified under three headings:

1. Information available on the organization of a customer

- ☐ The composition and roles of the specifying or purchasing group and the role each member plays
- ☐ The number and location of buying points in the organization
- ☐ Links with other companies whether through ownership or license arrangements
- ☐ The existence and nature of any reciprocal buying practices
- ☐ The nature of any quality approval standards and how suppliers achieve them

2. Information available on the products (or services) bought by a customer

- ☐ The applications for the products which are purchased
- ☐ The volume and value of purchases over a period
- ☐ The historical and future trend in purchases
- ☐ The purchase frequency
- ☐ The specifications and characteristics of the products
- ☐ The prices paid for the products
- ☐ Satisfaction with the products purchased and areas of possible improvement

3. Information available on suppliers to the customer

- ☐ The names and locations of the suppliers
- ☐ The share of business held by each supplier
- ☐ The products on which suppliers concentrate
- ☐ The length of time the supplier has been used
- ☐ The image of and attitudes to suppliers
- ☐ Factors which determine the selection of one supplier in preference to another
- ☐ Factors which will result in a supplier being dropped

There is no limit to the depth of information which could be sought under these headings. For example, every subject could be examined over a period of time and, from this trend, a forecast made of the future. The study of how and why a company makes a decision to choose particular suppliers is complex and may be as much due to subtleties such as a friendship between buyer and salesman as to some more logical influence like price, delivery or quality. Measuring customers' awareness and image of suppliers is another sizeable subject which is often of sufficient importance to merit a dedicated study.

The objectives of a study dictate its depth and breadth. If the purpose of the research is to win new business it should concentrate on how much is bought, what prices are paid and how suppliers are selected. A study which it is hoped will suggest improvements to a product will concentrate on the applications for the products and the satisfaction of the customer with them. Thus, although any information on a consumer is potentially useful, user surveys tend to focus on either image, buying patterns, supplier selection or some similarly narrow subject, for otherwise the subject coverage would be too broad and unwieldy.

How to obtain the information

Simple background information on customers or prospects can be obtained from directories; MacRae's Blue Book or Thomas's are adequate for the address, telephone number and brief description of what the company does. Thomas's provides a breakdown of products made and a description of the management structure. Specialized directories become necessary where a detailed picture is required of product range, subsidiaries, trade names and capital structure.

Large companies are analysed and commented on in the financial press. A general appreciation of a company's well-being can be used to determine the sales attention it receives while specific comments about expansion plans or recent large contracts could be a useful pointer to a salesman of a pending order for him. Press releases in trade journals also provide snippets which help the salesman talk sensibly and knowledgeably to the buying team.

Advertisements by the customer can provide a concealed message to a salesman. A recruitment advert may mention an expansion plan. A promotional message may provide background on how a product is made or give an astute salesman a line on how it could be improved.

Product data sheets and technical literature often give considerable detail on the construction of products, their specification and special features. Stripping down the customer's product itself can reveal what he is buying.

Government statistics, trade association figures or a copy of the company's latest accounts may provide a rough guide to the volume of annual purchases. An announcement in the press by a customer that he has won a contract will spell out his purchase requirements for the next few months.

Desk research can usually provide no more than a useful background to a customer. Detailed information requires a personal approach, usually by telephone or personal interview with observation playing an occasional supportive role. During a visit, sharp eyes can sometimes spot displays of the product range or photographs of important installations in the foyer. A flip through the visitors' book should provide a shortlist of competing suppliers who are already well entrenched, together with the names of the buying/specifying team who are being called on.

The collection of data through discussions with customers, whether over the telephone or face to face, can be structured using a formal questionnaire, or unstructured, guided by a checklist of topic headings. Information can be collected by company researchers or possibly the sales force, or a specially recruited market research agency. The approach depends on the objectives of the study. If the aim is to win one or two large customers it may best be handled by a delegation from the supplier who will be able to build in sales effort at the same time as collecting data. However, an analysis of the market for strategic planning purposes demands the objectivity of trained market researchers. A survey by salesmen may have some dividend in that it trains them to sell by questioning, but it brings with it the dangers of their predilections and the possibility of discord with the buyer.

The choice of telephone interviews or visits as a research technique is a balance determined by cost, speed and the amount of detail that is required. Where depth information and the exploration of attitudes are important, visits are essential, while simple fact collection is well suited to the telephone.

Summary

Information on customers or potential customers enables the market researcher to understand buyers' needs; it therefore ultimately helps his company sell its products or services. A wide range of information can be collected from customers, including data on the organization of the buying function, the products or services which are purchased, and the suppliers who currently enjoy the business.

Simple background data on customers, such as their address and product range, can be easily obtained from desk sources. Greater detail demands a fieldwork program of visits and telephone interviews which can be carried out by the internal staff or a specialist agency, depending on available resources and the objectives of the study.

Chapter 6
Information on Competitors

The importance of knowing the competition

If you are the manager of a successful soccer team drawn to play against a top European side in a vital match, how would you plan your campaign to win the match? Naturally, you would ensure that your men are at the peak of physical condition, but that alone would not be enough. You would need to know as much as possible about the opposing team — their strong and weak points, their characteristic attacking and defensive strategies; you would undoubtedly consider the skills and playing styles of each member of the team separately. You would now be in a position to plan your own game. Your players could be forewarned what to look out for; counter strategies could be worked out in advance. And how would you obtain all this background? You would take the trouble to watch one of their fixtures. You and your team would study videos of their matches. You would call managers of teams you know that have played them. You may go out of your way to get inside information from a player who has recently left the side. All these sources are easily accessible, perfectly legitimate and absolutely essential in order to obtain a competitive advantage.

In industry the competition is no less fierce than on the soccer field and yet companies often act as if they are in isolation. Many can, if pushed, recall the names of their major competitors and possibly tell an anecdote or two about them. A few may keep files in which they collect competitors' brochures and press cuttings. Still fewer, however, produce dossiers on the competition which are regularly updated and contain marketing implications and recommendations for action. Business is about beating the competition for an even larger slice of the cake. This does not mean to say that communications with competitors should be strained and warlike; quite the reverse. Every effort should be made to understand the way the competition ticks and there is no better way of doing this than constant contact with them. (And it is surprising how willing to talk most competitors are!)

Profiling the competition plays an important role in four decision making areas: product planning, setting future strategies, pricing and acquisition policy.

Product planning

In determining the product range, the marketing director needs a detailed knowledge of all the competitors' products and their prices in order that he can make comparisons with his own and determine ways of making improvements. This must, of course, be undertaken in conjunction with the technical and production departments who will wish to say what they think can be produced efficiently, but it must be the marketing department that gives guidelines on what will sell and for how much. Knowledge of the competition's new products before they are launched strengthens every marketing man's arm. This information need not be so difficult to obtain if the sales force is alerted to keep their eyes and ears open for news of products out on test.

Strategic planning

There is no point in drawing up fancy marketing plans which aim to increase market share unless it can be shown where the extra share will come from. An understanding of buying motives is a necessary input in arriving at this judgement but so too is a knowledge of the strengths and weaknesses of the competition.

Pricing policy

This is the one area where most companies have some knowledge of their competitors. There are, nevertheless, problems in making comparisons if heavy discounting takes place or if no price-lists are published. In these circumstances, it is important to treat with caution the glib assertions of buyers that they can buy for 10 per cent less — they are very likely exaggerating the price differential for their own ends.

Acquisition policy

Market share can be built up the long, hard way by fighting the competition or, alternatively, it can be obtained by a company acquisition. Determining which companies are most attractive potential acquisitions needs more information than can be found in financial statements. The image of a competitor in the eyes of the users and the relationship it has with its staff and distributors is equally important as this could materially influence whether or not it is a suitable candidate for a takeover.

Information which can be acquired on competitors

Given an indefinite period of time there is no limit to the information which can be obtained on the competition. Eventually, the researcher will chance upon an ex-employee (his own company may well recruit one) who is prepared to divulge all he knows. Piece by piece a jigsaw can be built up covering the competitor's total operation.

Researchers seldom have the luxury of unlimited time and must, therefore, set out to collect as much information as possible within the set confines. The researcher needs to formalize his search for information and this is helped if he has an advance plan of what information is required.

A number of topics which should be featured in a typical competitor survey are:

Products and turnover
Companies build up product ranges and assemble these into divisions so that the turnover declared in their profit and loss accounts is only a guide and a ceiling to their sales of a particular product range.

The researcher must first establish the breadth and depth of the competitor's product range and then attempt to break down the turnover, by product, for both home trade and exports. Spares often make up a significant proportion of the turnover and these should be separated out.

Performance over time
The turnover of the competitor provides an easily available barometer for measuring sales performance over the years but it is frequently deficient in being too general on those repeated occasions when the product constitutes only a small proportion of total sales. Nevertheless, if a product has consistently had a small share of a company's turnover, this is itself significant and could be an indication of low interest or neglect. Just as turnover can be plotted over time, so too other financial data and trends can be established for exports, profit margins, return on capital, stock turnover, etc. The historical sales performance of the competitor can be related to past market sizes to produce a trend in market shares and thereby illustrate to what extent the company has gained (or lost) strength.

Customers

The competitor profile should seek to include a list of end-user industries and customers so that it becomes evident where the company obtains a large proportion of its business. This analysis will highlight dependency on certain customers and strengths and weaknesses in user sectors. As much detail as possible should be assembled on customers, the type of products they buy, the number of years they have dealt with the supplier and the prices they pay, so that eventually a picture emerges of how the business has been obtained and how it is being nurtured.

Pricing

Price-lists and discount policy should be obtained on each competitor to compare with one's own. If published lists are not available the pricing may have to be pieced together from examples provided by end users.

The timing of price increases and whether they show a tendency to follow a lead or be instigated independently could help in the development of counter offensives.

Delivery

The reliability of competitors' deliveries provides a benchmark against which one's own company can be measured.

Image

The awareness and image of competitors is a standard against which other suppliers can be judged. Image can be assessed as a total view or it can be split into constituent parts such as price, quality, delivery and service.

Promotion

Estimates can be made of the size of competitors' promotional budgets both in terms of media and below the line expenditure. 'Hidden' methods of promotion, such as direct mail, are hard to assess and the researcher may have to be satisfied with a very rough judgement as to the extent of its use. Competitors' exhibition policy is very visible and reasonable estimates can be made as to levels of expenditure on it.

Selling methods

The size and organization of competitors' sales forces should be assessed as this is one of the most powerful tools for achieving marketing success. If additional background on the sales force can be discovered, so much the better. Is the sales force arranged geographically, on products or markets; what is the range of products which is sold by each salesman; what are their call rates; what are the methods and value of remuneration; what is the turnover of sales staff; what are their qualifications?

Company organization and philosophy

The management structure, parentage, filial relationships and any reciprocal buying practices should be logged. Based on the knowledge of competitors' organization and marketing, an attempt should be made to arrive at a statement of business philosophy or what 'makes the company tick'.

Production facilities/capacity

It is usually difficult for an outsider to obtain details of a competitor's production facilities and capacity except by chance. Unless the market researcher has a technical or production background it may be difficult to make little more than a cursory statement on this part of a competitor's activity. For example, determining production capacity depends on the number of shifts which are worked and the number of idle machines which are tolerated during so-called full production.

How to obtain the information

It is not necessary to be devious to obtain information on the competition. Sources abound which are legitimate, cost little to tap and are usually easy to find.

A good starting point is the customer. He constantly receives calls from competitors — some he will be dealing with, others may only be courting him. Only occasionally are buyers reluctant to talk about their suppliers: usually they are more than pleased to discuss them, rightly believing it to be in their best interest to foster competition. Buyers are likely to be among the first to hear of new products; they have free access to competitors' prices, they frequently visit competitors' works and may have seen their production lines in operation. Over a period of time, buyers develop an image of the competition and form views on their strengths and weaknesses.

The biggest problem most managers face in tapping the customer as a source of information is the fear of asking questions. Of course, there is a right and wrong way to do it. Representatives who have built up a good relationship with their customers need to use diplomacy when seeking data on competitors; a brash approach could offend. A formal market research survey is a tried and tested method but clearly it requires a program of interviews and is therefore costly. A sales force that is asked to report regularly on critical questions (see box below) would not perhaps produce the objectivity of an independent survey but it would provide free information and arm the representatives with information helpful in their selling effort.

FOUR QUESTIONS ABOUT COMPETITORS
reps should regularly ask their customers

1. What are their current prices, discounts and offers?
2. What are their deliveries (promised and actual)?
3. What news is there of any new products or services?
4. How does the buyer rate the quality and design of their existing products?

Between companies in a similar industry there is much job mobility — especially in sales, marketing and general management. These people carry with them a wealth of information on competitors — and often they do not realize the depth or significance of their knowledge until it is drawn out of them.

Ex-employees of competitors are very much a hit-and-miss source of data as they may have worked there many years ago and, even within short time-scales, memories can prove unreliable. It is important, therefore, that whenever the opportunity presents itself to talk to an ex-employee, he should be questioned and the data committed to paper.

Customers and ex-employees are valuable sources but they are likely to generate uncoordinated data, not always at a time which suits the researcher. A direct approach to the competitor is well worth a try as long as no aberrant purpose is invented as justification for the study. Competitors are more likely to be helpful than not. They will be eager to learn the depth of the researcher's knowledge and curious as to the purpose of the study. Most will cooperate in the belief that they stand to gain from an exchange of data.

General directories show companies' addresses, product ranges, approximate size (in number of employees) and management structure. There are, however, many hundreds of specialist directories which can be consulted to find the name of the parent and subsidiaries (the *Directory of Corporate Affiliations*), or financial background (Dun & Bradstreet) or specific details on products (one of the many trade directories).

Having established the basics it now becomes necessary to measure the performances of the competition. This requires piecing together financial information from a number of sources. Dun & Bradstreet will provide a search on a private company for a fee. If the company is quoted, it must file a 10-K report with the US Securities and Exchange Commission and this is made available to a researcher on request.

Unless great detail is required from the accounts (as would be necessary for an acquisition study) it is useful to edit the accounts and produce a summary profile showing five years' figures of total sales, exports, net profit and net assets. In this way a trend is obtained of all the key operating statistics and ratios. An estimate of sales in the particular field of interest may provide a measure which can be cross checked against those derived from other sources. It is always worth while studying the accounts in some detail — especially those of earlier years. In a UK survey of the metallic strapping industry, for example, it was found that Textron (in whose accounts are consolidated the Signode strapping division) used to show a breakdown of divisional sales though this practice has now stopped. This early split was unlikely to have changed dramatically and it provided a good point from which estimates could be made of current sales by applying the earlier proportions of the product sales to the most recent turnover.

Financial accounts are an excellent guide to company performance but they suffer from being out of date (two years is not unusual) and they cannot provide that all-important 'feel' for the company. This can often be obtained from a company's sales promotion. Sales promotion is the outside face of a company. It is a reflection as well as an instrument of marketing policy. Aggressive adverts usually indicate aggressive selling methods and ambitious plans. Old fashioned advertisements undoubtedly reflect a 'gin and tonic' low key sales approach. So, too, modern letterheads and logos are more likely to be associated with modern marketing methods than an old-fashioned fussy logo and a letterhead cluttered with membership details of archaic engineering federations.

Take, for example, the series of ads which the pneumatic tool company Desoutter have run for many years on the front page of the British newspaper, the *Daily Telegraph*. They feature a caricature of a man with a handlebar moustache who is supposed to resemble Roger Desoutter, the company's managing director. The ads shout out (but not in words) 'We are a family firm, we pride ourselves on this, we have a reputation to live up to.' Research has shown that this image is being conveyed to the market. Desoutter have a high reputation for good quality and service. Such a feel for a company's marketing policy can be transmitted by any type of promotion — whether letterhead, advertisement, exhibition stand or brochure. An examination of each type of promotion will show the reader how easy it is to obtain a wealth of more specific competitive data — straight from the horse's mouth.

Every marketing man is interested in the size of his competitors' promotional budget — it tells him what he is up against. That part of the campaign which consists of ads in journals or newspapers can be assessed for only a modest expenditure of effort.

Done to a turn.

A bitter lesson from Desoutter.

Productivity in creases.

Telling it like it is. Those Desoutter ads which have occupied the
Daily Telegraph *front solus, from, it seems, time out of mind,*
project the image of a friendly, family run business —
which research has indicated Desoutter to be.

In consumer markets life is made comparatively easy by the publication of media expenditure. This does not cover advertisements in trade and technical publications and, since this is where most industrial ads are placed, it is of little use to the industrial market researcher. Screening the technical media to tot up the number and size of advertisements by the competition is not the onerous task it initially appears. Most industrial products are aimed at selected sectors, and appropriate media which are targeted at these can be identified in the monthly *Standard Rate and Data*. Examining the advertisers' index of a few back numbers of each potential trade journal will confirm whether it is a vehicle for any of the competition's ads. Thereafter, the approximate spend of the campaign can be calculated by applying the rate charge from *Standard Rate and Data* to the size and frequency of insertions (after making an allowance for any series discounts).

No doubt there will be a few omissions resulting from those hidden away in obscure journals. Within the overall scheme of things these hardly matter. The exercise will have rewarded the researcher in telling him:

1. the seriousness of intent of the competitor in promoting his products (indicated by the monetary value of the campaign);
2. the sectors in which his push is taking place (as reflected in the choice of media).

The advertising content itself is worth scrutiny as it is likely to contain valuable data. Ads can variously reveal:

☐ the competitor's product range
☐ the product's claimed technical advantages
☐ the price
☐ the number of products which have ever been sold
☐ the sales of products over a period
☐ the number and location of factories; their size and prospective resources
☐ the position of the supplier in the market place
☐ the number and identity of distributors stocking the product
☐ the R & D support which backed the product
☐ major customers (customers may well be the centrepiece of the ad, as in a testimonial)
☐ methods used to service customers.

Of course, advertisers often exaggerate or even misrepresent their position. Terms such as 'leader' or 'number one' are too vague to be taken literally — they could mean number one or leader in a narrow field of activity. Claims for research and development expenditure which have backed the launch of a product may include man hours valued at current commercial rates rather than actual costs, and in any case such figures are not easily substantiated independently. It is up to the researcher to read behind the ad and piece together as true a picture as is possible.

The most obvious sources of product, service or corporate ads are newspapers, trade journals and directories. The advertising content may well reflect the source. Journal ads attempt to stimulate immediate action as their life is short. Directory ads will be designed with staying power since they will have a shelf life of one or possibly two years. Recruitment ads are often full of information. The position which is being advertised may itself tell a story while the preamble could describe the history of the company, its current position and even its future aspirations.

When a company goes public, it must advertise its prospectus, which can also be obtained from the banker handling the issue. Such advertisements provide a potted history of the company, its sales and financial performance to date, a forecast and a description of the management structure. Researchers cannot hope to be fortunate enough to have a competitor they are profiling go public at the very time they are seeking information; however, knowledge that a company was floated in the last year or so would enable a back issue of a newspaper to be consulted at the library, and much of the material would still have value.

Data sheets, brochures, house journals, service manuals and technical literature very often contain intelligence which is useful to the marketing man. The specification and data on the products will show their performance and enable comparisons to be made with others. Photographs of the factory and cut-away diagrams of the products may provide a clue to the methods used in production. Examples of the products in use, whether as photographs or in the narrative, are likely to reflect those in which the company is strongest; they may even mention customers' names and thereby give an artful competitor a sales lead.

House journals or company newspapers (if you can get hold of them) abound with inside information. News of sales coups, whether intended to boost employee morale or impress prospective customers, may also tell the researcher how well the company is performing, where their sales efforts lie and the extent to which it will be tied up on contracts in the future.

Exhibition stands are fair game for the researcher. On the stand will be the usual array of brochures and data sheets while display photographs may show the market strengths and provide names of customers. The latest products will be on show together with a helpful informant if the researcher is cheeky enough to ask. The exhibition manual should not be ignored. It will contain a collection of ads and write-ups which at the very least will provide a pointer to the principal components of exhibitors' product ranges.

One marketer's successful PR placing is another's source of market intelligence. Unlike ads, whose media schedules have some logic and can therefore be anticipated by the researcher, PR mentions are almost random. Usually, however, the editors of the journals used for the ads find the press releases of relevance and so a search through selective back numbers is rewarding. Diligence is required; but given a thorough search, something useful will undoubtedly be found — even on the most obscure subjects.

There is no central source from which PR mentions can be garnered. However, Predicast, Dow Jones Information Retrieval and Trade and Industry Index handle selective searches for press comments.

Summary

Business is about beating the competition for a larger slice of the cake. It is, therefore, essential to know as much as possible about the competition.

A competitor study should aim to show the company's total turnover broken down by product group, trends over time, major customers, pricing policy, delivery performance, image, promotion, selling methods, company organization and production facilities.

Data on competitors can be obtained from customers, ex-employees and the competitor itself. A variety of desk sources can be used for a quick and inexpensive profiling of the competition. Of great value to the researcher are the advertisements, brochures and press releases put out by the competition.

Part Two:
The uses of market research

Chapter 7
Developing the Marketing Plan

What is a marketing plan?

Every company should have a business or corporate plan — a statement of where it is going and how it intends to get there. A business plan has a number of important elements:

☐ *The marketing plan* which shows what sales and marketing position the company holds now, what it believes it can achieve, where it will be placed in the future market, and the steps it intends to take to accomplish its targets.

☐ *The production plan* which maps out the company's investment intentions in terms of facilities which are required to produce the goods efficiently.

☐ *The finance plan* which shows what funds are necessary, where they will come from and what the fiscal results should be.

Production and finance plans are dependent on the marketing plan as it is the future sales of the company which determine its need for production and financial resources. The price at which those sales can be achieved is a key determinant of the future profitability of the company. The marketing plan must, therefore, be produced before the production and finance plans which are largely derived from it. If the marketing plan is wrong, the production and finance plans will be thrown awry.

The contents of a marketing plan

The time horizon of a marketing plan will be determined by that of the corporate plan of which it is a part. Throughout the 1960s and 1970s five years was the most commonly adopted time period for a plan, which was realistic given the steadier patterns of movement in markets and the economy. In the late 1970s and through the 1980s these patterns became

79

erratic and predictions beyond one, two or three years were difficult to make. Corporate plans still looked forward over the longer term of five to ten years but only took a general view. The detailed marketing plan and sales forecast is now commonly restricted to just three years and is reviewed every year or six months.

A marketing plan would typically contain the following sections:

1. The position of the company now

This is the benchmark from which all targets can be set. In describing the position of a company, it is necessary to show the strengths and weaknesses of all suppliers as these influence the strategies which can be devised. Data on buyers and their reasons for selecting or specifying suppliers, will similarly show how to convert more customers. Most marketing plans should include an analysis of the market and the company covering the following topics:

MARKET BACKGROUND

In this section information is presented which describes the market in which the company operates.

- ☐ A definition of the market and products used within it.
- ☐ An analysis of market size including segments such as product groups, end-user industries, geographical sales.
- ☐ Trends in the market and a prediction of market size (by segment) for the next three years (or the time horizon of the plan).
- ☐ An analysis of the distribution route.
- ☐ An assessment of the competition including their products, market shares, financial performance, marketing strategies and overall strengths and weaknesses.
- ☐ An analysis of the user industries including the identification of buyers, their size, their suppliers and how they make their buying decisions.

COMPANY BACKGROUND

In this section the company itself is described and analysed.

- ☐ The product range and new products under development.
- ☐ A sales history over the last five years by product group.
- ☐ A detailed analysis for the last year showing company sales by product group, end-user market, geographical region, and customer.
- ☐ Trends in company sales by product group, end-user market, region and customer.

☐ Marketing policy including sales organization, pricing, delivery, distribution, promotion.

WHERE THE COMPANY STANDS IN THE MARKET

In this third part of the statement of the position of the company now, the market background and company background are drawn together.

☐ The performance of the company in the market over the last five years.
☐ The strengths and weaknesses of the company by product group, end-user market, region, distribution and customer.

The data on the company and its markets enables the second part of the plan to be constructed.

2. Where the company intends to go

An old marketing adage says, 'If you don't know where you are going, any road will take you there.' The marketing plan should include a statement of where the company wishes to go and around this objective the rest of the plan will hang. It is important that the objective is stated in detail. To say that the company wishes to achieve number one position in a market, for example, is too broad. It needs to be qualified by a time horizon, a market share and target sales figures.

The statement of objectives at the beginning of the marketing plan could therefore be:

'to achieve market leadership in ducted air domestic central heating systems over the next three years. This will require an increase in sales from 7000 to 9000 units per annum and a rise in market share from 20 per cent at present to 25 per cent in three years' time.'

This statement of objectives has encapsulated five important elements:

☐ a description of the product (domestic warm air central heating systems)
☐ a statement of the overall goal (to achieve market leadership)
☐ a specific target to be achieved (9000 units pa)
☐ a time horizon (three years)
☐ a competitive outlook (market share to rise by 5 per cent).

The same five objectives are not essential ingredients in every statement of where a company should go but illustrate the need to be as specific as possible.

3. The company targets

Much of this part of the plan will emerge naturally from the preceding analysis. By relating the company sales to the market it will have been shown where there is evidence of under-performing and where additional sales can be achieved. An appreciation of competitive strengths and weaknesses will facilitate forecasts of trends in market shares, and from these a tentative sales forecast can be obtained. This can now be adjusted to take account of any factors which will further affect the competitive position or market demand, such as an investment in production plant which will provide a lower cost product, or one with improved reliability. The investment may, however, be in marketing, on promotions, extra sales force or a more comprehensive distribution network.

The company targets in this penultimate section of the plan differ from the objectives stated in the second section in detail rather than content. The sales targets may be broken down to show quarterly or even monthly figures; they may be split by representative's area, product group, user market and customer. The rationale for setting the targets must be justified, otherwise there is the danger of setting figures which are wishful thinking or, conversely, unrealistically low.

Besides the key sales targets there will be other marketing targets which must be spelt out. These could be:

☐ *A spreading of the customer base.* If a company is too dependent on a few customers or a narrow market, it may set a target to diversify. As always, this target should be quantified so that it can subsequently be measured and the strategy deemed successful or not. Thus the target could be expressed, 'to achieve over the three-year period no less than three new customers in the aerospace, avionics and electrical sectors with annual sales in each of $100,000, producing an aggregate additional turnover of $300,000 per annum'.

☐ *An increase in awareness.* A high level of awareness in the target market is an important requirement in the build-up of sales.

☐ *An improvement in image.* If a company suffers from a deficiency in any aspect of its image, such as sales service, delivery, product range or pricing, it must set targets to rectify it.

Even though image is subjective it can be converted to a measurement by asking respondents in an interview to attribute a score. As always the targets should be expressed in quantitative terms.

4. How the company intends to get there

The final part of the plan is the most important. It shows the steps which are planned to enable the company to achieve its goals. These steps will not be the same for every company but they could well include:

- ☐ *Product development.* Plans for new products or modifications to existing products with data for testing and launch.
- ☐ *Customer development.* Large customers may justify mini-plans dedicated to increasing the company sales. These can cover improvements in customer service such as more frequent call rates, educational programs for their employees, or special product modifications, etc. There is also likely to be a plan for converting prospects with large potential customers singled out for special attention.
- ☐ *Sales policy.* The targets may only be achievable with a larger sales force or the appointment of new agents. The sales team may have to be altered to include internal sales back-up working over the telephone, and a field force which becomes more heavily involved in servicing large accounts and prospecting.
- ☐ *Distribution policy.* Distribution layers may be introduced into or taken out of the company's sales network. Existing distributors may be pruned or expanded. The role of distributors may be changed, with some specializing in spares and repairs and others in new sales.
- ☐ *Pricing policy.* There are numerous permutations to the pricing strategies which could be invoked. They could focus on discounts, be aimed at selling into distributors, 'loaded' on spares and add-ons, based on contribution rather than total cost, etc.
- ☐ *Promotional policy.* This will be an important part of any plan and should be divided into public relations, advertising, exhibitions, direct mail and other below-the-line activities such as give-aways. The promotional strategy will itself be based on specific objectives already stated in the section on company targets. Typical objectives could be to build up awareness, generate enquiries or educate an audience – each requiring a specially tailored campaign.
- ☐ *Delivery policy.* Although deliveries are the problem of the production section, it is the marketing and sales staff who are responsible for them as they make the promises and are obliged to chase the work through production to ensure that it is on time.
- ☐ *Service and/or servicing policy.* In industrial marketing it is very often the service provided by one company that distinguishes it from another. Responding quickly and efficiently to sales enquiries, complaints and service requests very often determines whether sales are won and customers are kept happy.

The marketing plan, once prepared, submitted and agreed, does not become holy writ. A plan is a map of where the company is going and how it will get there, but intentions may change. A map allows a road

traveller to switch his journey plan if he hears that there is heavy conges-
tion due to road works on a particular day. Similarly, a new product or
price-cutting campaign from a major competitor may demand retaliatory
moves not envisaged in the original plan. The plan should be flexible. It
should be modified to take account of changes in circumstances and in any
case should be reviewed periodically, say every six months, to make adjustments for new objectives or a different environment.

The role of market research in the marketing plan

The division of the marketing plan into its four parts has shown that in
the first section — the position of the company now — a large number of
facts are necessary. It is here that market research is required to show the
size and structure of the market and the strengths and weaknesses of
suppliers. In this application, market research is at its most orthodox
with assessments required of:

- ☐ market size and segments
- ☐ market trends
- ☐ suppliers' shares
- ☐ suppliers' strengths and weaknesses
- ☐ the distribution network
- ☐ end-user market
- ☐ the buying/specifying decision.

The collection of data follows the usual paths for this type of market
assessment and analysis. Desk research and fieldwork will be employed
in differing degrees depending on the published information available.

The market researcher should aim to be involved in more than just
the collection of facts on the market. His training makes him eminently
suited to preparing the analyses of his company's sales and relating these
to the market assessment.

The researcher's role does not stop when the plan is finalized. The
constant changes in demand and supply should be monitored and made
available to the marketing management for their periodic review.

In particular the researcher will be required to monitor the specific
targets which have been set — market shares, awareness and image levels,
for example.

It is debatable whether the market researcher should also be involved in
determining the objectives of the marketing plan, establishing the targets
and designing the strategies which will enable these to be reached. Although
the researcher's views will be sought and valued, the setting of objectives
and strategies is more logically undertaken by the person who will be

responsible for their achievement. In most companies this person will be the marketing manager or marketing director.

Summary

A marketing plan is that part of the wider business plan which states the sales and marketing intentions of a company, its position in the market, the marketing targets and how these will be achieved.

There are four parts to a marketing plan:

1. the position of the company now
2. where the company intends to go
3. the company targets
4. how the company intends to get there.

A marketing plan must be flexible and reviewed periodically in order that it can be modified in line with changes in the environment in which it operates.

The market researcher plays an important role in collecting the factual data which shows the position of the company now. The setting of targets and determination of policies should, however, be the responsibility of marketing management.

Chapter 8
Improving the Competitive Position

What is a competitive position?

Few companies operate in isolation from competitors. Manufacturers of electro-pneumatic hammers such as Kango and Hilti compete on the one hand with each other and on the other with percussion drills, pneumatic drills, and even the humble hammer and chisel. Even the mighty suppliers of telephone services compete with legs, cars, couriers and the mail. It is necessary, therefore, that each supplier of a product or service maintains a competitive position. That is to say, its customers choose to stay with it and potential customers are converted to buy from it instead of some other supplier.

In marketing terms a competitive position does not demand that the company is profitable — though if profitability is consistently inadequate the company is, in the long term, dead. Rather a competitive position implies an ability to hang on to and win market share.

In ensuring that a company maintains a competitive position, the marketing management have to consider the factors which make buyers select a certain supplier and those elements of the marketing mix which help them sell. This chapter focuses on the way a company can manipulate its promotional efforts in order to achieve a competitive advantage. Chapter 9 extends the discussion through an examination of how buyers and specifiers select suppliers.

How suppliers can use promotion to influence their competitive position

Any promotional action a supplier takes which in some way steals a march on a competitor is improving its competitive position. Defining promotion in its widest sense this could include action as varied as taking a potential customer for a meal through to a large media campaign.

Promotion is a pressure which a supplier can bring to bear on the buying decision and, in industrial marketing, it is likely to be one or more of the following types:

Selling

This is by far the most important tool in industrial marketing as it provides the supplier with the opportunity of finding out the needs of the users and adapting his products or services to suit them. Selling by visits is the norm and is justified whenever the buyers' needs are large or complex, or the product on offer is expensive and technical. Telephone sales may well be sufficient for servicing simple products bought on a routine basis.

Above-the-line advertising (in journals, the press and directories)

A wide range of attitudes to the effectiveness of advertising exists among suppliers of industrial products and services. Those supplying specialized goods or services to a narrow range of customers may choose to invest their marketing budget exclusively in a sales force. By contrast, the large office equipment manufacturers face a broad market and need to spend heavily on media advertising to inform their target customers of the rapidly changing products and create a pull of demand for their sales force or their distributors.

Give-away promotions

The limited number of customers supplied by many industrial organizations has traditionally enabled suppliers to give generous presents and mementoes to keep their name at the fore and ingratiate themselves with buyers and specifiers.

Direct mail

Because the customer bases of industrial companies are frequently narrow and easily defined, direct mail has become a much favoured method of promotion.

Brochures

These provide support for salesmen and are used in direct mail campaigns. They give the advertiser the opportunity to describe the benefits of his products and their many features. Even today the quality of industrial brochures is poor, with a tendency to focus on the product and the producer rather than the customer and how the product will help him.

Exhibitions

Trade shows and exhibitions are more important in industrial markets than consumer markets. Professional buyers and specifiers have greater interest, money and time to travel, often some distance, to view a collection of products with which they want and need to be familiar.

Public relations

As with other below-the-line promotional techniques, PR is popular in industrial markets. It is relatively inexpensive compared with media advertising and the large number of specialized trade journals provide excellent vehicles for publicity. Because the press releases appear as editorials in the journals, they carry a note of authority and independence compared with paid-for advertising.

However, controlling what editors print and when and where press releases are published is difficult compared with above-the-line advertising.

Sponsorship

This can vary from boards at football grounds and sportspersons wearing a company's name, through to support of the arts. It is a subtle form of promotion which is successful in building awareness and winning support and respect from the fans of the activity which is being sponsored.

The use of market research in sharpening the competitive position

The marketing methods that have been described are all employed with the ultimate objective of persuading the customer or prospect to buy. They do so by moving the buyer from a state of unawareness through to a decision to purchase the product.

Determining the effect of these many elements of the marketing mix is one of the most difficult tasks of the industrial market researcher. The promotional methods usually require time to achieve a result, and yet, as time passes, buyers' memories become fogged as to how awareness was created and why certain courses of action were taken.

Also, the elements of the marketing mix seldom act in isolation and the buyer cannot distinguish the importance of each factor. Decisions to buy are made in steps or stages as awareness, comprehension, conviction and action are triggered off by the marketing methods. At each step there is an accumulation of promotional capital which is carried on to the next. However, the steps are not usually obvious to the buyer who may not be aware that he is being influenced by the promotion.

Because of the complex interaction of the elements of the marketing mix there are great dangers in asking the buyer directly which sales or promotional approach he prefers or believes is most effective. His view will be coloured by the approach he likes or the one which gives least hassle, rather than that which works best. Market research, therefore, concentrates on recording factual data such as awareness levels, numbers of visits from representatives, etc, and relating these to sales results. This is never straightforward as it is difficult to isolate any one company's attempt to influence the buyer from the activities of its competitors. A dramatic rise in market share may be as much due to the demise of another supplier as to positive action on behalf of the company. However, research which shows a correlation between a promotion and sales becomes useful in forecasting the effect of an increase or decrease in any investment in that method (see also Appendix 1). The relationship is, however, unlikely to be simple. Beyond a certain point there is little extra benefit from increases in the sales force or advertising appropriation. Once awareness levels begin to push 100 per cent, the cost of seeking new prospects exceeds the payback from their purchases.

Research can also be used to determine the best mix of the promotional elements. A survey may show that buyers are spread across a large number of industrial sectors and, as a result, read a wide range of journals reflecting their various interests. A media campaign designed to cover this spectrum would be very costly and could have a low impact. The buyers from these many industries may, however, attend two or three exhibitions each year and they could present a much more cost-effective opportunity of reaching people with a serious interest in the products.

In many industrial markets, products are moved from producer to consumer by a distribution network. Cable for house wiring is sold through electrical wholesalers to electrical contractors. Research has shown that contractors do not specify brands of cable when they order — they will accept anything that is made to a standard. The cable makers can, therefore, gain most competitive advantage by gearing their promotions to the wholesalers whose buying policy determines market share.

Image and its relationship to competitive advantage

Image is how others see us. It is created over time by the promotional process which first generates an awareness among buyers and specifiers and eventually builds up perceptions in their minds. It is obvious, there-fore, that for a company to possess an image, buyers must be aware of them: it is not vital that they should have had experience of the product or company. Although most people have never driven a Rolls Royce, they have heard of it and have formed an image which would influence the likelihood of their buying one should they ever have enough money. Because image is such a strong influence on the propensity to purchase, it is the root of competitive advantage. Out of a good image, sales will grow, higher prices can be charged and profitability and market share will increase. Conversely, a poor image leads to a fall in sales and a decline in profitability and market share.

What is a good image? This depends entirely on what face the management of the company wants to project. Bethlehem Steel may find it advantageous to be seen as a big manufacturer of steel plate. This image of size may place them in a position to compete for very large orders at home and overseas. Small specialist plate mills, on the other hand, may aim to build an image of flexibility: they can handle any sort of plate, in small quantities if need be. To them an image of size would be counter-productive as it would discourage the type of customer they seek: one who requires service and is prepared to pay a premium for it.

It is important that every company should ask themselves what image they wish to project and to whom. The image held by customers is a key factor influencing competitive advantage but it is, of course, possible that a management's chief concern is its image in the City, with employees, or even among the populace around its factory.

Customers and potential customers, being the lifeblood of a company, are the most common targets for image research. Actual customers should be considered separately from potential customers in an analysis of image as they are two very different groups. Actual customers have a first-hand knowledge of the company, its sales presentations, prices, product design, reliability and after-sales service. The image they have of it is likely to be the more accurate since it is born of experience. Potential customers may possess an image which, for all that it is not based on experience, is nevertheless real to them and likely to influence their inclination to buy from a particular company.

Researching image in industrial markets

Image is a relative measurement. Knowing a company's image is useful only against the benchmark of its obvious competitors. If a supplier believes that his company has a good image it may lead to complacency unless he is aware that a competitor has an even better one. It is this knowledge of strengths and weaknesses which makes image research so valuable. Given such information, the marketing team can advise how to improve the company's products and services, they can correct misconceptions about the company, make capital of its strengths and can hit competitors where they are known to be vulnerable.

Image research is only one part of attitudinal research, other elements being measures of awareness and experience. If, for example, one company has a 95 per cent awareness and another only a 20 per cent awareness, the latter is at a relative disadvantage assuming both companies are selling a range of similar products.

A feel for a company's image can be obtained from a qualitative approach such as group discussions or by a precise measurement following an interview program. The qualitative assessment of image can be useful despite the small base of respondents and one perceptive response can synthesize a general view.

Frequently, measures of image are taken to show where a company is positioned. The measurements could be on the total view held of the company or focus on one part of the face it presents — such as the quality of its products, the value for money it offers, its service, etc. Using pictorial scales or scores with numbers, it is possible to provide a figure which measures the image of a company across many dimensions. Surveys of this type repeated some time later allow the researcher to monitor the image and point to any improvement or deterioration.

Summary

A competitive position in marketing is the ability of a supplier to hold or increase its market share. Competitive positions are influenced by how the buyer buys and the seller sells.

Sellers can take aggressive action to win a competitive position by investing in any, some or all of the elements of the marketing mix, namely the sales force, media advertising, give-away promotions, direct mail, brochures, exhibitions, public relations and sponsorship.

Researching the factors which influence the competitive position is made difficult by the interaction of the factors and the build-up in their effect over time. Study of what influences the selection of a supplier is usually carried out by asking buyers to attribute rankings or weights to the factors which they take into consideration during the selection process. Determining the impact of advertising, salesmen, exhibitions and the like is achieved by measures of awareness and recall and, wherever possible, by drawing correlations between appropriation on the promotion with the resultant sales.

Image summarizes a buyer's or potential buyer's view of a company and has an important influence on competitive position. Image research can be qualitative or quantitative. Quantitative measures of image play an important part in showing where a company is positioned against its competitors, and comparisons of findings taken at different times enable the researcher to identify trends.

Chapter 9
Influencing the Buying Decision

The persons who influence the buying decision

Numerous studies have shown that the industrial buying decision is a complex process. It begins on the drawing board when the draughtsmen and designers decide how the product will be made and with which components. Depending on the tightness of the specification, the components may have to be secured from nominated manufacturers. This is especially so with materials used in the construction industry where the designer is a consulting engineer or architect. He takes care to specify details right down to the fasteners as it is he who shoulders the responsibility for the finished building. Similarly, the fabrication of power stations and aircraft is so critical that even the smallest components are specified.

In these circumstances the buying department's role is one of simple procurement from a specified supplier. Their involvement is to negotiate price and delivery and to chase the progress of the order. At other times, and especially where undifferentiated products are involved, the buying department carries more power and responsibility – screening suppliers, negotiating price, and setting up the terms of the order.

Production departments also have their say. They may make recommendations as to whose products and which materials can most easily be worked. They can despecify products by refusing to use or handle materials which give them problems in assembly.

In large organizations, the buying decision may be influenced by special standards departments which evaluate the performance of components and materials and set standards with which suppliers must comply.

The industrial buying decision is at its simplest in a small company. In the extreme example of a proprietor operating alone and making a product of his own design, all the buying and specifying responsibility is vested in one pair of hands. Where production is subcontracted, a company is large, or a product is of a high-tech design, there are likely to be many influences on the buying/specifying decision.

Table 4 summarizes the influences which different departments can have.

TABLE 4

The areas of responsibility of company departments on the buying decision

Department	Area of responsibility
Design/Technical/Standards	Setting standards; specifying suppliers
Production/Maintenance/ Stores	Specifying suppliers; despecifying suppliers; determining delivery requirements; determining order frequency and size
Sales/Marketing	Setting design parameters; specifying materials; setting selling price constraints and therefore manufacturing cost
Finance/Accounts	Approving terms of payment; agreeing budgets
Buying	Screening suppliers; specifying suppliers; negotiating price, delivery, specifications; obtaining quotes; placing orders; chasing progress of orders
Directors	Sanctioning sums for purchasing; approving choice of suppliers; setting buying policy (eg domestic source); setting overall design parameters (ie high quality/high cost or low quality/low cost)

It must be emphasized that the buying process is complex and dynamic and attempts to simplify it, as in table 4, must not be taken as categorical.

The persons involved in the decision-making unit may vary over time. For those companies where material purchases have a significant effect on the prosperity of the business, it is more than likely that the decision to approve a new supplier will be taken at board level. Once 'listed', the routine buying may be passed down to middle management who nevertheless have the discretion to alter the spread of their spend between the various suppliers.

The market researcher must be aware of the different phases in the buying decision in order to decide at what level he pitches his enquiry.

How buyers select suppliers

Using the term 'buyer' in a wide sense to include any person who has a responsibility for selecting a supplier, two buying situations can be recognized:

1. When a company is looking around for a new supplier because it is seeking a better price, quality, delivery, etc, or it is starting production of a new product needing materials which it has never used before.
2. When a company is not looking around for a new supplier but is approached with a new and tempting offer.

These two situations create different responses from the buyer. In the first case, quality may prove the most important factor; in the second, it may be price. This is a gross over-simplification as high quality at ridiculously high prices and with lengthy deliveries would not be tolerated, just as very low prices with cheap quality would not create a temptation to switch suppliers.

Buyers are, therefore, influenced by a package of benefits which the supplier puts before them.

Five factors dominate the buyers' minds. These are service (sales and technical), price, quality, reliable delivery and speedy delivery. Each factor covers a broad range and can be broken down into many component parts. Quality, for example, encompasses reliability, durability, finish and design, while price includes discounts, credit and allowances. If the limitations implicit in the broad headings are accepted, it is possible to compare their relative importance across a number of industrial products and services. Table 5 shows findings taken from a number of surveys in which respondents were asked which factors they considered important when selecting a new supplier.

These surveys were carried out in a period when most firms had underused capacity and, even though some suppliers were prepared to cut prices to obtain work, quality was ranked first almost every time. There are exceptions, of course, and these tend to be where products are undifferentiated, possibly because they are made to a common standard. Reliable delivery follows close behind price as the third most important factor in the buying decision and if the surveys had been carried out in the early 1970s when firms' production resources were stretched to the limit, it may well have been ranked second.

Ranking tells only a part of the story as there is usually a 'distance' between each factor which can vary considerably. This is demonstrated in table 6 where, using the example of an engineering raw material, a substantial gap is seen to exist between quality (ranked first) and reliable delivery (ranked second). Price comes a close third while speedy delivery, technical back-up and sales service lag far behind.

Although quality is important to many industrial buyers who are seeking a new supplier, it may not be paramount if a seller takes the

97

TABLE 5

Factors considered important by decision makers when selecting a new supplier

Rank: 1 = Most important 5 = Least important

Product/Service purchased	Shell castings	Finishing service	Rubber covered rollers	Brush wire	Shelving	Forgings	Sintered components	Investment castings	Luton box vans	Hose reinforcement
Factor required	Rank	Rank	Rank	Rank	Rank	Rank	Rank	Rank	Rank	Rank
Quality	1	1	1	1	3	1	1	1	1	3
Price	2	2	3	3	1	3	3	2	2	2
Reliable delivery	3	3	2	2	4	2	3	3	4	4
Speedy delivery	5	4	4	5	3	4	4	4	3	1
Service	4	5	5	4	5	5	5	5	5	5

TABLE 6
*Distance between factors which are considered important
when selecting a supplier of cold heading steel*

Factor	Factor weight*	Overall rank
Quality	100	1
Reliable delivery	84	2
Price	76	3
Speedy delivery	42	4
Technical back-up	31	5
Sales service	30	6

*All weights are expressed as an index with quality achieving the maximum score of 100.

initiative in an attempt to open a new account, and approaches a company satisfied with its current suppliers. A buyer usually requires an incentive to change his source of supply and, over the last few years, price has been the chief motivation. Table 7 shows that, to buyers of a finishing service, quality was mentioned as the most important factor *when seeking a new supplier*. When these same decision makers were asked which factors would *prompt them to change supplier*, price was most important, although it was often linked with another benefit such as improved quality or delivery.

TABLE 7
Factors which may prompt a change in supplier of a finishing service

Factor	Percentage of companies mentioning factor*
Lower price	71
Improved quality	61
Better deliveries	58
Would not change	3

*The column does not add up to 100 as decision makers may seek more than one benefit.

Still further qualification is needed to show how much lower the price must be and how much better quality and delivery service must be to prompt a change. Continuing with the example of the finishing service, it became clear in the survey that small reductions in price were not enough to result in a change in supplier. The pattern shown in table 8 is, of course, unique to the finishing industry though many other surveys confirm that industrial products are insensitive to discounts of 10 per cent or less.

TABLE 8

Price reductions required to change supplier of finishing service

Percentage reduction	Percentage of companies mentioning reduction
10	27
12.5	14
15	41
20	14
25	5
Total	100

Weighted average: 14.4 per cent reduction

Similar tables could be constructed to show the improvements in quality and delivery required to tempt a buyer to change.

It is not unusual in industrial markets to find that quality is the factor judged to be most important when buyers seek a new supplier on their own initiative and price the prime motivation which stimulates a currently satisfied buyer into making a change. Price cutting, however, has obvious dangers quite apart from the risk of starting a price war. Consider, for example, a product with a 25 per cent profit margin and annual sales of $1,000,000. A cut of 15 per cent off the price requires more than double the turnover to provide the original profit of $250,000 and involves handling two and a half times more goods!

Price cuts of 10 per cent are substantial in industrial markets and it must be reassuring, for existing suppliers at least, to know that most buyers will not change their source of supply unless the discounts are in excess of this. Buyers recognize that cut prices may mean a reduction in service or quality which could jeopardize their own production and profits. By sticking with what they know, decision makers have a measured level of quality, delivery and price which can be built into their production program. A new supplier may promise a better package which, from experience or fear, the buyer thinks may not materialize or be long lasting.

The buyer's chief motivation in selecting a supplier is therefore security — for his company and his job. A relationship builds up between the buyer and supplier and over the years, mutual trust develops. As a result, loyalty in industrial markets is extremely high and many examples exist of companies enjoying a chief supplier status for ten years or more. It is hardly surprising, therefore, that buyers only reject a supplier if they are repeatedly let down.

Research shows that the most frequent reasons claimed for rejecting an established supplier of industrial goods or services are failures to meet delivery and quality specifications — it is seldom price.

How the buying decision is made is one of the most difficult research problems faced by the industrial market researcher. The rational factors which influence the choice of supplier can be identified and measured in the manner described in this section but the importance of emotional influences must not be under-estimated, and are hard to uncover and weigh using straightforward interviewing techniques over the telephone or in structured personal interviews. A high level of inertia exists in buying decisions — it is easier for a buyer to stay with a supplier than change, even though change may be the logical thing to do. Empathy and trust between the buyer and supplier may count for far more than an alternative supplier's promise of lower prices, better quality and faster deliveries.

It is in such circumstances that the market researcher must bring his artistic as well as his scientific approach to the subject to bear. The rational aspects of the buying decision must be studied and weighed up but thereafter it is up to the researcher to superimpose his own knowledge of the market and apply his own interpretation. Evidence does not always fit the facts. Superficially, buyers may say they are prepared to move to new suppliers for better prices and yet history may show that they have stayed loyal to their existing suppliers during periods of price cutting. In these circumstances the researcher may feel it justifies a deeper qualitative study, perhaps using group discussions (Chapter 24) or depth interviews (Chapter 20) to establish the real motivations.

Non-differentiated products and their importance in industrial marketing

Companies that sell raw materials or simple components face a marketing problem — how to give their products recognizable benefits which differentiate them from competitors'. A popular tactic is to cut prices in the belief that this is the principal influence on buyers. The unfortunate result may be a price war, as competitors retaliate to maintain market share. Selling non-differentiated products chiefly on a price-cutting platform can be both economically disastrous and unnecessary.

For most purposes, non-differentiated products can be defined as those which are made to a common standard and where the consumer sees little difference or advantage between them. They are also often, but not always, characterized by a low service requirement, they tend to be purchased regularly, have a minimal superficial design content and a low level of brand loyalty. Perfect examples of non-differentiated goods are commodities which are graded for quality according to agreed international standards. Copper, wheat, cotton and coffee are all non-differentiated products whose prices are determined by supply and demand.

Industrial market researchers are usually interested in products which are one step beyond commodities and are marketed by companies rather than sold at exchange or auctions. The fact that a product is marketed means that an element of service is involved and a degree of differentiation is introduced. The reason for this is obvious: there are few circumstances in which buyers select goods for their own sake and pay no regard to delivery and service. Buyers find it hard to distinguish between a company's image and the product image. Thus, once a product is marketed, it or the company will develop a personality which to a greater or lesser degree can be differentiated from competitors'. For this reason it could be argued that there is no such thing as a non-differentiated product. In the harsh world of reality, however, most marketing men have faced situations where buyers consider the wares before them and claim they are no different from others in the same class.

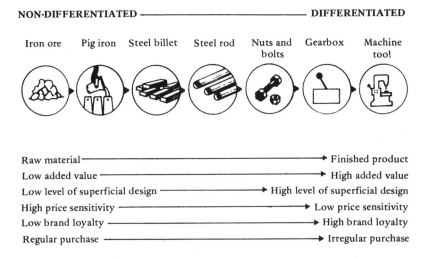

NON-DIFFERENTIATED ———————————————— **DIFFERENTIATED**

| Iron ore | Pig iron | Steel billet | Steel rod | Nuts and bolts | Gearbox | Machine tool |

Raw material ⟶ Finished product
Low added value ⟶ High added value
Low level of superficial design ⟶ High level of superficial design
High price sensitivity ⟶ Low price sensitivity
Low brand loyalty ⟶ High brand loyalty
Regular purchase ⟶ Irregular purchase

DIAGRAM 8
Non-differentiated products in the chain of derived demand

In the eyes of buyers non-differentiated products do exist, and marketing managers must consider every means open to them to avoid competing on price. Diagram 8 illustrates how the level of non-differentiation decreases through the chain of derived demand. At one end of the spectrum iron ore, pig iron, billets and rod are non-differentiated, whereas at the other end, machine tools are quite clearly seen as very different within their own genre.

Influencing the buying decision without competing on price

Manufacturing processes are seldom identical even though the end products appear the same. The first places to look for a differentiating feature are in the raw materials, the processing equipment, utilization of labour, or processing control. Sales pitches are not hard to find if every aspect of the manufacturing process is examined. For example, specially selected steel qualities guarantee uniformity in the manufacture of pressings; modern rolling plant ensures closer tolerance in rod production; a large inspection staff produces goods with fewer rejects. It is especially important in industrial markets to draw the buyer's attention to an element in the company's manufacturing process which suggests that its products are of a higher quality than those produced by competitors.

Decision makers whose job it is to specify which companies' goods should be purchased span a number of disciplines. Technicians are frequently represented in the decision process and they are especially concerned with quality. Professional buyers stake their reputation on their suppliers and so, while more concerned with price than are the technicians, they nevertheless recognize the importance of quality — to them it represents value for money and job security. Even buyers with the largest of purses, such as those employed by the motor vehicle manufacturers, believe it is imperative to obtain components in the right quality and quantity with price ranked third as an influence on their decision.

Product differentiation

The marketer does not need a unique feature in order to differentiate his product from the competition's. Indeed, the feature which is sold to the customer could be imaginary as long as it is seen as a benefit peculiar to that product. Motorists say there is little to choose between the quality of different brands of graded gasoline and yet many oil companies have managed to achieve differentiation with nebulous promises such as National's freedom of the road, Shell's economy and Esso's tiger in the tank. Thus, despite motorists' recognition of gasoline as a standard product, gasoline stations on the freeway, which offer a choice of brands at the same price, show a pecking order with the best advertised brands leading the field and those which are less advertised trailing behind. The moral is simple: look for a selling proposition, spend time and money telling your market why your product is special, and eventually it will become differentiated from its competitors.

This process of building up brand consciousness is well recognized in consumer markets, much less so in industrial sectors. Nevertheless, a few industrial companies have achieved a very high level of product awareness. Most buyers of glass fiber think first of Fiberglass. Steel shelving, aluminium profiles, chemical products and fixings all have their generics. In each case the product is undifferentiated and yet many buyers regularly place orders with these market leaders, despite price cutting by competitors. Buyers are thought to be totally rational in their selection of suppliers, whereas in practice habit, loyalty, security and ignorance plan an important part.

Manufacturers of undifferentiated products are frequently their own worst enemy. In the belief that products are bought chiefly on price, they employ order-takers rather than a professional sales force. The lack of sophistication of the representatives in the field means they are unable to counter pressure exerted by buyers to reduce prices and the result is lost business or a trimming of margins to the bone. Those companies which invest in a high quality, well-trained sales force carry with them an image which rubs off on the product, while their sales ability ensures that business is not lost on price without a fair fight.

There may be an opportunity to differentiate products by making design changes which in no way affect performance. Esso, for example, introduced a blue dye to their kerosene and Aladdin colored theirs pink. These standard products become immediately distinguishable from their competitors'. The scope for changes of this kind in industrial markets is great. Traditional dove grey steel shelving could be brightened by coloring it orange, and would cost no more. Industrial overalls would be more attractive, more noticeable and therefore safer if they were made in distinctive colors.

Differentiating consumer goods through the use of packaging is well understood. Industrial companies should not ignore its many possibilities. The Japanese were quick to identify a problem that faced companies purchasing large coils of steel wire on returnable spools — the normal method of packaging used by UK manufacturers. The traditional spools are large bulky items to manhandle, require expensive storage space and involve both supplier and consumer in much paperwork. Japanese manufacturers designed a lightweight tubular version which reduced transport costs, made handling easier and could be discarded after use.

Service is another common and highly desirable feature which is used to differentiate products and companies. Buyers select a package when they opt for a supplier, and one element is service. This is often given a low score when buyers are asked its ranking of importance in the decision-making process.

However, service is taken for granted and is only noticed or appreciated when things go wrong. Service is a broad concept but in reality it describes the ability and willingness of a supplier to bend over backwards to help. It includes the speed and efficiency of sales staff in dealing with enquiries and orders, delivery performance and the supply of technical help, should this be required. The possibilities of differentiating products by selling service are endless.

A manufacturer of chain link fencing instigated a programme of back-selling to local authorities as a service to his distributors with a resultant increase in sales and customer goodwill. A fiberboard supplier held one-day seminars in numerous cities to educate his customers in the technicalities of the product's manufacture and also to raise its image.

Industrial products are seldom totally undifferentiated. Buyers choose suppliers after considering the complete package offered to them, and even then many decisions are made on emotional grounds. Suppliers of undifferentiated goods need not compete on price, although at first glance it would appear this is the key motivation influencing the buyer's choice of brand. An examination of the buying decision shows that there are many alternatives open to marketers before resorting to price cuts. Diagram 9 summarizes these options.

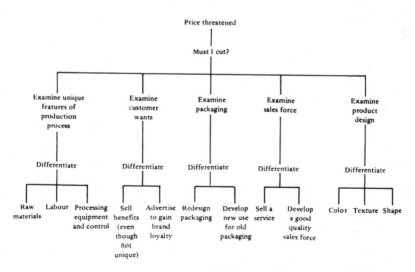

DIAGRAM 9

Product differentiation as an alternative to price cutting

Summary

Industrial buying decisions invariably involve more than one department and frequently there are three.

When a company seeks a new supplier it often considers quality to be of overriding importance. However, if a supplier wishes to break into a new account, it must offer an inducement and this usually has to include a lower price. Price cuts under 10 per cent may well be ineffective.

Many industrial suppliers produce goods to a standard and their products are undifferentiated. Traditionally, suppliers of undifferentiated goods compete on price. There are, however, many alternatives to price cutting by focusing on unique aspects of the production process, promotion, examining the packaging, selling service or cosmetically modifying the product's design.

Chapter 10

Evaluating New Products and Services

What are new products and services?

Innovations are the growth force in any company. A failure to innovate is often associated with the demise of a company or industry. The British machine tool industry made their products like tanks but they lacked the sophistication of other European and Japanese products which bristled with gadgetry even though they had only a mere 10 to 15 years' life. Buyers of machine tools welcomed the benefits of the innovations and, as they wrote the tools off in 10 years or less, saw no disadvantage in their shorter life. The British companies which survived the widespread collapse of the industry were those that responded to the competition by meeting or beating their designs.

Innovation brings improvements — to efficiency, reliability, service-ability, utility and appearance. Occasionally the pressure to launch a new product as fast as possible results in teething troubles which create scepticism.

In the construction industry, the architects and consultants who specify building components are understandably cautious about new products. Failures in construction are lethal and very public. On the other hand, fashion designers who specify materials for clothes can afford to be more adventurous with new materials and processes since, for them, a failure could be quickly rectified with no loss of life, and at the worst a dent to their reputation.

Three classes of innovation can be recognized in industrial markets:

1. Modifications to existing products or services

Commercial vehicle manufacturers seldom launch a new chassis and engine together. They believe it better to move their customers forward in smaller steps, building up trust in one feature at a time.

Most industrial innovations are of this type. They are modifications to existing products rather than completely new revolutionary ideas and occur so frequently they are hardly noticed by customers. They may involve a change in layout which makes a product easier to handle, a faster and more powerful motor, faster warm-up times, a lighter and smaller construction. They are the type of improvement which manufacturers customarily build into their products each year for their new model launch. The basic construction of the product remains the same. The customer can, therefore, easily focus on the improvements and adjust to them in the knowledge that the fundamentals are unchanged. As a result, these small changes are easily related to and are the factors which manufacturers have used to win reputations for being progressive.

2. Innovations which are substitutions

Some new products are direct replacements for ones long established. Automatic stapling replaces nails, adhesives replace both. Plastics have taken over from metal in many car components, especially in interior and exterior trim.

Equipment to produce lettering for artwork has seen the substitution of quills and dip pens to special mapping pens through to instant lettering (diagram 10).

In some cases substitution is straightforward with no gain or loss of benefit. Glass produced by the float glass method made a fortune for Pilkingtons but, to the consumer, the difference in the finished product was hard to distinguish. Plastic knobs instead of metal knobs, synthetic instead of natural fibers, are all substitutes where the effect on the end user is marginal.

There are some differences in the application or use of the product resulting from the innovations but the consumer finds them easy to adjust to as, functionally, the old and new products are similar. Because the consumer sees relatively little change, it is easier to predict the future potential for the innovation. Respondents can evaluate the innovation and confirm its acceptability. They can give a view on their willingness to buy it, given guidelines on the new price, delivery and consistency of quality.

Substitution, though in theory a simple matter, can, for many reasons, take a number of years in industrial markets. Loyalty is strong to suppliers of the traditional products who may stem their loss of sales with aggressive marketing policies. On occasions, the replacement of an old product by a new one may make machines redundant and require changes in manufacturing practices which have been inbred over many years. From the date a buyer becomes aware of an industrial innovation, capable of simple substitution for another product without any snags, at least one year is required for a significant level of penetration to be made. More typically, the substitution period in industrial markets could be between three and five years.

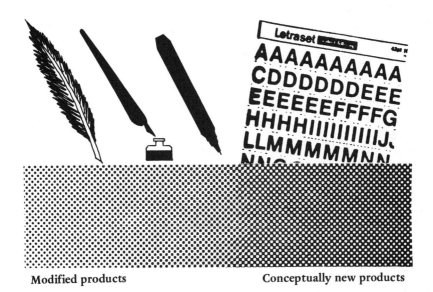

Modified products   **Conceptually new products**

DIAGRAM 10
Innovation by substitution in artwork lettering

3. Innovations which are conceptually new

Revolutionary designs or new concepts are what most people associate with innovations. These are the innovations which most often fail and yet, when they are successful, are the most remarkable: the Xerox process, the jet engine, the microchip, penicillin. When they were invented the true potential could not be envisaged as the user must first experience the products, enjoy the benefits and allow demand to be created, and this takes time. Thus, conceptually new products take a long time to reach commercial take-off.

Acrylic plastics, discovered in 1901, took 30 years to reach the production stage. Steel fibers for reinforcing concrete have still made little penetration, despite the fact that they have been marketed for several years and were discovered in the early 1960s. Carbon fibers, invented in 1965 and brought to production in the 1970s, seem still to be many years

away from making a significant impact in industrial markets. As a general-
ization, industrial innovations which are totally new in concept are likely
to have at least a five-year time lag between invention and initial production
and possibly the same lapse of time again before sales build up to commercial levels. The time period is, however, getting shorter as development
programs are speeded up with more sophisticated testing equipment.
Also it differs considerably from product to product. In the electronics
sector, innovations are expected and eagerly awaited, whereas in engine
design, users are likely to respond more cautiously.

The role of market research in evaluating conceptually new products

Some would argue that success in business is dependent on the ability to
innovate; so too is that success dependent on the ability to avoid launching
innovations which fail. The cost of failure comes high given the large
expenditure on research and development, plant and promotions needed
to bring a product to market. Any technique which can be used to reduce
the chance of failure is, therefore, to be welcomed. Market research is
often sought as such a tool and yet is criticized just as frequently for its
inability to provide adequate answers.

Market research faces a number of problems in assessing the potential
for innovations. There are the built-in prejudices and fears of the researcher
himself on whose judgement may depend a colossal investment. He recognizes the inadequacies of the tools at his disposal, he may lack the
confidence to make recommendations on his vague interpretations and
play safe by writing a damning report or one that is over-cautious. It is
hardly surprising, therefore, that of three consultants commissioned
independently to research the future for an early model Xerox copier,
two were against the launch and the third forecast sales of 8000 units over
six years. Xerox ignored the advice, launched the copier and within three
years installed 80,000 units.

The research failed because the users who were asked for their opinion
did not know how they would react. Nor could they be expected to know
until they had experienced the promotion and the product. With conceptually new products, potential buyers need educating and their imagin-
ations need firing. This is a process of conditioning which cannot usually
be speeded up. A presentation of a new product and its benefits in depth
interviews or group discussions provides insufficient time for respondents
to adjust to it and decide whether or not they would buy.

Researching conceptually new products must, therefore, be highly
interpretative. The researcher has to consider all aspects of how the

potential buyer operates at present. He attempts to uncover any problems that exist in the user's *modus operandi*, how he costs his products and the extent to which he recognizes the limitations of his current practices. The researcher can then relate the innovation to the environment and rationalize the extent to which it could fit into it. It is, therefore, the researcher and not necessarily the potential buyer who identifies the latent demand (though the buyer may be asked for his comments as one element of the research input).

Assessing the future demand for industrial innovations is particularly hazardous for two reasons. First, a high level of perspicacity is required on the part of the researcher, and as a result the findings are open to the very obvious possibility of human error.

Second, because innovations take such a long time to reach commercial fruition, the demand environment, competitive products or even the innovation itself may be modified beyond recognition by the time it comes to market. It would therefore be unrealistic for the researcher to make a narrow prediction as to the future demand. More realistically, the forecast should be much qualified and demand levels given between minimum and maximum bands. The lack of precision need not detract from the value of the exercise. Because the researcher takes a critical, rational and unbiased view of the future for the innovations, the risks in developing the market will be minimized.

The role of market research in assessing modified or substitute products

When an industrial product is improved, it is launched as a new product. Assessing the demand for such improvements is relatively simple compared with that for new concepts. The improvements can be clearly understood by the respondents and they can make assessments as to how useful or otherwise they will be. These assessments can be converted into measurements by questioning target buyers on the likelihood of their buying a product with the proposed features or their willingness to pay a specified premium for it.

Researching the demand for new products which are substitutes has its own problems. It is possible to study the demand for the established product but it is the determination of the rate at which the innovation will replace this product which presents uncertainty. The rate of substitution is as dependent on promotion and sales effort as it is on price incentives or other product benefits. Customs, practices and investments in plant which are dedicated to using the old product may have to be scrapped or changed. Labour may have to be shed. A good idea can, as a result, be more slowly accepted than logic would suggest. The researcher must estimate these substitution levels based on his understanding of the barriers which are faced.

Very often, new products are launched across the world at different times. Silicone foam used to plug holes around pipes in nuclear power stations was introduced in the USA in the early 1970s and came to mainland Europe in the late 1970s. The growth in demand in these territories provided a test market or model which researchers could use to predict demand in the UK. Products do not always travel, however. The front-loader waste disposal truck which lifts bins above the cab to empty through a hole in the top of the vehicle has long been established as the standard refuse truck in the States. It is unacceptable in Europe, except in specialized applications, as the narrower streets and tight access to city centres favour the shorter rear-loading dust-carts.

Though most market research cannot produce new ideas out of a hat, there are formal approaches which, over time, will generate suggestions for innovations.

Customers are a fertile source of new ideas. They use the products and suffer their inadequacies often to the point where they make their own modifications to improve them. Regular contact with customers, especially feedback from trained sales engineers, is perhaps the best source of new ideas. A product improvement which is developed in collaboration with the customer has the added advantage of locking him in as the two companies work together and a specification is drawn up which favours the entrenched supplier. The use of sales engineers in generating new product ideas will only work if it is given the constant encouragement of management. It will not work as a one-off exercise for, as already stated, innovations usually occur at the end of a lengthy period of technical development.

Competitors too can stimulate new product ideas. Companies so often fall into a routine, resulting in designs and production methods which are seldom challenged. The examination of a competitor's product and internal questioning by the technicians who strip it down and analyse it may beget new ideas. It is important that the technicians have an open mind, are prepared to criticize their own practices and accept that there is almost certainly a better way of making their product.

Summary

In order to grow, companies need to innovate. Innovation is accompanied by a high risk of failure.

Innovations, whether products or services, can be simple modifications or something conceptually brand new.

Innovations which are conceptually new are difficult to research as potential users need time to gain awareness and experience. Consumers' reluctance to change and researchers' in-built caution can produce negative results. Research into conceptually new products should study the environment in which they will be used and findings are thereafter determined by interpretation.

Researching the demand for *modified products* can employ conventional interviewing techniques during which potential customers evaluate the new features while recognizing that the fundamentals of the design remain the same.

Researching an innovation which is a *substitute* for a product already on the market is best carried out by assessing the demand for the established product and predicting the rate and ultimate degree of substitution.

Occasionally, the earlier launch of a new product in another country can provide a model of the likely growth pattern elsewhere.

Chapter 11

Making Promotions Work Harder

The industrial promotional mix

Promotions in the context of this chapter are any paid form of non-personal presentation of goods or services by a company.

Industrial promotions are usually a very mixed bag. Budgets are small in comparison with those for consumer products and they are often controlled on a part-time basis by a sales or marketing manager who shoulders many other responsibilities. The result is messy, unprofessional and wasteful. Table 9 lists 11 commonly used types of promotion from which the industrial marketing man can choose.

Though each type of promotion may have a specific role (such as awareness or image building) the ultimate purpose is to help the company sell its goods or services. Some promotions are directly aimed at the financial markets to bolster share prices, to fight or defend a takeover, or they may simply be as a matter of public record only. These are highly specialized and rarely involve the industrial market researchers.

The promotional task is, therefore, aimed at transmitting information, creating an awareness and an interest, finally resulting in a desire to buy (see diagram 11).

In practice, no single promotion works in isolation and each type, including selling, should be part of a grand design in which one reinforces the other.

Though the ultimate aim of promotion is to sell goods or services, there may be a number of short-term aims. These could be to:

1. build awareness of a company or brand
2. build a certain image
3. inform and educate
4. build brand loyalty
5. stimulate enquiries
6. stimulate orders.

115

TABLE 9

Eleven types of industrial promotion

Type of industrial promotion	Where used
Media advertising (press, radio or TV)	Suitable for image building, or where education or supportive messages must be conveyed to large, diverse audiences. Ephemeral.
Trade journals	Suitable for building awareness, image, and stimulating a response among specialized groups. Ephemeral.
Directories	Suitable for educating and building awareness over the long term, again usually to specific industry groups.
Direct mail	Suitable for converting customers by aiming at key individuals in selected companies and industries. Ephemeral, with a longer-term effect where mail shots are filed by the recipient.
Public relations	Suitable for image building in narrow or broad sectors. Ephemeral.
Exhibitions	Suitable for educating and converting customers within a specific industry. Ephemeral, but some long-term effect from directories and literature.
Brochures/sales literature	Suitable for educating and converting customers. Ephemeral and long-term influence.
Give-aways	Suitable for cementing relationships. Longer-term effect, especially with diaries, pens, calendars, clocks, etc.
Sponsorship	Suitable for building awareness and image building. Long-term effect.
Audio visual	Suitable for educating and converting customers. Ephemeral.
Competitions	Suitable for creating interest and awareness and converting customers. Ephemeral.

Unaware   Aware   Comprehension

Conviction   Action

DIAGRAM 11
The role of advertising on the buyer/specifier

Every promotional plan should have one or more promotional goals. Further, each goal should have a target which is expressed quantitatively. Without a measured objective, it is not possible to state whether the promotion has been successful or not. Setting targets for promotions when no benchmarks exist presents a real problem, as the actual results could be way off beam and so disappoint or create false euphoria. Even so, it is preferable to set some quantifiable target than to launch a campaign with no measurable objective.

The relationship between promotion and sales

Industrial companies generally use a mix of different types of promotion which can make it difficult to determine the impact of any one element on sales volume.

The relationship needs proving under test conditions. One promotional variable is altered in a geographical area and compared with a control area where that variable is kept at a known constant or zero. The sales performance over the period of the campaign can then be compared between the two areas and a correlation can be established with sales.

This approach is possible in industrial markets where products are sold to a large number of consumers — cable to electricians, cement to builders, copying paper to offices. It cannot be applied to markets where there are a small number of buyers — heavy cranes, large machine tools, petro-

117

chemical plant, or where the media used are national rather than local. Even where the product and user industries lend themselves to test marketing, other influences can have an effect which, as much as possible, should be taken into account. Retaliatory action from competitors is perhaps the most serious interference factor but others could include local holidays or strikes.

Research to provide promotional messages

Industrial advertising all too often focuses on the seller and his product. It shows pictures of the factory, the production process and the product. Research has repeatedly shown that buyers are not interested in these for their own sake — they want to know what benefits they will obtain if they buy the product. They want to be assured that if they do buy the product it will prove reliable and be backed by excellent service. Pictures of the product, the factory and the process do not convey that message. Detailed performance tables and a description of the product's features may help, but they should be reinforced by a seductive presentation of benefits.

Market research can provide useful advertising platforms for the creative team. Most usually this data is obtained from depth interviews or group discussions with users which probe why they buy products and what they expect from them.

Research to isolate the media for a campaign

Media planning is concerned with the selection of newspapers, journals, television and radio as sources for promotions. The aim of the media planner is to make a selection which achieves the greatest impact for the budget.

In consumer marketing, media planning has reached a high level of sophistication with the press, TV and radio providing potential advertisers with a detailed breakdown of their audiences. There is no similar data for industrial media. Some journals have small circulations but high readership; some are free issue; some are aimed at narrow markets and some at specific job functions. Controversy is often associated with claimed figures for readership as journals may be received but not read.

Market researchers can design surveys to question buyers and specifiers on their readership, viewing and listening patterns and this can help in planning where to spread the appropriation.

It can also present the planner with dilemmas, as the buyers/specifiers may be exposed to many journals and papers with no single one reaching more than 10 to 15 per cent of the target audience. The decision must then be made as to whether the appropriation is spread thinly across a wide range of titles or concentrated in just a few. Almost always the decision to concentrate promotion is the right one as this results in repetitive exposure and only in this way can promotional capital be built up. Awareness grows, recognition is achieved and finally, conviction and action take place. The best time to advertise is at the beginning of a buying season, not in the middle of a seasonally quiet period. Research can be used to pinpoint the optimum time to launch a promotion by studying the buying patterns in the market.

Research to show the impact of different types of promotion

The problems of selecting media for a campaign are greater in industrial promotions than in consumer campaigns. So too is the problem of choosing between the different available elements of the marketing mix. These vary from promotions in journals to direct mail, personal selling or exhibitions.

Research can be used to question buyers and specifiers to show the extent to which they have visited exhibitions, read journals, referred to brochures and attended sponsored events. Such studies will as much reflect the efforts which the sellers have put behind each type of promotion as their potential impact. If people do not attend exhibitions, it may be because no suitable or convenient ones are held rather than because they are ineffective.

Research to test advertisements

Before advertisements or brochures are launched, they can be tested to determine their effectiveness. Ads can, for example, be tested to show their impact, clarity and durability by measuring how easily they are noted among competing text and ads, the level of comprehension of the message and the degree of retention of that message.

TV campaigns can be tested by showing respondents graphics in the form of a story board or a cartoon style film which forms the basis of the envisaged ad. Ads and brochures can be mocked up and tested on their own (say, for comprehension and retention) or mixed with others (for impact).

The testing of ads is carried out by direct observation and questioning – showing the respondent the ad and measuring his awareness (visually or with a blink meter) and discussing his associations and empathy with it, his understanding, recall, likes and dislikes. The interviewing can be individually or in groups. Groups play an important role in advertising research, especially in the study of motivations, but they may not be suitable if the respondents need to be kept isolated in order to obtain individual views untarnished by any interaction.

Research to test the effectiveness of promotional campaigns

Earlier in this chapter it has been shown how the effectiveness of promotions can be tested by comparing two geographical areas in which one is held as a control. Another approach is to carry out studies before the promotion and after it to measure the effect it has had. This is referred to as pre- and post-advertising research and is used to show shifts in awareness, attitudes and action among the target audience.

In industrial market research this type of study is only applicable where the target audience is large and the promotion is judged sufficient to create a significant impact. One-off or limited advertising would not justify measurement and in any case is unlikely to have an effect which can be measured. Usually, a campaign which is worthy of measurement will be sustained for two months or more, with sufficient time and exposure to have had a repetitive effect.

Great care must be taken with the sample construction and its size in a pre- and post-advertising study. If the sample in the first study consists of a certain number of respondents selected from specific industry groups, the second sample should be similarly split. The actual respondents, however, should not be the same, as the very fact that they have already been interviewed will have conditioned them, perhaps to look more closely and be more critical of adverts in the forthcoming period.

The number of respondents in the pre- and post-studies must be sufficient to produce results which have statistical significance as otherwise a shift in response could well be a sampling quirk. Two hundred interviews is a reasonable size for each study but it should not be much less. The interviewing can be by telephone or, if visuals need to be shown, it must be personal. The size of the sample and the need to carry out two batches of interviewing make pre- and post-advertising tests expensive.

Attempts to save on the research budget, or simply because time precludes a pre-test study, can lead to a single research exercise after the promotion. Post-advertising studies can generate useful and interesting data on why the buying decision was made, where adverts were seen, what was remembered, awareness levels and attitudes to suppliers. Unless they are preceded by an earlier study they cannot, of course, show shifts in awareness or buying intentions as no pre-campaign benchmarks exist.

To that extent, therefore, they cannot be used as objective measures of effectiveness.

Promotions which test themselves

For most individual products, advertising is too insignificant to make the testing of it worth while. In any case, many advertisements are designed to elicit a response and here they test themselves. Enquiry cards which are returned from promotions in trade journals or clipped coupons from the adverts provide a measure of whether the advertising is working and where the response is best. A greater response from a certain journal or class of respondent could provide a pointer as to how the future advertising could be sharpened.

Direct mail is widely used in industrial marketing because it can be aimed at selected respondents in an industry and also because it allows the facility to enclose a pre-paid card which is returned as a sales lead. The cards provide marketing information useful in its own right, such as which sectors or lists achieve the best response. After the card has been followed up, a further analysis may show which sectors generate the highest conversions.

Competitions are another promotion which produce a response that indicates its effectiveness as a pull and as a novel means of building up awareness and market share. Unfortunately, the response to competitions is not always a true indication of their success, as is illustrated by a short case history.

A manufacturer of barbed wire and field fencing once faced a new season with warehouses full of his products. He reviewed the strategies open to him. These were fairly restricted in his particular market since:

1. All fencing is made to a British Standard and there is little difference in quality or design between the products of the three major UK manufacturers;
2. The objective is to sell as much as possible to the key distributors (who sell on to small agricultural merchants, who in turn supply the farmer).

The manufacturer could increase his distributors' discounts but this might provoke retaliation from competitors and thus lower profits. He could step up his salesmen's efforts, though in practice they were doing all they could, and excessive pressure in this genteel market might boomerang.

He finally decided to differentiate and promote his product by offering a prize to the farmer who best completed a simple competition; there was another prize for the merchant who sold the lucky winner the fencing.

Access to the competition could be gained only by enclosing a label from one of the fencing products along with the entry form. The advertising agency's views were sought and they checked out the idea with *Farmers Weekly*. There appeared to be no doubt about it, farmers were suckers for competitions. The idea had to be a good one.

The promotion was launched with cut-out entry forms in *Farmers Weekly* and loose forms available from the agricultural merchants. Sales to distributors rocketed — at last they had something different to sell. The agricultural merchants sold the fencing out to farmers, and without doubt the campaign was a great success. It had achieved the objective of building up market share.

Unfortunately, the story doesn't end there. The ads had worked, but could they have worked harder? The company's advertising manager certainly thought so: fewer than 100 farmers actually entered the competition — yet *Farmers Weekly* sells (in the UK) 128,000 copies a week. And a few weeks earlier it had carried a competition which, with a smaller budget, had generated thousands of entries. In an attempt to get to the bottom of the mystery he commissioned some market research.

The findings were revealing. The prize for the successful competitor was a Mediterranean holiday for two. Farmers, with a year-round work-load, saw the prize as a disincentive and did not enter. They had, nevertheless, bought the fencing because it was easily available from the merchants; and their awareness of the fencing manufacturer and his brands had been raised. They had at least read the advertising copy.

Nevertheless, the increased market share that had been gained clearly owed more to push by the distributors, who had stocked up, than to the pull of direct demand by farmers. A more attractive prize would have yielded more entries, and hence a still larger increase in sales and market share.

With hindsight, the reason for the competition's failure to draw a satisfactory response appears obvious. At the time the choice of a prize was being considered, however, it seemed a good idea to offer the farmer a chance to get away from it all. None of the many experts involved in designing the campaign was aware of the pitfall because at no stage did any of them consult the farmer.

Summary

Industrial advertisers usually work with small promotional budgets which they spread across many different types of promotion. The selection of promotion is usually by judgement based on past experience.

Market research can be used to sharpen the effectiveness of the promotional spending by showing which messages have impact and which media should contain most of the spend. Where advertising budgets are large, market research can be used to test the ads prior to publication. Research studies before and after an advertising campaign will show shifts in awareness, attitudes to the product and supplier and buying intentions. The effectiveness of advertising can also be determined if it is possible to compare sales between two areas where one has had a campaign and one has not.

In many cases, industrial advertisers choose methods of promotion which test themselves, such as coupon responses, direct mail or competitions.

Chapter 12
Guiding Acquisitions and Investment Policy

The traditional approach to acquisitions

The sizeable sums involved in acquisitions, and the dire implications they have on a company's future, demand that these decisions be in the hands of the board of directors. The chairman plays a leading role, assuming a high level of responsibility for directional changes, group growth and corporate strategy.

A decision by a company to expand through acquisition usually takes it into discussions with its merchant bank who search for candidates. A portfolio of financial and background information is assembled on each acquisition to guide the deliberations. Visits by senior directors of the suitor company take place to look over the works and gain a view of the effectiveness with which the company is managed. Through the shrewd experience of the acquisition team, a decision is made as to whether the company would be suitable and a bid is proffered.

The weakness of this traditional approach to acquisition strategy is the relatively small emphasis given to the company's market position. The production resources are there to touch and observe; the finances are documented and can be plotted and analysed. Customer lists are sometimes made available if the acquisition believes that to do so will help the sale.

Nevertheless, the possibility of the deal not going through makes management at the acquisition company understandably taciturn about too high a level of disclosure. This means that acquisitions usually proceed with little knowledge of the customers, the marketing philosophy and the company's standing in the market. Acquisitions are made with only a cursory understanding of the company's market strengths and weaknesses and yet it is these which have most influence on its future. Outdated machinery can be replaced, new sources of finance can be found but a bad image, a narrow customer base or a poor distribution network can take a long time and much management effort to rectify.

The role of market research in acquisition studies

Market research has three roles to play in acquisition studies:

1. identifying areas of opportunity and companies within them;
2. screening potential acquisitions;
3. in-depth studies of nominated acquisitions.

In the first of these capacities, market researchers require some limits within which to work. These may be geographical, products or industries. A fine balance must take place between a brief that is too wide and, therefore, in danger of spreading the research effort too thinly, and one which is too narrow, in which case the researchers are harnessed, perhaps at the expense of finding opportunities on wider horizons.

In general, however, the tighter brief proves the easier to handle. A more fruitful result can be expected from a brief which requires the researchers 'to examine the opportunities in engineering companies servicing US petrochemical installations' than one which says 'to examine the opportunities in industrial servicing in the US'. The latter gives the researcher some direction but not enough. The subject of his studies would in this case encompass services as wide apart as catering and consultancy. If an engineering company seeks an acquisition in a business where it has some understanding, it is unlikely to be interested in industrial catering. Even within the narrower definition which specifies the engineering industry, the scope for the researchers would be wide, involving leak sealing, valve lapping, fire protection, pipe installation, etc. The search for opportunities may produce acquisitions with high market shares, strong management teams, good growth and profit prospects or new products. Because the term 'opportunity' within the brief is broad, it may be advisable to narrow the definition down to just one of these favourable conditions. In this way a screen is applied which eliminates all companies which do not meet the acquisition profile.

Shortlisting acquisitions by screening is made difficult if the screening factor needs detailed or privileged knowledge. If, for example, the screening factor were to eliminate all companies with a lawsuit against them, it would occupy the researchers in considerable work. Although potential acquisitions facing lawsuits are risks which should be avoided, such detail can be picked up at an early stage in the depth investigations.

Screens which are often applied by researchers in acquisition studies are:

☐ Product: eliminate all companies which do not sell a specified product.
☐ User industries: eliminate all companies which do not sell to specified markets.

☐ Market share: eliminate all companies with a market share below a certain figure.

☐ Ultimate market potential: eliminate all companies operating in a sector with a ceiling on sales of $x million.

☐ Growth prospects: eliminate all companies with growth prospects below x per cent over five years.

☐ Size: eliminate all companies over/under a certain size (measured by number of employees or turnover).

☐ Exports: eliminate all companies which have an export content of more/less than x per cent.

☐ Profitability: eliminate all companies which have a return on capital employed of less than x per cent over the last three years.

☐ Location: eliminate all companies which fall outside a defined geographical area.

The importance of these screening criteria will vary depending on the ambitions of the suitor and the market in question. An established supplier of green sand castings may want to acquire a company with a similar product group to close it down and fill his own works with the order book. A cash-rich conglomerate may seek an acquisition to take it into high technology, and their interest is in a company with unique products and growth prospects rather than one which is currently large and profitable.

The screens can be applied at different times. A coarse screen at an early stage may eliminate those companies where information is obvious and easily available — they produce the wrong products; are located in the wrong geographical location; they are the wrong size. A secondary screen can then be applied more discriminatingly, so reducing the high research costs involved in studying market shares, growth prospects and strengths in user industries.

The final, and possibly the most important, contribution market research can make in acquisition studies is the depth study of the company. When a quoted company is to be studied, special precautions are necessary to preserve secrecy which, if lost, could lead to speculation in the share price. A code name for the company is almost always assumed. The acquisition of private companies is in many respects easier for the researcher as it usually takes place with cooperation from the firm which speeds up and allows a more thorough appraisal of customers and markets.

Where access to the acquisition is not directly possible, there will be restrictions on the depth of data which can be obtained on the company. Nevertheless, by piecing together information gained from discussions with other suppliers, distributors, customers and desk sources it is almost always possible to provide sufficient information to guide the acquisition team. The most critical restriction is invariably the time available to collect the data.

Information which is sought as background to the acquisition and its internal management can be summarized:

☐ *History of formation*	This helps in understanding the position of the company today; it provides a benchmark and a perspective.
☐ *Product range*	Of obvious importance, especially the unique/special features, its modernity, breadth of range, prices, discounts, delivery, competitive position.
☐ *Sales turnover*	By volume and value for as long a period as possible to show trends and provide a pointer as to the future. As much detail as possible is required on sales including breakdown by export territories, by salesmen's regions, by product groups.
☐ *End-user markets*	This will indicate the spread of the company, its vulnerability to recession or opportunities for growth.
☐ *Customer analysis*	Especially a listing of the top customers (say top 50) together with their turnover as an indication of the dependence on a few key accounts.
☐ *Financial performance*	Five years' accounts is usually sufficient, paying close attention to key ratios such as sales margins, return on capital, acid ratio, stock turn.
☐ *Management structure and employment*	A tree for the whole company (with ages of the managers) will help show the strength of first and second line management.
☐ *Marketing organization*	The distribution network and description of the sales force shows the strength of the company's sales operation. Included here should be a description of its promotional budget and philosophy.
☐ *Licence/ technical links*	These can be indicative of a valuable asset or, in some cases, reflect low R & D/innovative resources.
☐ *Production resources*	Market researchers should not attempt to report beyond the limits of their knowledge but they may usefully be able to provide a catalogue of key plant, show where the products are made, list chief suppliers of raw materials, describe important features of the production process, and estimate production capacity against output.

Besides the information on the internals of the acquisition itself, data must be collected on the market to provide an industry perspective and customers'/potential customers' views of the company.

☐ *Market size*   With this measure the researcher can see the ultimate potential for the company.

☐ *Market segmentation*   By breaking the market size down into product groups and end-user sectors, it is possible to show the performance of the company in narrower but possibly more meaningful niches.

☐ *Market shares*   The size of the acquisition is set against its competitors to show relative positions. The movement of market shares over time indicates winners and losers.

☐ *Growth prospects*   Trends in the market are an indicator of the prospects facing the acquisition.

☐ *Image*   Often neglected, this measurement should figure high in determining whether the acquisition goes ahead, as a good image compensates for many other deficiencies while a poor image is very difficult to repair.

The researcher may be asked to carry out an acquisition study starting from the first stage of building lists of possible companies of interest to the second stage of screening and finally to a depth study of any one of them.

A reporting break between each stage is normally built in to allow the findings to be digested and the objectives modified where necessary. Each stage of the report should contain a conclusions section with recommendations for action. At the end of stages one and two the conclusions may simply summarize the companies worthy of further consideration while the final stage would include recommendations to proceed (or not) with the acquisition, the need for any corrective action of the company and the opportunities it faces for short- and long-term expansion.

Research to guide investment

As an alternative to acquisition, a company may decide to expand by means of some other investment route. This could be:

Expansion of existing plant capacity

Here the researcher produces a study to establish if the market can accommodate the extra capacity by natural growth or if it must be attained by stealing share from a competitor. Of course, most firms can flex their production departments and temporarily stretch themselves to meet a

129

peak in demand. Longer-term expansion programs, however, present the opportunity to build up production resources well beyond current order levels, and so marketing information becomes necessary to show the sales which can be achieved and sustained over a future period.

Green field venture

A company may decide to set up its own firm to distribute or manufacture goods rather than acquire a going concern. Because the company is starting with a 'green field', the production process and technical know-how can be bought in or developed internally. The market researcher is employed to show how quickly such an undertaking could obtain business, how the sales will build up over a period and the way in which sales will be achieved. Because a green field venture involves launching a company into a new market (for it), there is likely to be more uncertainty of success than in an acquisition or an expansion programme. Market research becomes all the more necessary because of the high risk and the large sums of capital that are involved.

Investment in a company normally increases efficiency or the capacity to supply more products or services. Research to indicate if the investment is viable should, therefore, be designed to show if and how sales can be increased by the required amount. Investment market research studies focus on:

- ☐ *Market size* Is it big enough now or in the future to accommodate the proposed expansion?
- ☐ *Competition* What are their strengths and weaknesses; which companies can market share be stolen from; which companies will be the most formidable competitors to the new or expanded company?
- ☐ *The buying decision* How can buyers be switched to buying from the new/expanded company rather than traditional suppliers; which potential customers are likely to show the most rapid rate of increase in the future and how accessible are they?

Technology transfer

A company can aim to short circuit the technical development time required for a new venture by taking on a licence or buying outright the manufacturing rights to a product. Specialist companies offer data banks or use their connections to marry companies which have technology to offer and those which want to acquire it. The advantage of using these specialist technology transfer brokers is their speed and 'relatively' low cost. They can, however, suffer from out-of-date data banks full of producers or brochures which have been listed for six months and which nobody wants.

The market researcher can play a role in technology transfer by systematically screening the market for either a potential licensee or licensor. He must, however, have a number of guidelines from his board of directors, otherwise his study could spin off in wasteful directions. Say, for example, a company wants to find an electronic product to manufacture, the researcher would need to know in advance of designing the study:

1. Some parameters about the technical complexity of the product which is being sought. Should it be a simple product consisting of a few components and capable of assembly by a semi-skilled workforce or should it need highly skilled electronic engineers?
2. Whether the product being sought should be a finished assembly or whether a subcomponent would be acceptable.
3. Whether the product should hold a unique position in any market into which it is sold.
4. Some indication of the scale of business which it is hoped to build up. Is the company hoping for a modest sized business with sales of between $1 and $5 million per annum or is it looking ultimately for a much larger turnover?
5. Some indication of the markets it wishes to sell to. Is the company looking for a product which it can sell worldwide or will it accept restrictions on the countries available to it?

Even with these guidelines, the scope of a study to find a suitable electronic product would be very wide and, for this reason, may have only a limited likelihood of success. The larger the number of guidelines, the tighter the brief, and the more constraining the study is, but equally, the greater the chance of finding a suitable product. The project would be carried out in stages with reviews at the end of each.

Stage 1. A list of products is built up for consideration as being of possible interest to the prospective licensee. Against each product it is necessary to provide a description of its function and use, key aspects of its assembly, selling price, the method of selling and approximate market size. Broad answers are good enough at this stage, as succinct information is sufficient to enable a review committee to decide if a product looks interesting and is worth pursuing.

Stage 2. After cutting back the list of products to a manageable number (perhaps between five and ten), more detailed information

131

is collected to show a precise market size, the shares of the competition, buyers' attitudes to the different products, etc.: all the components of an orthodox survey, except that much more emphasis will be given to building up profiles on companies that could be approached with a view to technology transfer. Data would be collected on the names of executives who deal with such matters, whether licensing deals exist with other companies and, if so, the nature of them.

Stage 3. Finally, an approach is made to those companies from which a technology transfer is sought. Because the implications of a technology transfer are likely to be of great importance to both companies, contact is usually by senior executives at board level.

Technology transfer studies are usually very costly and it can take three to six months to carry out all the stages. The first two stages of the project comprise, in fact, a number of surveys of products and may well involve the researchers in overseas travel in their search for data on potential licensors.

Summary

Acquisitions are traditionally vetted by a high-powered team of senior managers who make their decisions after assessing the production and financial resources of the company under consideration. The marketing resources of acquisitions are less tangible and yet any weaknesses here can only be rectified over a long term and at great expense.

Market research has three roles to play in acquisition studies. It can identify areas of opportunity and companies within them; it can be used to screen lists of potential acquisitions; finally, and most importantly, it can be used to produce a profile of potential acquisitions. Depth studies of acquisitions should provide a detailed background on the company's history, sales and customers. To put these into context, it should also position the company in the market as a whole.

Market research which guides investments is needed to show if and how the extra sales capacity can be sold. Investment is likely to fund an expansion of existing plant or a new venture. New ventures are especially risky and require market research to show if entry can be achieved and with what ultimate success.

Market research provides a logical and thorough means of identifying technological opportunities. In spite of its being time-consuming and expensive, it provides a faster and more secure means of diversification.

Part Three:
Organizing the project

Chapter 13
Problem Definition and Research Design

What is a marketing research problem?

Research is almost always undertaken to solve a marketing problem. Occasionally studies are carried out for no other justification than 'it would be nice to know', or 'to confirm suppositions'. Usually, however, there is a catalyst. It is essential to identify the true reason for undertaking the research and, while this may seem a naive edict, it is often hard to spot the underlying problem which has sparked off the enquiry. Without a clear statement of the problem it is not possible to design a research program which will lead to a solution.

Consider, for example, a company which manufactures industrial springs. After many years' profitability it makes a loss. Sales are falling, competition is fierce and the market itself could be shrinking. In this situation is the problem that:

1. it is making a loss?
2. the competition is stealing share?
3. the market size is shrinking?
4. its sales are declining?

The losses incurred by the spring manufacturer are not the problem, rather they are the effect or result of it. Nor is the fierce competition or market size the problem — though they may be a cause of it. The problem is the decline in sales which is a reaction to the harsh marketing environment. The problem can be more neatly defined as a market research objective: *to examine reasons for the fall in sales of springs and to recommend if and how these can be reversed.*

After the problem has been identified, the cause and effect can be recognized, an objective established and a research plan designed to meet it. In the example of the spring maker, the broad objective of the survey has been set and it is important to keep this in the forefront of the mind throughout the project. There will, however, be a host of sub-objectives which must be fulfilled before the broad goal is achieved. Again to revert to the spring maker, these may be:

- ☐ to establish the trend in market size over the last 10 years
- ☐ to explain the trend
- ☐ to identify factors which will influence future trends
- ☐ to forecast the market size for each of the next five years
- ☐ to assess the share of each supplier to the market
- ☐ to show which suppliers are increasing their share and which are declining
- ☐ to analyse why each supplier's share has changed.

The achievement of these sub-objectives may in itself require a detailed investigation. For example, the last of the sub-objectives listed above would need a study of the sales and promotional methods used by each company; their pricing, product and delivery strategies; and any concentrations they have on certain user markets or particular customers.

The market researcher cannot assume that, when he receives a brief, the problem will be identified for him by the sponsor. If the manager who delivers the brief cannot adequately define the problem, the responsibility must remain with the researcher to do so. It is most important that the final document which the researcher produces is one which leads to effective decisions. In order to achieve actionable research the researcher must, together with the sponsor, answer the following four questions.

1. What is the problem?
2. What is the cause of the problem?
3. What information do I require to find a solution to the problem?
4. What are the possible courses of action I could take when I am armed with the information I want?

The approach to problem solving can be widely applied in industrial marketing and some examples are illustrated in table 10.

Pressures which influence the design of the research programme

Three factors must be weighed before the research plan can be formulated:

Cost

If there is a budget which limits the scope of the study it must be known at the outset. The researcher should be pragmatic in his choice of research method recognizing that, beyond a certain input of effort (and therefore cost), the increase in volume and accuracy of information which can be

136

TABLE 10
*Questions to ask before commissioning research—
and some specimen answers*

What is the problem?	What is the cause of the problem?	What do I want to know?	What will I do with the information when I have got it?
Insufficient turnover	My sales are limited to certain industries	Market size and segments	Push into new segments
Insufficient turnover	We sell only in the south east	Location of demand through the UK	Increase sales effort in other areas
Sales and profit are falling	Product is entering 'old age' on life cycle	Future market size	Invest or sell off plant
The profit on sales ratio is falling	Our prices are too low	Price sensitivity	Adjust prices and relate them to profitability
The advertising budget is out of hand	We don't know where to get the best return	Advertising effectiveness	Modify advertisements to suit the market
Sales are falling	Our product has a quality problem	Users' levels of product satisfaction	Redesign products or introduce a new range
Sales are falling	Competition has become more aggressive	Market shares and factors influencing choice of supplier	Sharpen up the marketing mix
Costs are rising	The cost of representatives has risen dramatically	Effectiveness of salesmen	Implement controls
Sales are static	We suspect we are regarded as old-fashioned	Company image	Influence by means of advertising and/or PR campaign

garnered becomes marginal. Determining that point in advance of a research study requires judgement. As will be shown in Chapter 18 on sampling, the industrial market researcher can seldom apply probability sampling techniques which enable him to state the accuracy levels. The researcher must also be prepared to stand up to management in circumstances where he knows that budget constraints will result in a poor job.

Poor research may be worse than no research, as it could mislead management and potentially will prejudice them against ever using marketing research again.

The cost of carrying out a market survey is easier to determine if it is undertaken by an agency, as quotations stating the cost of the exercise are submitted in advance. Estimating the cost of a project carried out internally is a worthwhile discipline, even if sight of those costs is not required by management. Researchers must acknowledge that research is only justified if the payback is greater than the cost of the project. Even if the findings lead to a recommendation not to enter a market, the sponsor may be saved a considerable sum in investment and management time which could otherwise have been wasted. The estimation of the cost of a research project before it takes place gives a perspective against which the expected benefits can be measured.

Time

Just as there are normally cost limitations to a market research project, so too there are time restraints. Having decided that information is necessary, the findings may well be summoned immediately. Researchers bear the responsibility of explaining to management what can and cannot be achieved in certain time-scales in order that they can decide whether they are prepared to accept the inadequacies which result from a punishing timetable. Yielding to the screams of management for the results yesterday could, like a scant budget, produce incomplete, mistaken findings.

Objectives

The scale of the business decision which will be based on the research findings must ultimately determine the input of the research time and cost. A large investment as a rule needs a thorough and costly study; a small investment can only merit a limited study. As always the rules are never simple. Management may be forced to make decisions by a certain date, as is frequently the case with acquisition studies. The choice may realistically be no marketing information or as much as can be found in the allotted time. As long as any deficiencies in the information are qualified, the researcher must learn to live with the constraints of time and cost. He may be jaundiced by management's long and seemingly unnecessary procrastinations which delay the start of a project and squeeze the time-scale for its completion; he may be disturbed by research reports, commissioned in haste, which gather dust and moulder. His reaction should be to advise and educate management as to the uses and misuses of research and above all to produce actionable and clearly presented findings which can easily be used.

Selecting the research method

Market research surveys can be classified into two categories, depending on the nature of the information to be collected:

1. quantitative
2. qualitative.

Most industrial market research projects are made up of a mixture of both.

Quantitative studies
These require the findings to be expressed in measures or quantities and typically include:

- ☐ market size and analysis of segments
- ☐ forecasts of market size
- ☐ market shares
- ☐ price/volume relationships.

Since quantitative research encompasses any finding which can be factorized and quantified, it can be applied to the motivations and attitudes which are the very essence of qualitative research. It is possible, for example, to show how price, quality, delivery and sales service are the four factors which buyers weigh up when selecting a supplier. A large number of interviews will produce a finding which shows that a certain percentage ranked quality first, price second and so on. In this way the qualitative data is converted to a measure and becomes quantitative. Similarly, quantitative studies can be undertaken of:

- ☐ awareness of companies, products and brands
- ☐ image and attitudes to companies, products and brands
- ☐ buying practices
- ☐ selling practices
- ☐ advertising recall.

Most quantitative research, however, centres on the analysis of what buyers do.

- ☐ what they buy
- ☐ how much they buy
- ☐ when they buy it
- ☐ how often they buy
- ☐ who they buy from.

Clearly the questions can be manifold but they are usually concerned with a factual recording of what actually takes place. Frequently, this factual base on buying procedure is used to calculate market size and market shares.

Quantitative market research need not originate from fieldwork. Statistical data drawn from published sources may be the basis for the report. A survey of export opportunities for a product in an overseas territory would usefully be preceded by a search for published data on imports, exports and the country's internal consumption and production. A domestic survey on the future for the market in wooden pallets may be partially solved by plotting published output statistics of all the pallet manufacturers and correlating these with sales of fast-moving consumer goods and bagged products — two major categories of products which are moved around on pallets.

Quantitative research is normally associated with the collection of raw data through structured interviews. By definition, quantitative research requires a large base of interviews in order to arrive at an acceptable measure. These are achieved by visit, telephone and postal response. The occasions which are suited to these techniques are discussed fully in Part Four. However, the circumstances favouring each approach are summarized below.

TELEPHONE INTERVIEWS

☐ Where simple factual information is being collected.
☐ Where the timetable is short.
☐ Where the budget is limited
☐ Where the respondent is relatively inaccessible geographically or as a result of security factors (eg, a manager in a nuclear power station).

FACE-TO-FACE INTERVIEWS

☐ Where the questionnaire is lengthy (over 10 to 15 minutes' duration).
☐ Where there are a large number of open-ended responses or complicated questions.
☐ Where the respondent may need to refer to his files or some other person at the establishment.
☐ Where it is necessary to show the respondent prompt cards or a sample product.

POSTAL QUESTIONNAIRES

☐ Where the budget is limited
☐ Where the respondent is interested in the subject and likely to respond (eg, recent car buyers).
☐ Where access to the respondent is difficult for geographical reasons or he cannot easily reach a telephone.

Quantitative research is typically carried out to assist in investment decisions such as what course of action should be taken; is an investment justified; where can growth be achieved?

The information which is needed to solve one of these problems is not wholly quantitative. For example, to decide whether a company can grow at a faster rate may need a detailed analysis of the market size and competition as well as buyers' attitudes to the various products and brands on the market.

Qualitative studies

Qualitative research is concerned with the thoughts, feelings and attitudes of buyers. It is quite likely that the buyer may be unconsciously acting in a certain way and it is as a result of careful questioning that the researcher is able to interpret his actions. Qualitative research places a heavy responsibility on the researcher, as his empathy, sensitivity and creativity to responses are likely to be as important as logical deductions in arriving at the true answer.

Findings which may emanate from the qualitative side of a study could include:

☐ buyer behaviour and the importance of factors influencing the buying decision
☐ attitudes to products or suppliers
☐ the acceptability of a new product or concept
☐ satisfaction with existing products or suppliers
☐ future buying intentions.

In the section on quantitative research it was stated that attitudes can be factorized and measured. It is possible, for example, to measure satisfaction on a five point scale and quantify the response for buyers who have had experience of different manufacturers' products. The true qualitative research approach would go deeper than forcing a single response into one of the five boxes on the questionnaire. It would attempt to get under the skin of the subject and explore satisfaction by finding out whether the buyer has ever faced problems in using the product, how these are resolved, whether he has thought of buying an alternative product or how he believes the product could be improved. Qualitative research studies the subject in greater depth than quantitative research. It therefore requires a technique such as face-to-face interviews or group discussions which allows detailed probing and, especially with technical subjects, demands a highly skilled interviewer. In qualitative research the interviewer may follow a route of questioning which requires him to respond and redirect the discussion spontaneously. This discretion is not permissible in quantitative research as the same line of questioning must be used with every respondent.

The depth nature of qualitative research places a limit on the number of interviews that are possible. In order for researchers to build up the detailed insight into why buyers respond in the way they do, the interviewing team must be small and well coordinated. A qualitative research program is commonly carried out by one, two or three interviewers. A large-scale quantitative study may use many more interviewers, especially if interviewing is face to face and spread across the country.

The choice between the two qualitative research techniques of face-to-face interviews and group discussions is not clear-cut. They are often applicable for the same objective and it is not unusual to design a research program which incorporates both.

Generalizing, the following circumstances favour face-to-face interviewing in preference to groups.

FACTORS FAVOURING FACE-TO-FACE INTERVIEWING IN PREFERENCE TO GROUP DISCUSSIONS

- ☐ When respondents are widely separated geographically, and logistically are difficult to bring together.
- ☐ When the subject of the discussion is sensitive — for example, the outlining of production processes, buying agreements or recent trends in technical research.
- ☐ When a detailed response is required from each and every respondent (groups give individual respondents much less aggregate talking time than face-to-face interviews).
- ☐ When it is necessary to obtain respondents' private reactions as opposed to those which may be put forward within the public environment of a group.
- ☐ When it is necessary to control the sequence of questioning formally.
- ☐ When there is a possibility the respondent will have to use his files to answer questions.

In turn, group discussions may be favoured in the following circumstances:

FACTORS FAVOURING GROUP DISCUSSIONS IN PREFERENCE TO FACE-TO-FACE DISCUSSIONS

- ☐ When respondents need time to digest and develop ideas (in a group respondents have ample time to listen and think about what has been said).
- ☐ When the line of questioning is somewhat uncertain and the application of a number of minds is more likely to see an answer.
- ☐ When the interviewer needs to be provocative (it is easier for the

interviewer to be provocative in the neutral territory of a group venue than in a respondent's office)

☐ When large or cumbersome displays must be shown to respondents (films, photographs, products, etc).

By way of example, a number of qualitative objectives are listed below, together with a suggestion as to whether they are suited more to face-to-face interviews or groups.

Objective	Suggested approach	Main reason for selecting approach
To examine road hauliers' attitudes to engines	Groups	To explore an unknown line of questioning
To explore managing directors' attitudes on development areas	Face-to-face interviews	Difficulty in convening a group of widely spread managers
To decide why buyers of steel sheet choose a supplier	Groups and face-to-face interviews	Both techniques are possible and will reinforce each other
To evaluate the opportunity for a high-powered desk-top computer	Groups	To allow respondents time to digest ideas
To determine the opportunities for a new biscuit-making machine	Face-to-face interviews	To safeguard secret processes used by respondents
To establish attitudes to a crane safety device	Face-to-face interviews	To obtain a private reaction to safety
To explore the opportunity for the hover principle in lifting industrial products	Groups	To have the benefit of many minds on a nebulous concept

Deciding on the size of the research program

Time and cost normally determine the size and nature of a research program. Information needed to guide a forthcoming board meeting may necessitate a quick telephone survey when the problem would be better solved by face-to-face interviews. Similarly, cost constraints may force a researcher to choose the telephone rather than visits or a few individual interviews instead of a group discussion.

Almost every survey has some time and cost limitations. Even given unlimited resources of time and money, the researcher owes it to his management to select a package which is most efficient, taking into consideration the importance of the decision which will be made. The researcher is, after all, the expert, and his recommended approach is usually accepted without demur.

Deciding the size and scope of the research program makes the novice researcher feel most vulnerable. Although he may be able to select a suitable research technique — say some visits backed up by telephone interviews — his problem is deciding the size of the sample. Equally, group discussions may be selected as the technique to provide the answers, but how many should be carried out? The researcher will gain little comfort from knowing that there is no established formula for deciding on the numbers of people to interview or groups to hold. The decision is usually based on experience — a similar problem previously faced by the researcher in a related field very often guides the size and structure of the program.

If the proposed study is to provide a quantitative analysis of respondents' buying patterns, a 'large' sample is necessary in order that the results carry some authority. In a universe such as electrical contractors or garages, a 'large' sample may be 200 or more companies. Such universes have similar characteristics to consumer markets in that there are many respondents all of similar size and structure. Even 200 interviews may be too small if certain cells of respondents are to be drawn out for special analysis, for example, by geographical region or because they have certain buying characteristics (eg, they have had experience in a product). Caution is required for cell sizes of 50 respondents or less and so, assuming there were 10 cells in total, the sample size would be 500.

The industrial market researcher is often confronted with a universe that is neither large nor uniform. There may be only 50 or so consumers of a product and these could include five or six which dominate purchases, 15 to 20 medium-sized buyers, with the rest quite small. Here, a carefully selected sample of all the large companies, and a few of the medium and small ones, could result in a sample size of less than 20 companies in total but one which accounts for over 80 per cent of the purchases.

The number of qualitative interviews, even in a large uniform universe, need only be small. Thirty depth interviews should provide a consistency of response in most markets and sometimes the number could be much less. Where, however, a market is segmented into end-user segments, each with different buying patterns, the segments themselves should be regarded as universes in their own right. Rivets, for example, are used in a wide range of industrial sectors from commercial vehicle assembly through to architectural metalwork. As each sector has its special needs, a survey of buyers' motivations on riveting systems requires a suitable number in each — say no less than 15. Thus, a qualitative survey of the market for

144

rivets across the eight or ten major sectors that use (or could use) the product could need 100 to 150 interviews.

The number of group discussions that must be carried out to meet a survey's objectives is similarly variable. Where the characteristics of the respondent companies invited to the groups are the same (as with plumbers) then two or three groups may suffice. Even so, this must be considered a bare minimum, as some geographical spread should be attempted with groups held in different parts of the country to establish if there are regional differences in attitude.

Where the universe is made up of companies very different in character, more groups are required. Groups held among builders should represent those that only do extensions, those that build houses, those concentrating on industrial and commercial properties and, finally, the civil engineering contractors. A research study focusing on the simple brick may be able to mix these groups of respondents as each uses the product in much the same way — the nature of their business is unlikely to influence their attitudes to bricks. Three or four groups convened in different parts of the country would be a minimum while more than eight or ten groups would be overkill. If the subject of the study was the attitudes to cement mixers it might be necessary to view each class of builder separately, as small jobbing builders are likely to have different cement mixing needs from civil engineers. Three or four groups held with each of the four classes of builder raises the minimum number to (say) 12.

An option open to the researcher is to carry out the study in stages. Each stage provides a breathing space in which the researcher and, in particular, the sponsor, can consider the findings before proceeding. Staged studies have some important advantages:

Advantages of a staged study

□ It allows the sponsor an opportunity to cut off if the early findings suggest barriers to success.
□ It allows the researcher a chance to reflect on the research method and propose a modified second or third stage in the light of the findings.
□ It staggers the sponsor's financial commitment to the study.
□ It focuses the researcher's mind on objectives. Most goals are achieved by meeting sub-objectives which can be placed in order along a critical path. In a single study the global objective may overshadow the importance of a critical sub-objective which must be achieved early in a study to justify its continuance.

Disadvantages of a staged study

- ☐ It is more expensive, as extra time is required for reporting and discussing findings.
- ☐ It takes longer than a single stage study.
- ☐ In some circumstances it is not practicable, as the respondents contacted in the first stage could, with little or no extra expense, have provided much of the information to answer the objectives of stage two.

The staged study need not involve the formal, written reporting of findings at the end of the first part. A verbal discussion may be sufficient to inform the sponsor of progress and enable him to decide whether he wishes to proceed.

Summary

Researchers must identify the real problem which has given rise to the request for a study. Having established the research problem, it is necessary to determine what information is required and what action will be taken when it is obtained.

Most surveys require the researcher to collect quantitative and qualitative information. Quantitative information is obtained by desk research or, more usually, a fieldwork program of telephone or face-to-face interviews and, in special circumstances, self-completion postal questionnaires. Qualitative studies are based on depth interviews or group discussions.

The types of fact collection used in a project are a balance determined by the objectives, the time, and the money available to carry it out. The number of interviews which will provide reliable data can vary from many hundreds for a quantitative survey of a heterogeneous universe through to a handful of companies in a qualitative survey of a narrow industrial sector. The number of group discussions that are needed to provide qualitative information can be as few as two or three for uniform universes through to a dozen or more where the cells of respondent companies have different characteristics.

Studies carried out in stages can provide the useful advantage of a cut-off point. The extra reporting at the end of the stages adds to the time and cost of the study but this can be kept to a minimum by a verbal rather than a written presentation of findings.

Chapter 14
Taking and Giving a Market Research Brief

The importance of a research brief

A research brief is a statement from the sponsor setting out the objectives and background to the case in sufficient detail to enable the researcher to plan an appropriate study. As a general rule, a market research study is only as good as the brief. The brief is important to the researcher: it educates him and influences his choice of method. It gives him the objective to which the project is geared.

The brief is no less important for the researcher working in-house than for the agency. Research carried out by company personnel is frequently treated less stringently than where it carries the price tag of the external agency. The in-house researcher does, however, have the benefit of close and constant access to other internal staff who can fill him in on background and product details. Though the brief is less formal, it may well be (and should be) as thorough as any delivered to an agency.

The research brief should be a dialogue. It is expected that the sponsor has thought through his problem and set objectives for the study, though these may be modified as the briefing session develops. Nor are briefs irrevocable. Information discovered during the research programme may alter the complexion of the problem and prompt a change in direction. Progress reporting is therefore a vital part of every study.

What a research brief should contain

Some sponsors prefer to deliver their brief orally, developing points of detail during the initial discussion with the researcher. Alternatively, the brief may be fully thought through and perhaps committed to paper. This can be especially important when a number of research agencies are invited to submit proposals. A written brief provides a standard which is the same for all contestants.

147

Whether written or oral, the research sponsor should pay regard to a number of subjects which constitute a good brief.

A background to the problem
This may be a short chronicle of the events which have led up to and precipitated the study. It gives the researcher a perspective and a better understanding of why the project is to be commissioned.

A description of the product (or service) which is to be researched
The researcher needs as much detail as possible. The greater his understanding of the features, benefits, construction and uses of the product (or services), the more closely he will be able to tailor the study to what the sponsor wants. It can be helpful for the sponsor to state which products he is not interested in as well as those in which he is. Technical data sheets and product literature are a big help.

A description of the markets to be researched
The researcher must know which geographical territories the study will cover and whether or not it will be limited to certain end-user markets.

A statement of the objectives
The sponsor may feel inhibited by his uncertainty as to the limitations of market research. He should not worry about these at the time of briefing, and state the objective of the study as he sees it. The responsibility then lies with the researcher to interpret the brief and give his view on what can be achieved.

Timing and budget constraints
The researcher should be told of these whenever they exist. Otherwise he may waste his time designing a detailed model of a study which is subsequently turned down as unaffordable.

The sponsor may also be able to suggest, within the brief, a research method, though usually this is left for the researcher to propose.

Finally, there may be special aspects of the study which the sponsor needs to mention in his brief. These could cover his wish to remain anonymous, reporting requirements and progress meetings, or the need for direct access to the consultants.

It is always helpful for a researcher to see a demonstration of the product or service that is being studied, if practicable. A visit around the manufacturing plant or to a customer to see the product in use can provide that important 'feel' which researchers get from direct contact.

The role of the researcher

The researcher cannot assume that he will receive a detailed and well-considered brief. In many instances, management know that they face a problem but identifying what it is, its cause and the research solution are left to the researcher. With no formal brief the researcher must dig out the necessary background data himself.

Table 11 contains a checklist of questions which could be used by the researcher to draw out the background he needs to design a research program.

TABLE 11

Checklist to guide a researcher when taking a brief

HISTORY

How long has the company been established?

How long has it concentrated on its present product range?

What was the company's product range originally, and 10, 20, 30 years ago?

Has the company always been sited in its present location?

What factors have influenced its location?

COMPANY BACKGROUND

What is the principal business of the company?

What are its subsidiary activities?

What is its total turnover: (a) USA, (b) exports?

Describe any holding companies/subsidiary companies.

How many employees are there at the establishment?

PRODUCT DETAILS

What are the important products in the range (by size, capacity, shape, material, etc)?

What proportion of the total turnover in these products does each of the above groups account for?

To what extent are the products standard/custom built?

What proportion of an assembled product is made in-house or bought out?

How important are spares in terms of revenue *v* profit?

Are any of the products built under license?

PRICING

What are the prices for each of the important products
(are these prices trade or retail)?

How do prices compare with those of the competition?

Is there a published price-list?

What is the discount policy?

What power does the salesman have to alter prices?

How price sensitive are sales in the product thought to be?

SALES FORCE

Number of representatives?

Are they a general or a specialized sales force — in what way
are they specialized?

How many calls a day do they make?

Do the reps bring back orders or are they sent in
independently?

Are agents used — if so, where and why?

MARKETS

What are the major markets for the products?

What is the proportion of total sales to each of these markets?

Are any markets known for the product where the company
currently does not/cannot sell?

Which markets are believed to offer the greatest scope for
expansion of sales?

Who are the major customers? What share of sales do the
top 20 account for?

DECISION MAKERS

Who are the key personnel in a company who decide whether
this type of product should be bought? What roles do they
play?

Who are the key decision makers in a company who decide
who the supplier of the product should be? What roles do
they play?

What do decision makers look for from suppliers?

PROBE price, quality, delivery, sales service.

QUALITY

Where does the product fit against the competition's in its quality?

What are the special features of its quality?

Where is it weak on quality?

How long will the product last?

When it finally fails, why will it do so?

DELIVERY

What is the current delivery period?

What is the competition's delivery?

What is the ideal delivery?

COMPETITION

Who are the most important competitors? Where are they based?

What is their rank order/market share?

What are each company's (including the sponsor's) perceived strengths and weaknesses?

To what extent do competitors rely upon this market for their turnover and profit?

DISTRIBUTION

How is the product distributed?

What proportion goes direct/indirect? What is the policy which leads to this split (eg, size of account; original equipment manufacturer *v* replacement etc)?

What are distributors' margins?

What other products do distributors sell?

Do distributors actively sell or just take orders?

Who are the major distributors:
  (a) used by the company?
  (b) not used by the company?

What is the average size of a direct account and a distributor account?

PROMOTION

How big is the promotional budget?

How does this break down between:
  (a) media, (b) exhibitions, (c) PR,
  (d) print, (e) direct mail, (f) others?

Which media are used? Which are most successful?

What proportion of sales leads comes from promotion? How many? What is their quality?

Which exhibitions are attended? What is their perceived value?

OTHER DATA

Full details of names (with initials) of persons present at briefing; date of briefing; address of company; address to which proposals should be sent.

How many copies of the proposal are required — to be sent separately or *en bloc*?

Preparing the research proposal

Having received the brief, the researcher, whether in-house or from an agency, must submit a written proposal to his sponsor which states his appreciation of the problem, the objectives to which he will work, the research method and the timing. If an agency is preparing the proposal, a statement of cost must be given. An in-house job may omit this but many managers still like to see an estimate as a benchmark to compare with other surveys and as a perspective which they can relate to the size of any decision which may be taken.

If the proposal is accepted it becomes the contract between researcher and sponsor. The nature of industrial market research is such that it is seldom possible to know in advance whether the objectives or research method will remain fixed. Invariably slight modifications need to be made. These should always be documented and copied to all parties so they can react to them and, in the event of any later argument, refer back to whatever was agreed.

There is no rigid formula for a research proposal. It could be written on one page or run to over 20. A useful format, irrespective of length, would cover the following elements:

Background to the research in which the researcher states who is the research sponsor, what his problems are and how they have developed historically. The date and nature of the briefing (face to face or by letter) should also be given. This section is more than just a preamble. It shows the research sponsor that a full understanding of the problem has been achieved.

Research objectives. Here the objectives are laid out. It is useful to all parties if the section can begin with a one or two sentence summary of the overall objectives. This reminds both sponsor and researcher why the study is being undertaken and can usefully be referred back to for direction if there is ever a danger of straying down interesting but not so vital alleyways. A discussion follows of the many detailed objectives which must be fulfilled. For example, the broad aim of a survey may be 'to assess the potential for a new industrial adhesive and to suggest targets and marketing strategies over the next three years'.

To reach this goal a number of sub-objectives must be fulfilled, such as:

☐ To assess the market size in 1985 for industrial adhesives in volume and value and segmented by product type and end-user sector;

☐ To plot the trends in the market over the last five years and to identify reasons for these trends;

☐ To identify major suppliers of adhesives to the market and to assess their current market shares;

☐ To profile the suppliers of adhesives in terms of their products, prices, delivery, sales and marketing activity, financial performance and dependence on adhesives or other products;

☐ To profile end-users of adhesives in terms of their applications, annual consumption, order size, price, delivery, quality and after service expectations;

☐ To show how and why the decision is made to:
(a) select adhesives as a fastening method
(b) use one supplier in preference to others;

☐ To measure satisfaction of users of adhesives with existing products and suppliers and to identify areas where improvements could be made;

☐ To show factors which would prompt a change of adhesive supplier;

☐ To establish future trends in the consumption of adhesives and to forecast the size of the market for each of the next three years.

There may be other additional objectives such as testing reactions to a new adhesive or finding companies with whom a testing program can be established.

The fulfilment of the above objectives would culminate in a conclusions and recommendations section of the final report which would cover such topics as:

- [ ] attainable targets by user market (and possibly customer)
- [ ] product policy (range and future developments)
- [ ] pricing policy
- [ ] delivery policy
- [ ] promotional and advertising policy
- [ ] sales policy.

Research methods. In this section the way in which the research will be carried out is described. If desk research is to be employed it should be stated with what aim. The number and type (telephone or visit) of interviews should be given and in many cases further details should be provided, such as any quotas of size of companies or position of respondents to be questioned. Where interviews are to be carried out with competitors these should be described separately. A table should be drawn up to show how the time allocated in the project will be split between the various activities. Table 12 illustrates a time allocation which may well have accompanied the adhesives study.

TABLE 12
UK adhesives study: allocation of research time against activity

Activity	Allocation of researcher days	Estimated number of interviews
Commissioning and progress meetings	3	—
Questionnaire design and sample frame construction	2	—
Desk research	2	—
End-user interviews (telephone)	6	50
End-user interviews (visits)	5	10
Analysis and checking back	2	—
Report preparation	5	—
Presentation	1	—
Total	26	60

Also under the heading of research methods, the research team should be briefly described, though a more detailed curriculum vitae may be submitted as an appendix. It is especially important that the sponsor has some background on the qualifications and experience of the senior researchers and the structure of authority between the team members.

Research timing. The timing of surveys is critical. Clients are just as

154

concerned with an assurance that a report will be delivered on time as they are about the speed with which it can be finished. The researcher should include within his proposal a timetable to show how the various parts of the study dovetail together and when each will begin and end. This justifies the time-scale to the sponsor and enables him to see where the study will be at any date. Diagram 12 illustrates a typical timetable, again based on the adhesives study.

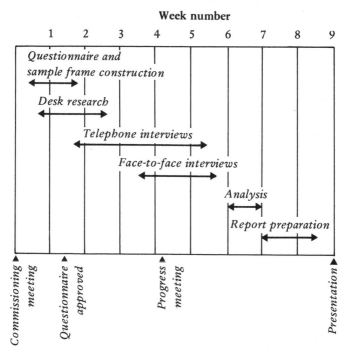

DIAGRAM 12
Proposed timetable for adhesives study

Research cost. A section on costs is a critical part of a proposal submitted by an agency. It should state:

☐ The fee, whether inclusive or exclusive of expenses. If exclusive of expenses, an estimate should be given of the likely range. It could be a percentage (eg 15 to 25 per cent of the fee) or an absolute sum.
☐ The terms of payment, including any deposit or stage payments; the arrangements for paying expenses; length of time allowed for payment of invoices.

Research experience. This is an optional part of a research proposal.

Sponsors usually value a description of a researcher's experience, especially that related to the subject in hand. It gives a boost of confidence in the team and creates a level of respect which eases the progress of the study and the submission of the findings.

Commissioning a research agency

When a market research agency is commissioned to carry out a project the sponsor must be more formal in his briefing than if the project is in-house. The sponsor must first draw up a shortlist of companies from which he wishes to receive proposals. The companies shortlisted may be screened against some criteria which are believed critical to the successful execution of the job. For example:

- ☐ experience in certain products and end-user markets
- ☐ special facilities such as linguistic or technical skills
- ☐ size (a large company may be preferable for its resources, a small company for the personal attentions of the senior staff).

An obvious starting point for building up the shortlist are the many directories of agencies and marketing consultancies. Advice from colleagues and trade associations can be helpful in narrowing down the list to two or three companies which will be briefed and invited to propose. A brief discussion on the telephone prior to the briefing session should establish that the agencies are all willing and able to do the work.

The research sponsor may prefer to brief the agencies at his offices where he can call upon other colleagues and, if relevant, organize a factory visit. He should, however, aim to visit the preferred research agencies prior to concluding his decision to meet the research team and obtain a feel for how well he and they gel. The chemical reaction between researchers and sponsor is not to be derided and many a project has suffered through personality clashes.

So far as possible, the briefing given to each agency should be the same. However, the researchers representing the agencies will inevitably ask different questions and have varying interpretations of the problem. How these are played back to the sponsor in the research proposal will become one of the most critical factors influencing the choice of agency. Three agencies working from the same brief will almost certainly present different research plans. The emphasis could be on value for money and push a large number of telephone interviews; others may opt for a small number of visits and seek depth. Some may include competitor interviews, client counselling and desk research. The variation in method from three professional agencies is a reflection of the wide range of approaches to solving the same problem and all may have their merits. If the sponsor has preconditioned views on the research method, this should be specified at the briefing. Assuming there are no confines on methodology, his selection between different proposals must be based on value judgements. He should ask himself which agency:

- ☐ has best shown an appreciation of his problem;
- ☐ appears to have selected a research method which it has argued is best for the job (not necessarily the easiest or one most suited to their resources);
- ☐ does he have most empathy with?

It will be noted that price and research experience do not figure within these selection criteria. Price alone is not the best method of selecting an agency. Of course, this is not to say that it is irrelevant, but a price difference of 50 per cent or more is quite possible given the wide range of methods an agency can select.

The price should always be related to the number of consultant days allocated to the job and the number of interviews that are promised. Research experience is frequently uppermost in a sponsor's mind as a selection criterion and so often this unnecessarily restricts his choice of agency. Every industrial market research agency worth its salt should be able to acquire technical knowledge quickly. It is better to look for specializations in broader classes of industry such as construction, steel, chemicals, agriculture, etc, than to demand precise experience in a narrow product range.

Summary

A brief is a statement from a sponsor to a researcher of the problem he faces, the background to it and what he seeks from the proposed study. The more thorough the briefing, the more able is the researcher to design an appropriate research plan.

A research brief may be oral or in writing. It should comprise:

- ☐ a background to the problem
- ☐ a description of the product or service to be researched
- ☐ a description of the markets to be researched
- ☐ a statement of the objectives
- ☐ any timing or budget constraints.

The researcher cannot rely on the sponsor providing him with a detailed brief. He bears the responsibility for questioning the sponsor and drawing out sufficient information to prepare a suitable research plan. All research should be preceded by a proposal prepared by the researcher and sub-mitted to the sponsor for his approval. A proposal should contain:

- ☐ a statement of the reasons for the study
- ☐ the research objectives
- ☐ the research method
- ☐ research timing
- ☐ research costs.

If an agency is to be commissioned to carry out the work, three proposals should be obtained. It is quite likely that the approaches of the agencies will differ, even given the same brief. The selection will be based on a judgement of who has understood the problem, suggested a research approach which suits the problem and who the sponsor believes he can best work with.

Chapter 15
Administration of the Project

Finalizing the timetable

As soon as the go-ahead is received to start the study the researcher should seek a meeting with the sponsor. This commissioning meeting serves to fine tune any aspects of the proposal and is an opportunity to discuss the timetable and detailed points which should be built into the questionnaire.

During the preparation of the proposal the researcher will have laid out the framework for the timetable. With an instruction to go ahead he must now produce one in greater detail. At this early planning stage the critical path should be identified and plotted through the timetable to ensure smooth progress and completion on time. Some tasks must follow in sequence while others can be undertaken at any time. The order of the components of research will vary depending on the study. Sometimes desk research is a prerequisite to gaining an understanding of the market and facilitating subsequent interviewing. In other surveys desk research can be fitted in at any time prior to report writing. Generally, however, the survey would follow a sequence as shown overleaf. Desk research usually begins at an early point with the collection of statistical material. It could continue well into the campaign as literature and reports are mailed to the researcher.

It will be noted that if overview interviews are to be carried out, perhaps with competitors, they follow the user interviews. This is to provide the researcher with a picture of the market which he can use as a platform for discussion with the overview respondent. Lacking this background, he is vulnerable to misunderstandings, being deliberately misled and has a weak position because he has no information to trade.

Dates can be set against the different constituents of the study. Arrangements can be made for progress meetings. Each task must be assigned to a person who should agree that he can carry out his work within the defined period. The names of the persons written on the timetable against the job allocations will show with whom the responsibility lies for action at any point in time.

Sequence of a typical industrial market research study

Questionnaire design

↓

Sample frame construction

↓

Preparation of briefing notes

↓

Briefing interviewers

↓

Interview program with
end users/distributors

↓

'Overview' interviews

↓

Analysis and checkbacks

↓

Report writing

↓

Report typing and checking

The finished timetable should be circulated to the sponsor and each member of the team in order that all are aware of their own and each other's duties.

Briefing the field force

Surveys involving a large number of interviews (and in industrial market research this may be anything over, say, 50) will require a number of interviewers to help in data collection. These interviewers may be full-time employees within the researcher's firm or people brought in to help. In the latter case, they must be booked early for the dates of the fieldwork program. Outsiders could be freelances contacted independently or arranged through a fieldwork agency.

Before booking the inteviewers, the research controller needs to know their experience and technical ability. Too often, excellent interviewers, trained to administer consumer questionnaires, flounder in industrial interviews where questioning is semi-structured and depends on a technical appreciation of products and processes. The controller also needs an assurance that the field force he is booking can complete the project on time.

In turn, the field force needs to be advised on the types of interviews they will be expected to carry out, how many there will be, where they will be located, how long they will take and how the work will be remunerated.

The field force must be briefed and, though this can on occasions be carried out by letter, tape or telephone, it is normal practice in industrial marketing to do it personally. The briefing given to the interviewers is rather different from that between sponsor and researcher. For example, interviewers may not be told the true purpose of the study — in an acquisition study such disclosure could be dangerous. The interviewers need to know only enough for them to perform the task, which is to elicit certain information from respondents. To do this job well they must be thoroughly briefed on the product, the processes in which it is used, the types of company which buy it, the positions of the persons involved in the buying decision, the products or processes against which it competes and as much background as possible on the competing suppliers. There will be occasions when some of this detail cannot be provided; indeed, the study may be designed to extract such data.

In some surveys the field force will have no discretion as to who they interview and will be provided with names, addresses and telephone numbers of companies and contacts. When interviewers are told which companies to interview but no contact is known, a suitable respondent must be found. At the interviewer briefing it is worth spending time on this subject, as failure to contact the right person results in suspect findings. The interviewers need guidance, therefore, as to whether they should be aiming to speak to the person *buying* the product or service (eg, the purchasing officer), *specifying* it (eg, the technical manager), *using* it (eg, the production manager), *selling* it (eg, the marketing manager) or *paying* for it (eg, the accountant).

All too often the decision to specify and buy a product is made by a number of people representing different operating divisions within the company. A single respondent may only be capable of answering some of the questions and yet contact with other members of the buying committee may be impractical. The interviewer must be briefed on how to deal with this situation by, for example, concentrating on the key decision maker and topping up by telephone those with a subordinate influence.

The interviewer may be given the responsibility of selecting the company to interview. Here too a consummate briefing is essential. Control may be necessary on the size of company to be interviewed, the type of products it buys or makes, the type of production processes it uses, its location or its suppliers. Choosing within these controls ensures that the sample is representative.

All interviewers should keep contact sheets (see diagram 13) which record where an interview has been attempted, with whom, at what time and with what result. It is advisable that the researcher controlling the project designs his own contact sheet in order to standardize the system of recording. At the end of the survey the data from the contact sheets will show the ratio of interviews to contacts and provides a valuable finding in its own right. It is also needed as a control and perhaps for calculating the rate of pay.

Explaining the questionnaire will occupy a considerable proportion of the interviewer briefing. The researcher must take the interviewer through each question, describing its purpose and showing how it should be asked. One of the best ways of ensuring total familiarity with the questionnaire is to test it out on a fellow interviewer.

Role-playing is not always sufficient. In a large, technical survey it is important to train the field force on the job. Accompanying interviewers on their first visits and listening to them during telephone interviews may be necessary.

The technical content of questionnaires is different in every case. There are, however, aspects of questionnaire structure which remain the same and are worth emphasizing at the briefing:

Completion of all sections. It is not superfluous to point out that all sections of a questionnaire should be completed. Too often they are returned without the address of the company contacted, the position of the respondent or with no response against key questions. If a respondent cannot answer a question, this should be noted on the questionnaire, otherwise the editor is in doubt whether it has ever been asked.

Obeying instructions on the questionnaire. The questionnaire will contain instructions to interviewers which, according to questionnaire design convention, are usually in capitals. These instructions should not be read out to the respondents; they are intended for the interviewer alone and should be fully complied with. For example, the interviewer may be instructed to read out a list of names to the respondent and rotate them. The rotation instruction is important as it eliminates bias that would result from repeatedly presenting the names in a fixed order.

Giving meaningful answers. In the semi-structured questionnaires used in industrial market research there are many open-ended questions asking 'Why?' — 'Why did you buy this brand?', 'Why did you buy this size?',

Project: _____   Interviewer: _____

Company name	Address	Tel no	First contact Date	Time	Interview obtained	Other result	Second contact Date	Time	Interview obtained	Other result	Name of contact(s)	Position

DIAGRAM 13

Example of interviewer's contact sheet

'Why did you say this?' The respondent may well answer, 'Because it is best' or 'Because I have always bought it.'

These answers do not present the full story. The researcher wants to know *why* it is best or *why* they have always bought it. The interviewers must be instructed, therefore, to probe superficial answers until they determine the real reason.

Write clearly. A fully completed questionnaire which cannot be deciphered by the editor is of no use. The interviewer must complete the answers clearly — blue ballpoint rather than an H pencil — and legibly. If, as is the case with some interviewers, they find it difficult to write both fast and clearly, they must rewrite or type the answers on to a new questionnaire at a later stage.

Make margin notes and ask if in doubt. Questionnaires are never perfect, especially in industrial markets where there is a high variability of responses due to the spread in size and type of respondent. If the interviewer finds difficulty in classifying a response to a question, notes should be made in the margin or as an addendum. They could prove helpful to the researcher in interpreting the answer. It is inevitable in a technical subject that issues will be raised which the interviewer does not understand. Feigning comprehension will take the interviewer into deeper water. Respondents are only too happy to explain and are able to pitch their answers at the right level, if they know the limits of the interviewer's knowledge.

If, after the first interview, a question does not appear to be right, the interviewer must contact the researcher and seek advice. On no occasion must an interviewer proceed if uncertain about any questions or the response that is being achieved.

The briefing of interviewers should always be accompanied by briefing notes. If the briefing is face to face, the notes can be simple, short reminders of the key issues. Wherever the briefing is by telephone, tape or through the post, the need for thorough notes becomes essential. The notes should cover all topics — the objective of the fieldwork, a description of the product, the markets, how the sample will be selected, which person should be interviewed and explanatory remarks on the questionnaire itself. Finally, the interviewer should be given instructions on when and how to return the completed questionnaires, how to claim payment and expenses and the name, address and telephone number of someone to contact should the need arise. If questionnaires are to be returned by post, the researcher may prefer to give interviewers stamped-addressed envelopes (interviewers find it difficult to obtain stamps and large envelopes after 5.30 pm when dashing to get completed questionnaires in the last post).

Briefing notes should not be verbose. They are most effective when written in a curt and concise style to achieve impact and so that the interviewer can quickly assimilate the message.

When the survey is in the field the researcher must check that interviewers have started on time and work is progressing. A field force that is left to get on with it is more likely to make mistakes and could take short cuts. A healthy interest from the researcher as to how many and which interviews have been completed and what problems have been met will result in a positive reaction. Interviewers need to be assured that what they are doing is important and a constant show of interest from the researcher will provide this conviction.

Briefing desk researchers

If the people who are to undertake the desk research have no experience of sources, it will be necessary to point them in precisely the right direction, stating what information is required and where it can be found. Too much detail cannot be given on what and where. Sales rather than output, volume not value, a five-year trend not a single year, could be typical instructions. Guidance on where the data can be found should cover the name of the statistical source and where this is accessible – the government department, library, trade association or whatever. The person who is being briefed also needs instruction on how to report the data – by verbatim notes, summary notes or photocopied pages. Finally, it must be emphasized that all data needs to be attributed to a source and so references must always be given.

If the researcher has had desk research experience, the briefing can be more general: in this case he needs to know the objectives of the study, the expectations of the desk research and how they will key in with other parts, how he should present the data (photocopied pages and working notes or fully written up), when the information is needed and to whom it should be given. If sources of data are known to the person responsible for the briefing then, naturally, they should be passed to the desk researcher to save him time.

Briefing recruiters for group discussions

Interviewers recruit people for a group or a clinic using a simple questionnaire designed to determine their eligibility to attend. Ownership or experience of a product, responsibility for specifying or buying, functional position, may all determine eligibility. There may be a quota of size of company or type of company that also affects recruitment.

The recruiter must be briefed on the use of the recruitment questionnaire together with special points which are not normally a part of conventional interviewing.

Incentives. Respondents who come to groups or clinics are usually offered a gift which they receive on attendance. The recruiter should be briefed on what this gift is in order to mention it during recruitment as an incentive.

Date, time and location of group. The recruiter needs precise details, including instructions on how to get to the venue, should anyone ask.

Invitation cards. An invitation card may be left at the time the respondent is recruited or a letter may be sent subsequently confirming the details. The recruiter may be responsible for the administration, in which case she needs the necessary paperwork.

Contact sheets. Lists should be kept of companies and persons contacted and those where a successful recruitment has been achieved.

Hostessing. When the group meeting takes place, the recruiter may be involved in hostess duties. These could range from help with the coffee and giving out the gifts through to product demonstration.

Briefing analysts and report writers

Where there are tens and not hundreds of questionnaires the analysis of industrial interviews is often carried out manually rather than by computer. Each questionnaire tells an individual story and margin notes or special comments can be more enlightening if they can be attributed to a source.

When assistance is employed for the analysis, the researcher must state whether he wants each questionnaire transcribed on to a master tabulation or if a simple count of responses will suffice. Groups of users may be analysed separately to allow for comparison one with the other.

Help for analysis is best organized by breaking the work into stages and supervising each step before moving on to the next. Thus the coding frame would be designed and agreed, the responses to each question slotted in, the numbers counted and tables constructed. Discussion at each stage would permit special instructions for a new cross analysis or table if it appeared relevant.

Just as the analysis is best handled as a collection of separate but sequential jobs, so too is report writing. The first step is to brief the report writer on the subjects which need covering in the text. This list will be derived from the questionnaire coverage and the objectives in the proposal. The report writer should then draw up a detailed table of contents including subheadings and briefly state which topics will be discussed under each. When this is approved, the writing up of one section can begin. As a section is finished it should be read and ratified before moving on to the next.

Organizing a personally conducted research programme

Industrial market research, especially that carried out in-house, is frequently undertaken by one person who must cope with the whole exercise — designing the questionnaire, selecting the sample frame, doing the interviews, analysing them and writing the report. Though there is no field force to brief, it is important to marshal one's own resources efficiently.

Where the program is mainly telephone interviews there are few problems. Concentrating the interviews to fit in with cheaper call times may save money but it is worth testing to see if the more expensive period yields a higher strike rate. If peak pricing times are spent idly waiting for the cheaper rate, or respondents prove hard to contact during off-peak times, the efforts to save money are ineffective and possibly counter-productive. Local calls (wherever feasible) in the morning and distance calls during the afternoon would be a balanced program of telephoning.

Planning the personal visit interviews is a logistical exercise. It is useful to start with a route planning map on which can be plotted the proposed companies to sample, using a colour code to indicate vital interviews. Geographical groupings will emerge around which appointments can be made. Problems occur when, inevitably, respondents' diaries are incompatible with the researcher's. Small and medium-size companies can be substituted one for another but large and key companies must be visited. These, therefore, should be the first line of attack with all others arranged around them.

It is never possible to control fully the time spent on an interview; the respondent may, for example, accept interruptions such as telephone calls. Traffic delays and difficulties of route finding in strange areas can further disrupt a tight interviewing schedule. It is better, therefore, to leave the proposed time of the interview flexible, settling for early morning, mid afternoon, etc. A letter confirming the visit is a must — especially when the interviewer is travelling some distance or the company is a key respondent. Unfortunately, market researchers have a low priority in some respondents' eyes. Respondents will change their programs and may not be able to contact an interviewer who has telephoned without leaving a phone number. A letter confirms the interview and should restate the time and date of the proposed visit and give some indication of what the discussion will be about. Finally, the letter should provide a hook which will convince the respondent that he was right to grant the interview and that he himself will benefit.

At the beginning of a fieldwork program the researcher may not know all the companies he hopes to interview. His initial contact may, for example, be used as a source of reference from which leads are obtained. Inevitably, inefficiencies in interviewing will occur with some criss-crossing and backtracking. Also, towards the end of an interview program, there is usually the need to sweep up respondents who were unable to fit into the earlier dates. Individual judgements must be made at this stage as to whether a visit is essential or if a telephone interview will be acceptable.

Reporting sessions

During the course of the study the sponsor will expect an account of progress. The progress reports may be by letter, telephone or visit and should aim to cover the following points:

Work done to date together with an indication of whether the survey is on schedule or, if not, how far behind it is.

Work yet to do especially highlighting any of the critical areas which will result in a significant input of data.

Tentative findings. In some surveys it is possible to report back findings at an interim stage. The findings should be qualified if they require further work to substantiate them. Where there is a possibility they could be incomplete or misleading, they should not be given at all. Progress reports are for reporting on progress and not for presenting findings.

Suggested modifications to the program. The knowledge of the market which has been obtained in the study to date may suggest to the researcher an alternative approach. The argument for any modifications and the recommended changes should be spelt out in the progress report and approval obtained for the action.

Final reporting date. Confirmation is required in a progress report that the study will be finished on time or, if it is in advance or behind schedule, the revised date for presentation.

Summary

When a survey receives the go-ahead, the researcher must finalize the timetable, paying particular attention to the critical path which shows the research components that must be completed in order that work flows smoothly and on time.

In a survey with a large number of interviews, the researcher must brief the field force. Wherever possible, this should be face to face and accompanied by notes which cover product descriptions, instructions on the selection of companies and respondents, explanations about the questionnaire and details for returning the completed work.

Many industrial surveys are carried out by one person who must organize visits over a wide geographical area. Key companies should form the central framework and others be fitted around them.

Part Four:
Methods

Chapter 16
Desk Research (Domestic)

The uses of desk research

Desk research is the study of published information. That is not to say it is always carried out from a desk — it may involve visiting libraries, sending off for information, and speaking over the telephone to people who can provide data or say where to find it. It involves reviewing published information and relating whatever is relevant to the question in hand. Sometimes desk research is called *secondary research* to distinguish it from *primary research* which is the collection of raw data.

Desk research is an important starting point for most projects. There is no purpose in carrying out expensive fieldwork to solve a problem if the answer already exists in published form. Desk research costs little and is quick. It is easy to carry out and is possibly one of the most useful tools available to the researcher working on a limited budget.

Desk research plays a part in most projects to a degree. In the paragraphs which follow we describe the applications for desk research from its role in providing a general economic background through to profiling companies and the products they make.

Providing an economic background

A business plan, a market survey, or an industry review generally needs a backcloth of the economic environment. This is the macro scene, the broader picture. There will be circumstances when it is hardly relevant. Attitude research on coffee and tea does not require an economic backcloth as much as a study which considers consumers' views on banks and building societies.

The sources of economic data are legion. At the start of each year forecasts of the economy abound and updates are carried out at intervals. The results are published in the *Wall Street Journal* in the USA and the *Financial Times* in Europe. The US Department Of Commerce publishes an annual forecast on the prospects for 350 industries in its *US Industrial*

173

Outlook. The outlook is given for the current year and a prediction is made for the next four years.

Again in the USA, Forbes do an *Annual Report on American Industry* which is published in January. This covers broad industry descriptions such as chemicals, steel, etc.

In the UK, *Economic Trends*, published monthly by the government's statistical service, gives time series of data on indices of output, demand, unemployment and inflation. The weekly financial press such as the *Economist* and the *Investors Chronicle* contain useful articles on the health of the UK and other nations. Banks publish appraisals of the domestic economy in most countries throughout the world. They are generally happy to provide these free or for a small charge through their economics departments.

Assessing market size and trends

Every country publishes statistics on the output and sales of its major products and services. These publications may contain the market size information that the researcher is looking for. If they do not, it may still be possible to derive the market size from a known link with published data.

☐ In the USA the *Statistical Abstract of the US* published by the US Department of Commerce, Bureau of Census in Washington, is an annual record of sales and production. The performance of 50 States is compared, trends are given for recent years in both tabular and graphical form. Population statistics are available on the major metropolitan areas. Data is included on new and topical issues such as consumer credit, leisure, computers, etc.

☐ The Department of Commerce in Washington also publishes the *Census of Manufacturers*. This five-year census is the most detailed insight into US industry statistics one could hope to find. It shows the number of establishments by Standard Industrial Classification (SIC), the number of employees in the SICs (including an analysis by production workers), the value of shipments, the cost of materials, and the value added in manufacturing. A breakdown is provided by region, division and state. The only problem, and one that is associated with most census material no matter who produces it, is the delay between collecting the data and publishing it. Around five years is needed to get it all into hard copy though some data is available in advance on microfiche.

☐ In the UK, market size statistics are presented in a summary form in the *Annual Abstract of Statistics* published by the Central Statistical Office in London. In a similar fashion to its American counterpart, the *Annual Abstract* contains a wide range of statistical data going back many years. There is data on demographics, the economy, construction and industrial output.

☐ Another UK publication of the government's statistical service, this time from the Business Statistics Office in Cardiff, is the *Business Monitor*. This is a quarterly statistical report showing manufacturers' sales, imports and exports for every industry. It is the market researcher's bible, being comprehensive, reasonably accurate, and available just a few months (about six) after the data has been collected.

Government publications may not contain the information which the researcher is looking for, in which case he must look towards one of the many trade associations which publish statistics about their members. Trade associations arose out of a need to provide commercial information on the market for their members. Some of them still offer more detail and better accuracy than the official government sources. Apart from a few notable exceptions (the automobile industry is one), trade associations are lacking because they are not wholly representative of the industry, and the ever-changing membership makes it difficult to compare year-to-year figures. A researcher who is not working for a member of an association could find that the door is closed to his questions, the statistics being for internal circulation only.

If data is not available in official publications, it may still be possible to obtain an estimate of market size by derivation from other published figures. A researcher may need to assess the demand for overalls in the garage trade. A few interviews with garages would tell him the number of overalls mechanics typically buy each year. Census data or one of the annual abstracts would show the number of employees in the garage trade. A few adjustments may need to be made to ensure that only mechanics (and not staff) are included in the figures. The calculation of market size is now derived by simple multiplication of the number of employees and the use of overalls per mechanic per year.

Table 13 shows a worked example of how the market size for a chemical has been derived from the number of employees in each SIC. The statistics are for the UK but the same data is available within the USA.

Analysing market structure
The market structure is the warp and weft of the industry. It is the way that the manufacturers, the distributors, the end users and other players in the market fit and relate one to the other. Desk research can provide a picture.

Lists of companies supplying products can be found in directories. Trade associations publish lists of members and a few minutes over the

175

TABLE 13

Calculation of market size for a cleaning chemical
(Based on known ratio of employees to expenditure on chemical)

Standard Industrial Classification (SIC)	Average annual expenditure/ employee (pence)[1]	Total no of employees in sector (000s)[2]	Estimate of market size (£000s)
Food, drink and tobacco	10.40	688.9	71.6
Coal and petroleum products	3.15	32.9	1.0
Chemical and allied industries	6.80	376.9	25.6
Metal manufacture	20.00	424.6	84.9
Mechanical engineering	29.00	869.8	252.2
Instrument engineering	7.73	150.0	11.6
Electrical engineering	25.30	673.6	170.4
Shipbuilding and marine engineering	27.00	148.9	40.2
Vehicles	24.45	735.9	179.9
Metal goods not elsewhere specified	15.38	471.6	72.5
Textiles	2.80	435.3	12.2
Leather, leather goods and fur	1.96	35.4	0.7
Clothing and footwear	2.55	369.2	9.4
Bricks, pottery, glass and cement	3.22	239.3	7.7
Timber, furniture	2.14	247.9	5.3
Paper, printing and publishing	8.70	525.6	45.7
Other manufacturing industries	13.60	320.5	43.6
All manufacturing industries	15.33	x 6746.5	= 1034.5

1. From survey of customers   (rounded figures)
2. From *Annual Abstract of Statistics*

phone to one of their officials would indicate which companies, if any, are missing. Ads in journals broadcast the interest of companies and their product range. Using these sources a comprehensive listing of companies buying, selling and distributing products can be compiled. The researcher can quickly obtain a feel for the most important companies simply by virtue of the number of times they are noted in the directories or ads. The size of the major companies can be checked out by Dun & Bradstreet, McCarthy or Extel cards.

Desk research can only give an overview of a market. The proportion of a company's sales in a particular product group is difficult to establish without a detailed interview program. Desk research can, however, be useful in building up a background to the market from articles published in the press and journals. The subject could have been studied by a market research agency and be available as a multi-client report for a modest sum.

An important part of the analysis of market structure is an assessment of imports and exports. These show:

- [ ] the level of competition which is being exerted on the domestic market from overseas and which countries are the principal culprits.
- [ ] the opposite side of the coin is the opportunity that is being taken by domestic manufacturers to supply overseas territories. The export statistics will show where the sales are going and in what volume and value.
- [ ] by simple division of the value of imports by the number of units or tonnes, an approximation can be obtained of the average prices at which goods are entering the country.
- [ ] an analysis of the statistics over a period of time may tell a story about the activity of importers. By relating the figures to a variable such as the £:$ relationship, it could show the extent to which imports are affected by swings in exchange rates.

Import and export data are published in the US by the US Department of Commerce (exports are published in their *Schedule E* document and imports in their *Schedule A* document). In the UK the collection of import and export data is the responsibility of the Customs and Excise Bill of Entry Section, while the publication and presentation of data are carried out by a small number of private companies working to the specification of the Customs and Excise.

Obtaining data on companies

Desk research is an excellent means of building up profiles of customers, potential customers or competitors. Companies publish a great deal of information on themselves but it is usually produced at different times and aimed at different audiences. The researcher must do his best to draw it together.

The finance department of a UK company must submit a summary of its annual accounts to Companies House in London. The researcher can access these direct or through an agent for a small sum. If the company is quoted on the stock exchange, it must comply with the rules and regulations of the country which invariably requires some form of annual report. In the US, companies must file a 10-K report with the Securities Exchange Commission. The same report is available to any person requesting it directly from the company (it is not unknown for companies to drag their heels in complying, as the 10-K report is expensive and gives potentially useful information to competitors).

UK quoted companies must produce annual reports and accounts and these too will be sent, on request, by the company secretary. The accounts include a chairman's statement which can provide clues as to the strengths, weaknesses and direction of the company. The profit and loss account gives the latest turnover, profit and costs of the company. The balance sheet shows the capital which is employed in the company and how this is broken down between the fixed and variable elements. There is usually an historical review of turnover, profit and key operating ratios which show the trends. The financial ratios which are of most use to market researchers are illustrated in Diagram 14.

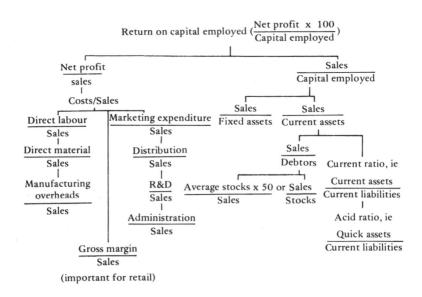

DIAGRAM 14

Pyramid of key financial ratios

Profiles on companies' financial status can be obtained from organizations such as Dun & Bradstreet. More details may be found in the US publications of *Standard and Poor's Register of Corporations, Directors and Executives* (a three-volume edition, the first containing 45,000 corporations, their annual sales, number of employees; the second contains 72,000 officers and directors; the third is the classification of the companies under 900 SIC headings). *Moody's Industrial Manual* covers in two volumes all the companies on the US stock exchange. It gives detailed financial profiles on each, including a history of the company's development, its products, its management, and its financial performance. Credit scores from Aaa to c are used to rate the companies as investment risks.

In the US and Europe, profiles on the large private and all the quoted companies can be bought from Dun & Bradstreet or on cards from McCarthy, or Extel. McCarthy provides a culling of the financial comment in the press on each company while Extel gives the history, profit and loss and asset statements.

The financial performance of companies can be conveniently compared in one of the ratio reports sold by companies such as Inter Company Comparisons (ICC) of London. These reports are undertaken on industry sectors and give a quick overview of their structure – the largest companies, their sales and profitability. They are based on the data available only within the accounts and so have limitations as a result. They do not, for example, show how much of the sales or profit of a company derives from particular groups of the products it manufactures.

Financial accounts are not the only source of information on companies. The promotions which companies pump out are designed to inform and full use should be made of them by the market researcher. Naturally, being the public face, promotions tend to gloss and puff up the company. They do, however, provide one of the best insights to an outsider of the company's culture. The ads in the press, in journals or on posters cry out what type of company it is. Old-fashioned companies have old-fashioned ads.

The advertising content itself is worth examining. It could provide answers to any or all of the following:

- the products which the company sells, with emphasis on those which are of current interest;
- the design of the products, especially the claims for any unique features;
- the way in which the products are made;
- the price of the products, and the philosophy of the company on pricing (whether it takes an aggressive or more reserved stance);
- the number of products which have ever been sold, and possibly the company's sales over a particular period;
- the number and location of factories, their size and resources;
- the position of the company in the market place (market leader; number one; number two; we are new, etc);
- the number and location of distributors selling or stocking the product;
- the R&D support given to the product, or that which was involved in its development;

179

☐ the company's major customers (testimonial ads feature only these);
☐ the company's approach to customer service.

The source of the ads is likely to influence the copy and the content. Ads in directories have to have staying power since they will be there for a duration. They may feature the location of service centres or name the distributors. Ads in journals and the press are more immediate and are therefore changed more frequently. They may give details of prices and of recent product launches. Recruitment ads can also tell a story. The very fact that a new marketing or production manager is being sought could be significant. The text in the ad may say what the company has done in the past and where it plans to go in the future. Recruitment ads often have a statement of the company's philosophy; important to the potential recruit, but a further piece of a jigsaw to the researcher.

In consumer markets it is comparatively easy to assess the weight of the advertising carried out by companies. The UK publication *Media Expenditure Analysis (MEAL)* shows the value of press and consumer journal advertising expenditure for important brands. (Figures are given at full rates, before discounts.) This source does not help the researcher trying to assess the value of a company's business-to-business advertising as these promotions are mainly in the technical and trade journals. A laborious task of screening trade media must be carried out to determine the number of ads placed. An approximation as to the advertising budget can then be arrived at by applying the rates for insertions as given in *British Rate And Data (BRAD)* for the UK or *Standard Rate & Data Service* for the USA.

The company brochure will possibly show pictures of the factory giving many a clue as to its production capabilities. It may include nuggets on the output of the products — how many have been made, what type of machinery is used in production, the square footage of production space, cutout diagrams of the product showing how it is made. Space devoted to different products in a brochure is a reasonable guide as to the importance of that range to the company (the exception is when a company is trying to build up a product and is giving it exceptional weight in its promotions).

Company or house journals can be a fertile field of information on companies to researchers. In between the recipes and retirement news there are likely to be reports of orders won and new investments at the plant. The editors of house journals make full use of the press releases which the company has put out over the recent period. Getting hold of a house journal can, therefore, save time trying to pick up all the press releases from a review of the press.

The public relations departments of companies churn out facts and figures on output. Open the newspaper on any day and it will be full of information on companies' plans and intentions. As this chapter is being prepared, the *Financial Times* of the day has a couple of columns on the investment plans of Craven Tasker — one of the UK's largest semi-trailer manufacturers. The article refers to Craven Tasker's £24 million turnover and sales of 2000 trailers a year. It mentions the size of the UK trailer market as 250,000 trailers; a figure which is being reduced by the more efficient use of equipment. A report is given of the company's recent investment of £500,000 in new trailer-making facilities at its Sheffield plant. Interesting information if you are a customer of Craven Tasker, but fascinating if you are Crane Fruehauf, making similar products.

Exhibitions are an opportunity for the researcher to take a look at all the companies in a market at the same time. Literature and sample products will be available on the stands with a company representative there to help further if need be. The exhibition manual will contain special articles of current interest and ads on the companies attending. It may prove to contain one of the best lists of companies in the industry.

Obtaining data on products and prices

The previous paragraphs have shown how desk research can provide information on companies. By definition, some of this information will also refer to products and prices. However, if price and product data is the target information being sought, the researcher can home in on specific sources.

In consumer markets the researcher has only to walk into a few shops or phone some outlets to find out the prices on the shelves. It doesn't necessarily tell him the discounts which preceded. Price lists may be published. This tends to be the case for products which have a high turnover and are consumables. Industrial products which are capital goods or specials are priced on request only.

Price indices are useful to measure trends in inflation. These can be obtained from the Bureau of the Census in the US or from the Central Statistical Office (refer to the quarterly *Business Monitor* or the monthly *Monthly Digest of Statistics*) in the UK.

Desk research as a means of sample selection

Desk research is often used for selecting samples. The 'sample frame' or the source of the sample may be one or more directories. Consumer samples could be selected from the domestic telephone book or from specialized brokers' lists (eg people who have purchased certain products, who have been on holiday to certain areas, who have written in to a journal asking for more details on products, etc). If a company is supplying products direct to the consumer, as in the case of mail order, it may be appropriate to sample from the customer list.

Industrial companies have a more varied, and usually less reliable, range of sample sources open to them. Trade directories, lists in buyers guides, ads of companies in journals, brokers' lists of specialized companies may all be used. As we shall describe in more detail in Chapter 18, industrial sampling is fraught with difficulties, not least because of the inadequacies of the sample frames.

Sources of information on desk research

There are thousands of sources of published information. There are special books just listing directories; others listing trade associations. There are books on sources of sources. Our aim in this section is to highlight the most important and readily available of these. As Dr Samuel Johnson said, 'The next best thing to knowing something, is knowing where to find it'.

Names and addresses of suppliers of directories, government departments and other useful contacts are provided in Appendix 1.

Sources on sources
There are a number of general guides to sources of information which are well worth owning by anyone who is likely to research markets more than once or twice a year.

The *Aslib Directory of Information Sources in the United Kingdom* is produced in two volumes. Volume 1 is for the market researcher. It is an alphabetical listing of all the important desk sources on science, technology and industry. Included are the names, addresses, and a short background on the larger companies, libraries, trade associations and what information one could expect to obtain from each.

A publication (one of many) from Gale Research Co of Detroit entitled *Statistics Sources* is useful to the researcher working in the US and the UK. It is a subject guide to data on industrial, business, social, financial, educational and other topics for countries throughout the world. For example, if you wanted to know the copper production in Bulgaria, you would look under the country name and find a listing of 'copper production' sources. You would now be in a position to direct your inquiry at the right sources.

Also from Gale Research Co is the *Encyclopedia of Business Information Sources*. This book gives an alphabetical listing of 1200 subjects. There is a short citation on each together with the address of the publisher and its price.

Government statistics
Governments collect statistics for their own use and, as a by-product, make most of them available to the public, usually at a nominal price. They are therefore the bread and butter of the market researcher, being

comprehensive, cheap and widely available.

GOVERNMENT STATISTICS IN THE USA

No other country in the world collects as much data or makes it as available as the USA. The most important organ of the government, responsible for data collection, is the Bureau of the Census. National censuses are carried out every five years to provide benchmark data on business, industry and agriculture. A ten-year census of the population produces demographic data down to neighbourhood level. The team of 4000 statisticians collect data on virtually every country in the world. The Census Bureau publishes information in printed reports, microfiche and computer tapes. Maps are also available.

It is to be expected that with an organization of this size, the Census Bureau can tell the researcher everything about anything. The publications that will cover most of his requirements are, however, the *Statistical Abstract of the US* (giving a statistical overview of the USA, trends, population estimates, etc) and the *Census of Manufacturers* (giving immense detail on industry by SICs).

GOVERNMENT STATISTICS IN THE UK

In the UK the official statistics are collected by the Business Statistics Office and the Office of Population, Censuses and Surveys. These two bodies are coordinated by the Central Statistical Office.

A valuable overview of the sources of UK government statistics is the *Guide to Official Statistics.*

Business Monitors are the most important source of data on the output of manufacturing industry. They are published quarterly by the Business Statistics Office and cover quite detailed products, usually using descriptions which correspond with the minimum list headings in the Standard Industrial Classification. The first *Business Monitors* were introduced in the early 1970s. Since that time their accuracy has been improved, so that today they are likely to embrace nearly every company employing more than 25 people in any industry sector.

Monthly Digest of Statistics and the useful yearly compilation, *The Annual Abstract of Statistics,* contain a wide range of statistical information with time series going back years on demographics, the economy and industrial output. They are a quick and easy source of information on trends or a base from which the assessment of a market can be made.

These sources for the USA and the UK are very much the tip of the statistical iceberg. In each country there are abundant statistics on agriculture, construction, mineral production, and transport. Special commissions sometimes look at an industry in depth to assess a problem such as long-term decline or the threat of imports. Reports by the Monopolies and Mergers Commission in the UK and the Anti-Trust Division of the Department of Justice in the USA are among the most comprehensive and detailed available to the researcher — if he is fortunate enough to be researching a sector which has recently been scrutinized.

Directories

Directories are used by market researchers all the time. They provide listings of companies operating in a market; they give specific data on ownership; they show who is managing the companies; they give financial backgrounds on them.

There are directories on virtually every subject: over 3000 in the UK alone. A good library will have all the 'standards' and many of the specialist directories. The appropriate one for the project in hand can be located in one of the directories on directories. In the UK good sources are *Current British Directories* from CBD Research or *The Top 1000 Directories and Annuals* from Alan Armstrong Associates. In the USA the *Directory of Directories* is the best source.

STANDARD DIRECTORIES ON THE USA

MacRae's Blue Book: from Business Research Publications, this annual directory is published in five volumes. These volumes incorporate an alphabetical listing of products under which are classified the companies, their addresses and size (measured by a turnover code). The product listings run from 'abrasives' through to 'zirconium sulfate'. Also from MacRae's are directories of manufacturers' representatives (sales agents in the UK) and firms which market their products through manufacturers' representatives.

Thomas's Register: from Thomas Publishing Co, there are 15 volumes of this annually published listing of companies. The first 12 give company details classified under products from 'abacus' to 'zonolite'. Volumes 13 and 14 provide company profiles, A to Z fashion with addresses, zip codes, telephone numbers, asset ratings and details of the management. Volumes 15 to 21 are a catalog file.

Standard and Poor's Register of Corporations, Directors and Executives: this three-volume register contains 45,000 corporations in the first volume (A to Z listing), management details on 72,000 people in the second volume and an SIC grouping of the companies in the third volume.

Ward's Directory: there are two popular Ward's directories for the researcher — *The 51,000 Largest US Corporations* and *The 49,000 Private US Companies*. Details are ranked by sales and employee size and within SIC industries. Full data is provided on name, address, chief executive, phone number, sales, number of employees, SIC code, etc, in three volumes — alphabetical, geographical and industrial.

US Industrial Directories: from Cahners Publications, thère are four directories: *The Product Directory* lists products and services organized by product; *The Address Directory* is useful for locating suppliers' addresses and telephone numbers from a company, trade or brand name; *The Literature Directory* has catalogs and literature on products; and *Fastfax* is a directory of cards which can be sent off to obtain information on prices, specifications, etc.

The National Directory of Addresses and Telephone Numbers: published annually, this directory contains details of all the larger US corporations.

Sheldons Retail Directory: provides details of the largest US department stores, women's specialty stores, chain stores, and the resident buying officers at these locations.

Forbes 500: an annual directory of the 500 largest US companies ranked in terms of their sales, assets, profits, and market value. It also gives the companies' names and addresses.

The Municipal Yearbook: this is a specialty directory, but since governments are so important as buyers, it is worth including in this 'standards' section. It gives details on city managements, government and local government, and has a directory of officers and their departments.

Trade Names Dictionary: another Gale Research publication listing 194,000 consumer-oriented trade names.

The Directory of Corporate Affiliations: from the National Register Publishing Company. This directory is a *Who Owns Whom.* The first section cross-references over 40,000 divisions, subsidiaries and affiliates with their parent company. Section 2 lists over 4000 parent companies, provides a short financial and management profile and also gives their subsidiaries and affiliations. There is a geographical as well as an SIC index.

Telephone books: the domestic telephone books and the Yellow Pages are standards for sampling. The Business Yellow Pages is a convenient compilation for up-to-date telephone numbers.

STANDARD DIRECTORIES ON THE UK

Kompass: this is one of the best general directories on UK industry. It lists over 25,000 companies in Volume 1, together with their addresses and product codes. Volume 2 contains expanded entries on over 30,000 companies, grouped by county and town and showing the address, telephone number, product codes, directors, numbers of employees and some brief financial data for each.

Kelly's: the *Manufacturers and Merchants* volume contains companies classified under product headings. Also within the same directory is an A to Z listing of 100,000 companies summarizing their main activity, address and telephone number.

Rylands: this is a directory of the engineering industry. It contains listings of the names, addresses and telephone numbers together with directors and brief details of the capital structure.

Stubbs: The National Business Directory. Published by Dun & Bradstreet, it has a listing of 90,000 companies with their addresses, telephone numbers and key activity. A *Buyer's Guide* divides the businesses into 2000 trade classifications. There is a separate guide to the offshore oil and gas industry.

Dun & Bradstreet: The Key British Enterprises is a useful listing of the top 20,000 companies in the UK. Each entry has details of turnover and the capital structure, the industry classification of the company and a full listing of directors and their function. A section of the directory has a grouping of the companies under SICs and is therefore useful for sampling purposes.

Who Owns Whom: this is the standard work for sorting out the tangle of company parentage. It gives a full listing of all companies which are part of a group.

Sells: Sells Products and Services contains an A to Z of companies and details on their addresses, etc. 60,000 firms are listed according to their products or services. There is a special section on trade names with over 10,000 names which can be linked back to companies.

Municipal Yearbook: this directory provides names and addresses of all the local, county and government offices in the UK. It contains useful sections on the power industry and general information on public services.

Telephone books: the 'white pages' and the Yellow Pages are the most comprehensive listings of private and business telephone numbers and addresses in the UK. This is despite the fact that the white pages, which list domestic (and business) subscribers to the telephone, only contain just over 80 per cent of the subscribers because of the large number of ex-directory customers.

Libraries
Libraries are a temporary home for the researcher working on desk research. In a good library, he can locate, examine, cogitate and copy (copyright permitting) information from directories, industry files, journals, the press

and statistical publications of the government and other bodies.

In the UK, local and city libraries are to very high standard, many with commercial sections. Librarians are capable of dealing with requests from businessmen and, as long as the question is reasonably straightforward, they are prepared to answer telephone inquiries.

The USA is rich in libraries but there is a greater emphasis on special ones than in the UK. In both countries, researchers are usually welcome in libraries run by business schools, universities, government agencies, companies, societies, trade associations, newspapers, etc.

The *Aslib Directory of Information Sources in the United Kingdom* provides a comprehensive listing of libraries in the UK. Gale Research's *Directory of Special Libraries and Information Centres* and the *American Library Directory* from R R Bowker are the equivalent sources in the USA.

Trade associations

Before governments undertook the job of data collection, it was the role of trade associations. Long-established industries had their own associations and produced excellent commercial statistics. Hence there were strong trade associations in steel, glass bottles, wire and textiles. The powerful motor industry was represented by an equally powerful trade association. The 'sunrise industries' of the 1970s and 80s do not have the necessity for commercial data collection agencies. There is no need for a trade association to collect data on computer shipments since this is undertaken by officialdom.

The fact that some trade associations still collect data is partly an historical legacy and partly because of the inadequacies of the official sources. The Society of Motor Manufacturers and Traders in the UK and the Automobile Manufacturers Association in the US are able to devote a resource to the collection of statistics which the government could not do. They can keep certain information confidential to members, sell other information and above all keep control.

The data collection services of some trade associations have their disadvantages. Membership is often incomplete. Large manufacturers and suppliers may choose to stay out of the association believing that they have more to lose than gain from the disclosure of data, even though it is consolidated along with that from other companies and not attributable to any single firm. Shifting membership over the years can make difficult the comparison of time series of data.

Finally, the reporting of data by the member companies is not always what it should be. The job of sending in data may be delegated and given little attention. Adjustments which should be made to make sense of peculiar circumstances could be overlooked because no one who understands the data is there to make the changes. It is not unknown for some

187

members to deliberately 'cook' their figures so that they do not give anything away and to confuse the competition.

Trade associations are not always open to market researchers as sources of statistical data. Much depends on the researcher's ability to charm the organization's secretary. Statistical data apart, the trade associations can be useful for obtaining an overview of a market and those with technical research facilities are generally helpful in providing pointers on future changes.

Guides to which trade associations do what are Gale Publication's *Encyclopedia of Associations* (for the US) and CBD Research's *Directory of European Associations* (for the UK).

Internal company sources

Sales figures on the researcher's own organization can be processed to reveal clues on the shape and structure of the market. They may show where the geography of demand lies (or where there are gaps); the typical customer classifications and purchasing patterns. Analyses of customers by rank can show if there is a dependency on a small group of firms or industries. Statistics on the company can be set alongside those for the market as a whole to show the share it holds. If data exists over a number of years, trends in the market can be identified.

The in-house market researcher working within a large company undoubtedly has a wealth of information available to him from colleagues. Salesmen's reports can give a picture of competitive activity and pricing. The salesmen and sales managers will have information and views on the market which are constantly being updated but which may not have been committed to paper. Talking to them can be extremely rewarding.

Technical members of staff may sit on standards committees and meet with their opposite numbers from other companies. They may have been on visits to competitors' plants to see special items of equipment. Publicity managers will hold files on competitors' literature. Managing directors may have played host to their counterparts in competitor companies and discussions about the market will almost certainly have taken place.

The in-house researcher is in a privileged position to interview and collect data from these people. They will provide a useful introduction at the beginning of the survey and can be used as cross-checks as the work progresses.

Market research companies

Many market research companies carry out studies on their own initiative which they subsequently sell as multi-client reports. The costs of these reports is far below that of an *ad hoc* commission. The price of the report will vary from less than $100 to over $2000 depending on the subject and the depth of coverage. Studies which cover a number of countries are clearly likely to be expensive, especially if they are based on a large field-work program.

The companies selling the studies will be happy to send details of the contents and a few sample pages. Some will allow sight of the report, though not in circumstances which would allow it to be photocopied.

Lists of multi-client reports, including their contents and prices, can be obtained from *The International Directory of Published Market Research* published by the British Overseas Trade Board in London.

Electronic desk research

The early 1980s saw the development of electronic communications, allowing the access of commercial databases via a modem and a personal computer. Once linked to the database, the researcher can search for information by means of special instructions, often simply a word or string of words which describes the subject of study. Whilst online to the database the researcher can review the information he is collecting and refine the search. Data is available on the screen of the VDU or an instruction can be given to send it offline by post.

The first databases covered mainly technical topics and were of limited use to the researcher. Today, databases are mushrooming on every subject. There are numerous marketing and business databases; some providing abstracts and references, others of optically read material which allows full text searching. The companies which host or own the databases run courses to train researchers in their use. Information on databases that are most suitable to market researchers can be obtained from one of the directories on the subject: Gale Research's *Encyclopedia of Business Information Services* contains online databases, as does the *Online Business Sourcebook* from Headland Press of London.

There is a temptation for the market researcher to see electronic desk research as the answer to his problems. Sitting in front of a computer calling up information beats getting a headache in libraries. However, online searching is expensive and there is a tendency at first to overuse it at considerable expense. (You pay by the minute for time in the database and, in some circumstances, selectively for information which you call up.) Lack of familiarity with the database search commands results in wasted time and frustration. Eventually the commands are learned and search strategies become second nature — but only after many hours of experiment. At the present state of the technology, it is probably only feasible to operate online databases economically if one person is trained to do the work. It is not something which can be played with now and then.

In the meantime, the market researcher will find that the conventional approach to desk research has great merit. It allows time to review and consider the data. Just being in a library presents opportunities to look around at other sources which may prove useful. The researcher has before him a wider range of material than is available on the database — maps, obscure directories, specialized journals, ads in magazines and the press, photographs and diagrams.

Online database searching has a useful role in desk research. It is quick and, as long as the necessary information is there on the database, it is more thorough than a tedious manual search. It is especially suitable for providing a bibliography of sources which the researcher can choose to follow up in the conventional manner.

TABLE 14
Action checklist to determine market size by desk research

Step	Action	If unsuccessful
1	Examine *The Statistical Abstract.*	Phone the Bureau of the Census, Washington DC. To step 2.
2	From leads provided by the Bureau of the Census search for other government sources of statistics.	To step 3.
3	Identify and contact relevant trade association from *Encyclopedia of Associations.*	Obtain leads from trade association. To step 4, 5, 6, or 7.
4	Search articles in trade magazines and press using McCarthy's or an abstracting service.	Phone relevant journals for leads. To step 5, 6 or 7.
5	Build up lists of sales of companies from Dun & Bradstreet, Extel, etc. Make estimates of proportion of turnover derived from product of interest.	To step 6 or 7.
6	Determine if any correlation exists with other products or employment. Seek data on that product or employment base as per step 2.	To step 7.
7	Check in directories of published market research for availability of multi-client report.	Consider fieldwork survey to discover market size.

TABLE 15
Action checklist to obtain product information by desk research

Step	Action	If unsuccessful
1	Write to company asking for brochures, data sheets, prices.	Contact distributors for same information.
2	Search trade journals and appropriate media for ads, editorial mentions, articles, product reviews.	Contact journals as a check. Try abstracting service. To step 3.
3	Search buyers' guides and directories for product specifications and background.	To step 4 or 5.
4	Buy or rent sample product for testing (obviously impractical for large or expensive items) or take photographs of products at dealers or end-users.	To step 5.
5	Search for exhibitions to visit where product may be displayed.	Consider commissioning study to find users of product.

TABLE 16
Action checklist to obtain information on a company or companies

Step	Action	If unsuccessful
1	Obtain accurate name, address and telephone number from a directory or buyers' guide. Phone reception to check on accuracy.	Question Directory Enquiries, competitive company, distributor, known end-user in case of change of name or address. To step 2.
2	Assemble basic data on date of formation, product range, subsidiary companies, parent, number of employees, directors, financial status, etc from directories. Build up list of distributors from ads in Yellow Pages or buyers' guides.	Check with distributors, competitors, other companies that may know. To step 3.
3	Check for Department of Justice Anti-Trust Division reports on the industry and industry reports published in *Wall Street Journal*. Obtain copies.	To step 4.
4	Write to company's publicity department for corporate brochure and literature.	Try sales department. Try distributor. To step 5.
5	Obtain largest Ordnance Survey map of factory site. Blow up to give plan of site, access, area for expansion.	Photograph site. To step 6.
6	For quoted company: write to company secretary for report 10-K.	Obtain accounts from Dun & Bradstreet, Extel, etc.
	For unquoted company: obtain financial profile from Dun & Bradstreet.	If 'non-trading' try to find trading company and obtain accounts. To step 7.
7	Search trade journals and all media for ads, articles and references including local papers close to works or head office. Record management appointments.	Try abstracting service. To step 8.
8	Check with trade association if technical symposia have included papers given by company. Obtain papers.	Consider fieldwork to profile the company.

Chapter 17
Desk Research on Overseas Markets

The opportunities in world markets

There are around 150 nation states in the world. However, only about a quarter are of a size, political disposition or state of economic development to warrant the interest of the market researcher. Indeed, of the 40 or so countries which are of interest to researchers, a half are in Europe while the largest single economy worthy of study is the USA.

TABLE 17

The important commercial regions of the world

Region	Percentage of world GNP	Percentage of population	Key countries
Western Europe	30	8	Benelux, France, West Germany, Holland, Italy, Spain, Sweden, UK
Anglo America	24	6	Canada, USA
South East Asia	18	55	China, Hong Kong, India, Japan, Korea
Soviet and Eastern Bloc	15	9	Poland, Romania, USSR, Yugoslavia
Near and Middle East	4	5	Egypt, Israel, Kuwait, Saudi Arabia
South America	3	5	Argentina, Brazil, Venezuela
Northern and Central Africa	2	7	Kenya, Nigeria
Caribbean America	2	3	Cuba, Mexico
Oceania	1	1	Australia, New Zealand
Southern Africa	1	1	South Africa
Total	100	100	

A concentration of marketing effort on Europe and Anglo America is, therefore, the most efficient way of utilizing a company's resources. Except that the largest industrial markets are also the ones with the highest levels of established competition. They are also mature and the prospects for growth may not match the economies of tomorrow: China, Brazil or India.

The developing countries have youthful, large populations and vast resources of minerals which present opportunities for growth far in excess of the developed West. Whether they are worthy of study by the researcher depends to a large extent on the products or services which are being offered. It could be inappropriate to try to market dishwashers and food processors to these developing countries whereas there is certain to be a demand for power stations and tractors.

Information which can be found on export markets

Information which can be found on overseas markets is broadly similar to that available on the domestic market. The accuracy of the data varies according to the statistical services of the country. As a rule, the more advanced the economy of a country, the better the information will be. Europe and North America are the best and easiest to research from desk sources. Japan, though economically mature and with excellent statistical services, is problematical to a Western researcher because of language difficulties.

The areas of information which a researcher should set out to cover in a desk research study could incorporate any or all of the following subjects:

☐ a background on the country in which the basics would be discussed — the language, the size of the country and its geography, the population and its demographics, the politics, the religion, the climate, the currency, the transport system, major ports and cities, the labor force.

☐ market size and trends: here the researcher hopes to show the demand for the product taking into account the domestic production, adding in the imports and allowing for exports which leave the country. In many countries the market is latent, in which case the potential needs to be indicated. This is not always easy to judge as is illustrated by the apocryphal story of the two salesmen who visit a desert island. One reports back to head office that there is no demand for shoes since everybody goes barefoot while the other says there is a massive potential on account of everybody needing a pair.

☐ the supply structure: a description is required of the domestic producers, the importers and the distribution routes used to get the products to market. Any information on the domestic suppliers would prove valuable, including their ownership and financial status, their production resources, their output levels and any production constraints, and their links with other companies, including any reciprocal trading arrangements.

☐ imports of the product: it is worth studying the imports into the country in some depth. This is an area of information on which there will be reasonable availability of statistics. An analysis of imports will show where the products originate, in what volume, at what prices (shown by dividing the money value by the volume), and the trends over time.

☐ the distribution network: a description should be given of the various ways in which the products are sold. Some may go through tiers of distributors, others could be sold direct. Some companies will have full-time representatives in the market while others will use agents (manufacturers' representatives in the USA).

☐ end-user markets and customers: the most important consumer groups should be described. All products have key consumers. Most cigarettes are smoked by the heaviest smokers; most whisky is drunk by the heaviest whisky drinkers. The same is true in industrial markets. The 80:20 rule applies uniformly. The market researcher must attempt to identify the major customer group in the export market and point out any characteristics which could be important in reaching them. Where are they located, what journals or press do they read, what do they like about the brands they buy?

☐ prices and discounts: these will vary according to the level of the distribution chain. Price information and discounts are critical to the would-be exporter as they determine the profitability of the market. In some emergent countries it will be necessary, if possible, to give guidelines on the importance of backhanders which are required to ease the passage of products through the customs and the distribution route.

☐ special features: the existence of tariffs, quotas, development regions and grants, political hot spots, permissible shareholding by foreigners, rates of pay, suitable sites for distribution or production points, etc. would all be suitable for inclusion in a desk study of an export market.

The aim of a desk study of an export market is to provide as detailed a picture as possible for as modest a cost as possible. There could be a wide gulf between what the researcher hopes to obtain and what he achieves. The information will vary in quality and availability from country to country. Nevertheless, it is worth aiming high for as much data as possible. The sources of the data are discussed in the next section.

Sources of information on export markets

The principles of desk research on export markets are the same as for domestic markets. The difficulties are created by language and accessibility. The researcher will need to study:

- ☐ directories
- ☐ yearbooks
- ☐ government statistical publications
- ☐ import and export statistics
- ☐ trade association statistics
- ☐ financial reports on companies
- ☐ journals, magazines and the press
- ☐ ads, company brochures and price-lists
- ☐ bank and other status reports on countries
- ☐ reports by independent consultants/research agencies.

It is not necessary to travel overseas to access any of the above information sources. They can be found in libraries in major cities, government departments, chambers of commerce and the offices of overseas embassies.

Libraries. The largest city and county libraries in North America and Europe contain statistical yearbooks and directories for most important nation states of the world. The libraries of the Census Bureau in Washington and the British Overseas Trade Board in London are amongst the best in the world for any researcher who can visit them. They contain up-to-date yearbooks and statements of trade on virtually every country in the world. The facilities are all the more useful because there are experts on hand who are familiar with all the sources.

Chambers of commerce. Each country has its own chambers of commerce with offices in the industrial capitals of the world. The overseas offices have commercial attachés who are happy to help with small and specific requests for data. The researcher who seeks information through this route should contact the chamber in the particular country by letter or telex with his request. The addresses of the overseas offices of US chambers can be obtained from the Chambers of Commerce in the United States of America in Washington and addresses of British chambers can be obtained from the Association of British Chambers of Commerce in London.

Banks. The large banks produce economic reports on overseas markets and status reports which show the credit risks of selling there.

Newspapers. National newspapers have libraries which can be used by researchers for a small charge. The *Financial Times* in London has a Business Information Service which, for a pre-paid sum, enables subscribers to request data on any aspect of UK and international business. The time spent on the request is debited against the fee at a standard rate per hour until it is exhausted.

Research organizations. The multi-client studies carried out by market research organizations could provide an economical answer to overseas desk research. The *International Directory of Published Market Research* from the British Overseas Trade Board lists 7000 studies (on all countries) carried out by 350 companies.

Online databases. Business databases are at their most useful in export desk research. They allow the researcher to screen foreign newspapers and journals with a speed and convenience that would not be possible by conventional means. If the researcher lacks the necessary familiarity with database searching he can commission libraries to undertake the work for a small fee on top of the search cost itself.

The time required to obtain data on overseas markets

If the researcher can find a library with most of the sources of data on export markets, he will be able to answer most of his questions in a couple of days. Much depends on the country and the availability of data.

A researcher carrying out a study of a market which is non-English speaking could find it takes much longer as time is spent translating the foreign technical terms. Libraries cannot be relied on as the only source of information. If the help of an overseas attaché at an embassy or chamber of commerce is sought, time must be allowed for them to deal with the request amongst the queue of other requests that they receive.

The use which can be made of overseas desk research

The researcher may set his sights high in his search for information on export markets, but could fail to find anything interesting because his subject of study is too narrow or the country has a poor statistical service. The researcher needs, therefore, to utilize his imagination to the full, drawing as many links and associations as possible with the data which is accessible to him.

For example, a researcher may wish to find out the market size for electric motors in India. If this information is not published (or if a cross check is required) an estimate could be arrived at by drawing an association with an independent variable such as the Indian production of electricity in kilowatt hours (this data is available for every country in the world). Assuming that the researcher knows the market size in another country, he can derive the market size for electric motors in India by the following formula:

$$\text{Market size for electric motors in India} = \frac{\text{Known market size in (say) USA}}{\text{Electricity production in USA}} \times \text{Electricity production in India}$$

Electricity production is a convenient indicator to use for the international assessment of market size as it is a fair barometer of industrial activity. It may not, however, be enough. A world survey of the test sieve market may need to derive a ratio from (say) the Gross Domestic Product and mineral production in each country, as sieves are used in industrial laboratories but especially those associated with mineral output.

In consumer markets there are many independent variables which could be used to derive market sizes. The size of the population itself, Gross Domestic Product, the number of telephones per head of population, the number of television sets per head of population, the number of refrigerators, the number of motor cars, etc. Statistics on all these variables are readily available for most countries.

TABLE 18

Checklist of questions for desk research country report

Subject coverage	Examples of sources of information
Background What is the Gross Domestic Product? What has been the trend over the last 10 years? What proportion of the GDP is from agriculture, industry, services? What is the population? What has been the trend over 10 years? What is the age profile? How fast is it changing? What is the climate, geographical area, the major cities, the transport, infrastructure, the neighboring states? What are the politics and how stable are they? What is the major agricultural base, mineral deposits, principal industries? What is steel output, electricity output, number of telephones per head and other barometers of economic development? What are exchange rates and trends? What are the tariffs on imports? How do they differ from 'knocked down' goods assembled in the country? What quotas exist on imports? What incentives exist as grants etc for investors?	*Libraries:* reference books, atlases, newspaper cuttings/surveys *Banks:* country reports *Statistical yearbooks:* economic indicators such as steel output, number of telephones *Chambers of Commerce/embassies:* tariffs, quotas, grants for investment
Products and services (ie for the product/service of interest) What is the range of products/ services sold? Who are the manufacturers of the products? How are sales organized in the country? What are sample prices?	*Embassies/Chambers of Commerce:* suppliers, prices, agents *Libraries:* directories, overseas journals

TABLE 18 *(continued)*

Subject coverage	Examples of sources of information
Market size What is domestic production, imports and exports of the product? What has been the trend over five years; ten years? What are likely trends over the next five years?	*Libraries:* Statistical yearbooks, Predicasts, overseas trade accounts at Bureau of Census library *Research organizations:* Multi-client reports *US Customs*
Suppliers Who are the main suppliers? Who are agents; who are direct importers; who are domestic manufacturers/assemblers? What other products/services do the suppliers sell? What is their dependence on the product in question? What is the financial status of the supplier? What links exist with any other companies?	*Libraries:* Financial and product directories *Embassies/Chambers of Commerce:* literature, individual reports *Banks:* status reports
End-user markets Which are the major end-user markets for the product? Which end-user markets are growing/declining/stable?	*Libraries:* Statistical yearbooks, journals, newspaper reports, special surveys *Research organizations:* Multi-client reports

Chapter 18
Sample Selection

Industrial and consumer samples compared

It is the subject of sampling which causes industrial market researchers twinges of inadequacy when they compare themselves with their counterparts in consumer fields. Consumer market researchers trot out jargon about quotas, stratification, probabilities and the like which is mumbo-jumbo to a high proportion of industrial market researchers. The industrial market researcher feels intuitively that the sophisticated sampling methods are not for him, but equally he is probably very conscious that his own techniques may be very hit and miss.

There are occasions in industrial sampling when circumstances resemble consumer markets. Mostly, however, they are very different. The difference is to be found in the nature of industrial and consumer buying. Consumers buy for themselves, their family or friends, and although each individual is unique, as individuals they are so small a part of the total market, their impact as buyers is infinitesimal. Collectively, similarities can be recognized in the purchasing patterns of these consumer buyers. By selecting randomly just a few of the consumers it is possible to build up a picture which describes the whole. That this is possible is based on a scientific principle which states that a large number of interviews will identify people with characteristics which vary. Since each person is such a small part of the total the individual effect is minimal and, added together, the variations will be in either direction tending to balance or cancel each other out. Thus in a sample of consumers that is plotted graphically, their distribution will be described by a bell shaped curve. (Diagram 15 shows such a curve.) This 'normal curve of distribution' or Gaussian curve (so called after the mathematician who first studied it) enables mathematical precision to be applied to samples, including the degree to which they are in error from the whole.

In industrial markets the member companies are more often than not of very different sizes. Unlike each single consumer, being infinitely small within the whole, a single industrial buyer may be extremely large and account for a high proportion of the purchases in his market. A random sample could fail to select one of these large buyers and would provide a distorted picture of the whole. Similarly, if the sample did by chance pick out the large buyer and treat it as 'typical' it would falsely distort the results. For this reason it frequently is not possible to apply random sampling techniques to industrial samples and, therefore, accuracy levels cannot be given.

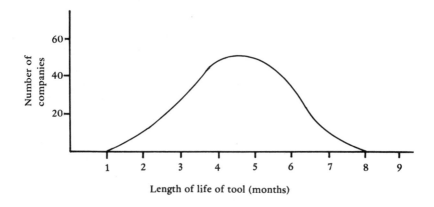

DIAGRAM 15
Normal distribution curve of life of cutting tool
in industrial establishments

Selecting the sampling method according to the universe

Before a sampling method can be selected, information is required on the 'universe' or 'population'. The industrial market researcher should ask himself two very simple questions about this universe.

☐ Is this a market in which one or a few companies dominate the purchases?
☐ Are the numbers of purchasers measured in 10s, 100s or 1000s?

Only a very broad view is required for the purposes of selecting the appropriate sampling method. At this stage it is not necessary, for example, to know who the big buyers are, only that some do or do not exist. Each type of sample can now be discussed in turn.

A universe with no companies dominating purchases

Typical of such universes are buyers of typewriters, twin and earth cable, copper pipe, fork-lift trucks, commercial vehicles, fertilizers and bricks. This is not to say that all the companies buying these products are small; on the contrary, many may be large concerns. However, none is so large that it accounts for more than 1 or 2 per cent of all purchases. Where industrial universes are homogeneous in this way they have great affinity to consumer markets and consumer sampling methods can be employed. This has advantages. Samples can be selected randomly and the error in the results can be calculated mathematically (see Appendix 1).

Of course, it is necessary to have some knowledge of the construction of a universe before it can be deemed similar to the mass populations typical of the consumer world. It may be necessary to obtain this feel for a market from people with an informed view or to carry out a pilot project to test the uniformity of the universe before the sampling method is finally decided. As a general rule, however, industrial universes which correspond closely to consumer universes in structure tend to have one or more of the following characteristics:

1. A high element of service in the sales package. Frequently the suppliers of the products and services operate within a limited geographical area (eg, plumbers, advertising agencies, van hire, garages).
2. The value of individual sales of the companies may very well be small (eg, engineers' merchants, motor factors). As a corollary, the value of the purchases by the consuming company also tends to be small (eg, items of office equipment, building materials, tools).
3. The companies supplying the products or services are frequently privately owned and proprietor managed (eg, caterers, builders, heating and ventilating contractors). Although large groups do exist in these markets, they tend to operate through local depots or subsidiaries which are similar in size to the privately owned companies with which they compete (eg, distributors of spare parts for automobiles).

The benefit to market researchers of homogeneous universes is the ability to select random samples and hence measure statistical error. Say there were 5000 electrical contractors in a number of states and a random sample of 500 showed that 20 per cent were prepared to buy imported cable. It can be calculated that the true proportion will be ± 3.5 per cent at 95 per cent confidence limits. In other words, there is a 95 per cent chance that the true proportion of contractors that would buy imported cable will fall somewhere in the range 16.5 per cent to 23.5 per cent of the sample. The confidence limits in market research are conventionally expressed at the 95-per cent level though they could be given at 90 per cent (in which case they would be narrower) or 99 per cent (in which case they would be wider). It is important to understand that the accuracy of any findings depends on the proportion of answers received to a question. If from the same sample of 500 electrical contractors, 5 per cent said that they currently bought imported cable, then by laying a ruler across diagram 16 it can be determined that this is accurate to ± 1.8 per cent (not, it will be noted, ± 3.5 per cent); ie, there is a 95 per cent chance that the true proportion lies between 3.2 per cent and 6.8 per cent.

The chart can be used to decide how big the sample should be. A sample size of only 100 would produce an error of nearly ± 10 per cent if 50 per cent gave a certain answer to the question. A sample size of 500 on the other hand would give an error of only just over ± 4 per cent on a 50 per cent proportion. The sample size must be selected, therefore, by deciding what level of accuracy is required in order to make decisions, assuming different responses for the sample result — at one end of the spectrum imagining the response to be only a few per cent (say below 5 per cent) and at the other, supposing it could be as high as 50 per cent. In practice, researchers prefer to work with sample sizes of around 200 or more as on most findings this gives an error of ± 5 to 6 per cent.

Random sampling, unfortunately, is expensive, and a comprehensive list of companies must be available from which to make the selection. Researchers, therefore, often choose to contain costs by multi-stage sampling. Multi-stage sampling starts with a list of companies which is segregated into groups according to a characteristic which they have in common. This grouping is known as a stratum. For example, in a survey of the replacement industrial filter cartridge market it would be necessary to draw up lists of strata of end users – ship operators, aviation fuel distributors, oil refineries, etc — all the sectors that use filter cart-ridges. A random sample would then be selected from each group or stratum. Equally, companies could be stratified according to size (number of employees is a simple and easily available measure) or geography.

The same strata of companies can be used as the basis for selecting a 'quota' sample. As the term suggests, the researcher selects a quota or proportion of companies from each stratum in which he wishes inter-views to be carried out. Say the objective of the survey was to compare the image of a company among small, medium and large buyers of a product. Lists would be drawn up (perhaps using the number of employees as an indication of size) and a quota of 100 or 200 (or whatever) companies selected from each stratum. The quota in this case would ensure that the same numbers of small, medium and large companies were surveyed to facilitate a comparison between the three cells.

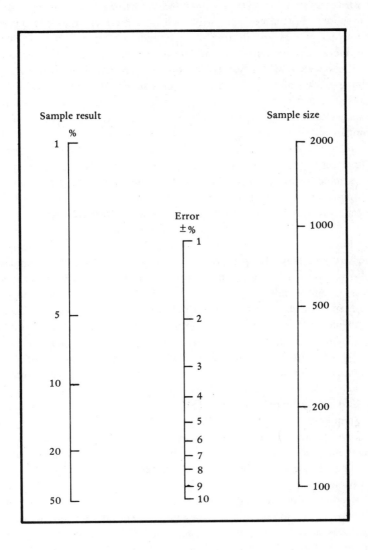

DIAGRAM 16
*Chart for measuring random sampling error
(95 per cent probability)*

A universe in which some companies dominate purchases

For those industrial companies that sell their products to a finite universe of buyers of widely differing sizes, a random sample would not work. Imagine a random survey of the 200 or so UK mining machinery manufacturers which by chance failed to select Gullick Dobson and Dowty Mining — two of the very largest — or a survey of the large and diverse fastener industry which missed the massive GKN group. The omission of such giants would seriously distort the results. Probably most industrial companies sell their products to a universe of less than 100 companies where the Pareto principle dictates that 20 per cent of firms account for 80 per cent of the volume consumed. In these markets it is vital to stratify the sample according to the size of the company measured by their purchasing power, so that all the large buyers (there may only be half a dozen) can be interviewed while a sample is taken from the rest.

Stratifying the sample is only half the problem: the researcher does not know at the beginning of a survey who is the largest and who is the smallest company. In practice, some desk research, such as studying advertisements in trade journals, entries in directories and articles in the press, should enable the researcher to sort the list crudely into 'possibly large' and 'possibly small'. Given a relatively small universe of 100 to 200 companies, the researcher can begin to fine down the list by selecting an initial sample from the 'possibly large' and asking each respondent, at the end of the interview, who else is likely to be a large buyer and worth contacting. This system of referral works well as each company contacted is likely to know its competitors and may be able to provide the researcher with an indication of their size before they are contacted in the survey.

Frequently, a two-stage sampling of smaller establishments is required if these run into hundreds. An extensive sample can be covered by a brief telephone interview to obtain key characteristics, thus enabling a subsample to be drawn up for a study of greater depth — perhaps by personal interviews.

Whether or not referral is used, the deliberate selection of companies, for whatever reason, means that the sample is not random and measures of statistical accuracy cannot be applied — it has become a 'judgement' sample. Judgement samples may actually be more accurate than random samples as the selection of companies could take in all the largest (thus carrying out a census of companies accounting for, say 80 per cent of the purchases) plus a certain coverage of the smaller ones — these having first been sorted out into pertinent strata according to the best knowledge of the researcher.

Managers commissioning research very often feel insecure with industrial samples as it is difficult (except with large homogeneous universes) to state the accuracy of the findings. Though their concern is understandable, it is also only partly germane, as accuracy can also be markedly influenced by the quality of interviewing and the interpretation of results. Even where the reliability and confidence levels of sampling can be calculated, these may bear little or no relationship to the accuracy of the results as presented in the finished report. The final arbiter must be whether the results check out as sounding sensible, whether they corroborate existing information which is known on the market, or if they can be validated by subsequent sales data that comes to light.

Choosing an industrial sample frame

Time spent on the construction of a sample is never wasted. Seldom is there an easy answer. An inexpensive directory may, on occasions, provide the ideal list from which the selection is made. At other times it may be necessary to buy a tailored list from a specialist in this business, or build one from customer records or a variety of sources.

Directories

Directories are the most widely used source for industrial samples. Directories which are in common usage are those which list companies alphabetically, geographically and by their industrial classification. MacRae's *Blue Book*, Thomas's *Register,* Standard and Poor's *Register of Corporations,* and Ward's *Directory* are all used regularly by industrial market researchers seeking data on names, addresses and managers of the companies (see also Chapter 16).

Kelly's Manufacturers and Merchants Directory provides a classified grouping of companies which, for most headings, is not as comprehensive as *Kompass.* However, it scores because in the same volume it has one of the most extensive A to Z listings of industrial companies (100,000 in all) together with full details of address, telephone number and a brief description of activity.

Yellow Pages provides comprehensive sources of company listings. Their big disadvantage is that they over-represent industry groups by including many wholesalers and fringe suppliers. Also, a sample frame built up from a national set of Yellow Pages would require great care to eliminate duplications, as many companies are listed more than once, and even within the same book they may recur under a variety of headings.

As well as general directories, there are thousands of specialist ones, some of which the industrial market researcher could find appropriate from time to time. No one could expect to have more than a passing knowledge of the more important of them, and indeed there is no need that he should. The *Directory of Directories* lists them all from business and industry through to sports and leisure.

Perhaps the easiest way of obtaining a quick introduction to the range of directories available is to pay a visit to the reference section in the public library of virtually any town. There will almost certainly be a good selection of up-to-date general directories which the library will probably sell off periodically at a fraction of the original purchase price.

Specialized lists

There are occasions when a researcher requires a specialized list of companies — either for convenience or because it is the best available source of buyers or specifiers. The list business has its roots in direct mail marketing and for this reason they are consumer-orientated and often inappropriate for industrial market research purposes. Frequently the lists are only available on rental and are bought 'unseen'. They are, therefore, of little use for any sampling that requires a telephone or personal contact.

List suppliers obtain their names and addresses either from publishers of journals (in which case the list comprises journal subscribers) or directories. Lists based on subscribers to journals must be treated with caution as they are a biased sample in that they ignore what could be a large number of non-subscribers with a different purchasing profile. Lists built up from single directories on the other hand, seem an expensive way of buying what is available, for little more effort, from the original source.

Customer lists

Very often researchers have excellent sample frames available to them under their nose. Customer lists may well be ignored in the belief that they are likely to be biased. Whether this is so or not can readily be checked against an independent list from a directory. Customer lists have the advantage of containing less waste than other sample frames since virtually everyone is by definition a buyer. Furthermore, it is quite surprising how, over the years, customer lists expand to encompass most large buyers.

Customers may have moved some or all of their purchases to the competition during this period, but their names are still likely to feature on the list and prove useful to the researcher.

In a survey of the wedge wire screen market (used for extracting water from various materials and separating the residues into sizes), it was necessary to obtain a sample of buyers of *welded* wedge screens. The company that had commissioned the survey made only *looped* wedge screens but, because it had been in business for many years, had attracted enquiries from companies that thought it might sell the welded variety.

This enquiry list proved an excellent starting point and provided dozens of welded wedge buyers that would otherwise have had to be found by expensive telephone sifting.

Referral

Seeking significant buyers in an industry can very easily be carried out by asking respondents whom they believe should be contacted. All that is needed is a starting point in any sector — just one or two companies taken from a directory or a customer list, and through referral, it is possible to identify the largest buyers.

Observation

One hundred and fifty specifiers had to be invited to a truck clinic. It was recognized that there was a limit to the distance respondents would travel to attend the clinic and so, by placing observers at busy intersections throughout the area, a comprehensive list of vehicle operators was obtained by noting the names and telephone numbers emblazoned on the sides of the trucks. Furthermore, the age, weight class and make of vehicle were known before the operator was telephoned to invite him to the clinic.

Observation can be used to provide lists on many other products. Glass packaging manufacturers can be identified by examining products on supermarket shelves and noting the unique punt mark which each moulds into the bottle or jar. Car component suppliers can be established simply by peering under the bonnet. Cable manufacturers leave their mark in a unique combination of thin coloured threads which can easily be seen by stripping back the insulant cover.

Self-selection

Occasionally the circumstances may be right to allow the sample to select itself. A project for a company that made canal narrow boats had the objective of determining narrow boat specifications from potential buyers. A self-completion questionnaire was taken in advertising space in *Waterways World* and a total of 1800 replies were received — 9 per cent of the readership of the journal. Most returns came from existing owners of boats and those thinking of buying one. Thus, although the sample was biased, it leaned towards those with a high interest in narrow boats and who were, therefore, key potential customers for the client.

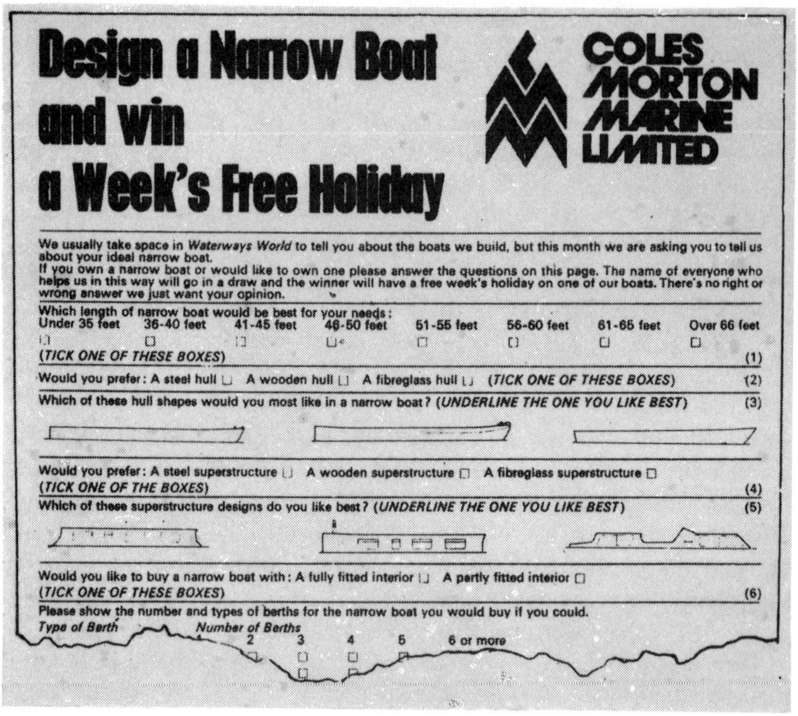

Design a Narrow Boat and win a Week's Free Holiday

COLES MORTON MARINE LIMITED

We usually take space in *Waterways World* to tell you about the boats we build, but this month we are asking you to tell us about your ideal narrow boat.
If you own a narrow boat or would like to own one please answer the questions on this page. The name of everyone who helps us in this way will go in a draw and the winner will have a free week's holiday on one of our boats. There's no right or wrong answer we just want your opinion.

Which length of narrow boat would be best for your needs:
Under 35 feet ☐ 36-40 feet ☐ 41-45 feet ☐ 46-50 feet ☐ 51-55 feet ☐ 56-60 feet ☐ 61-65 feet ☐ Over 66 feet ☐
(*TICK ONE OF THESE BOXES*) (1)

Would you prefer: A steel hull ☐ A wooden hull ☐ A fibreglass hull ☐ (*TICK ONE OF THESE BOXES*) (2)

Which of these hull shapes would you most like in a narrow boat? (*UNDERLINE THE ONE YOU LIKE BEST*) (3)

Would you prefer: A steel superstructure ☐ A wooden superstructure ☐ A fibreglass superstructure ☐
(*TICK ONE OF THE BOXES*) (4)

Which of these superstructure designs do you like best? (*UNDERLINE THE ONE YOU LIKE BEST*) (5)

Would you like to buy a narrow boat with: A fully fitted interior ☐ A partly fitted interior ☐
(*TICK ONE OF THESE BOXES*) (6)

Please show the number and types of berths for the narrow boat you would buy if you could.
Type of Berth *Number of Berths*
1 2 3 4 5 6 or more

DIAGRAM 17

Example of a questionnaire designed to select its own sample

Summary

Industrial samples differ from consumer samples in that industrial buyers vary considerably in their buying power and can account for a relatively large proportion of the market's purchases. Consumers, on the other hand, are individually inconspicuous within a market.

Where an industrial universe is made up of many small companies, it can be treated as a consumer universe and sampled randomly. Many industrial universes, however, comprise a small number of firms ranging widely in size. In these circumstances, it is necessary to identify the largest companies and interview them all, together with a sample of the smaller ones.

Industrial sample frames can be chosen from the many directories, special lists suppliers, customer lists, referrals from buyers, observations or even self-selection.

Chapter 19
Questionnaire Design

What is a good questionnaire?

A questionnaire is an assembly of carefully formulated questions designed to collect facts and opinions from respondents. It is an important tool of the market researcher's trade as it is used to generate the raw data on which findings are based.

The aim of the researcher in designing a questionnaire is fourfold:

☐ To obtain accurate data;
☐ To make the interview as interesting and stimulating as possible for the respondent;
☐ To be easily administered by the interviewer;
☐ To facilitate analysis.

Designing successful questionnaires requires considerable experience and, therefore, time. There are, however, a number of rules and routines which will shorten the apprenticeship. Taken in chronological order these are the formulation of the questions, the arrangement of the questionnaire layout and finally, the testing of the draft.

Formulating the questions

The style and construction of questions for a questionnaire depends in part on how it will be administered. A postal questionnaire is completed by a respondent without any possibility of his seeking clarification or advice from an interviewer. Great precision is, therefore, necessary. In contrast, a loosely structured interview carried out by a market researcher fully conversant with the subject he is studying, may be suitably guided by a checklist of topic headings which serve simply as a reminder of what to cover.

In formulating the questions the researcher must try to envisage the difficulties the respondent will face when answering them. To do this, he must have a good feel for his subject; otherwise, when data is collected, it may be found, too late, that foolish mistakes have been made.

The researcher should begin by working through the objectives of the survey listed in the proposal and jot down all the points on which answers are required.

Thus, if one objective is to assess the market size, a question must be posed which establishes the respondent's purchases of products over a given period. If another objective is to measure the market shares of suppliers, a question must be asked on the respondent's sources of purchase. The rough listing of questions should be comprehensive and may well include at least the following basics:

- ☐ What are the respondent's purchases of product in volume and value per year?
- ☐ Who are the major suppliers and what share do they have of his supply?
- ☐ What is the image of a selected number of suppliers?
- ☐ What factors influence his choice of supplier and how important are they?
- ☐ How are purchases likely to change in the future?
- ☐ What are the factors that will influence this change?
- ☐ What factors are relevant to classify the company and perhaps be used for cross analysis?

Clearly, the actual list will be much longer as it will contain specific questions geared to the needs of the survey. All the questions in the rough listing should now be scrutinized to establish whether they are vital to the survey, since the longer the questionnaire, the more taxing it will be for the respondent.

The difficult job of converting the rough questions to ones which a respondent can answer must now be tackled. In the process the researcher must avoid a number of pitfalls.

Questions open to misinterpretation

In some circumstances the respondent may believe that he knows what the interviewer is trying to find out and arrive at his own interpretation of the question. For example the question, 'How often do you buy steel sheet?' may be thought by the respondent to mean, 'How often do you buy steel sheet in normal times of trading?' He may, therefore, provide an answer which does not reflect his current purchases. The question should be pinned down with a qualifying statement such as 'over the last three months'.

The use of vague and ambiguous words is another cause for misinterpretation. The words 'last year' will, to some people, mean the last calendar year from January to December, others may assume it refers to the previous 12 months from the time of questioning. Words like 'frequent', 'good' and 'useful' are open to misinterpretation unless qualified. The question, 'Do you buy castings frequently?' could elicit a yes from two respondents though one may buy every week and the other once every two months. It must not be assumed that the respondent knows the meaning of words like 'salient', 'infrastructure', 'margin' or 'mark-up'. There is always the danger that what the respondent does not understand he will guess or attempt an answer based on the overall context of the question.

When a question is loaded with information it becomes especially open to misinterpretation, or the respondent may forget one part of it or mix the statements up. Similarly, questions which pose concepts can produce difficulties for respondents if they are not used to thinking in such terms. 'In what way could the product be improved?' may force the respondent to think in minutiae and draw suggestions such as building in the odd switch or changing the colour or shape. While these changes might have some relevance, they could have been forced by the question and actually be inconsequential in terms of the buying decision. The respondent may be unqualified to make any profound suggestions or find it so difficult that he settles for the easier option and mentions trivia. Equally, a question may pin down the respondent too tightly so that he makes his own interpretation and widens it. Questions such as, 'Which marketing journals did you read last week?' may encourage the respondent to widen the word week to fortnight because he feels deprived of being able to answer the question if by chance he missed his read last week. He is distorting the question to fit his experience.

Questions which are difficult to answer

The researcher may want to find out what the market size is for a product and aim to do so by grossing up a sample of annual purchases of companies. Unfortunately, buyers may not think in annual terms as they buy weekly or monthly. They may order their products in numbers of units after having negotiated the price of each product. It may be more acceptable to ask purchases per week or month — whatever the normal period for the industry. This may not be without problems. When he gives the weekly figure the buyer may think in terms of the last few orders he placed which are still fresh in his mind. These may be unrepresentative of the rest of the year and would therefore provide a false total picture. If it is vital that an accurate response is achieved to this question, it may be better for the researcher to design a series of questions which take the respondent through his purchase routine and end with a check.

Q1   Thinking back over the last 12 months, how often do you order flour? _____

Q2   And how many kilos/hundredweights of flour did you order each _____ ?
(STATE ORDER FREQUENCY MONTH/WEEK ETC) _____

Q3 (i) What price per kilo/hundredweight did you pay for flour over the last 12 months? _____

  (ii) IF RANGE OF PRICES IS GIVEN ASK:
What would you estimate the average price of flour per kilo/hundredweight over the last 12 months? _____

Q4   Excuse me a second while I work out the value of flour you ordered last year.
FROM ORDER FREQUENCY, WEIGHT ORDERED AND AVERAGE PRICE, CALCULATE ANNUAL VALUE OF FLOUR ORDERS.

I make that $ _____ of flour ordered over the last 12 months. Could it have been less or more than that figure?;

Less   [   ]   What figure do you think? _____

More   [   ]   What figure do you think? _____

Same   [   ]

Qualitative questions can be more difficult to answer than quantitative ones. With a quantitative question the respondent either knows or does not know the answer (although as has been shown there are ways of making the questioning process easier and more accurate).

A respondent may lack the confidence to give an answer to a qualitative question or he may not have thought about the problem sufficiently to give a considered opinion. The question, 'What will your purchases of sheet steel be over the next two years?' may be unfairly addressed to a buyer if his role is simply to reorder quantities of materials when stock falls to predetermined levels. Qualitative questions may be asked in open-ended fashion to obtain a top-line unbiased view but they almost always yield more if they are prompted.

The question, 'What do you think of Dormer as a supplier of twist drills?' may produce a vague response such as, 'Very good'. If the interviewer administering the questionnaire does not probe deeper, the researcher will be left wondering what 'very good' means. It is far better to pin the respondent down by providing him with a scale and introduce other companies as benchmarks. Hence the question becomes:

218

I will now read out a list of brands of twist drills.
READ LIST.

Going through the list again, which have you had experience of?
WHERE EXPERIENCE OF BRANDS EXISTS, ASK FOR EACH BRAND.

Thinking about <u>BRAND</u> would you give them a score out of 5 for their speed of delivery, where:

    5 is excellent
    4 is good
    3 is neutral
    2 is poor
    1 is unacceptable

IF DON'T KNOW CODE 6.

REPEAT QUESTION FOR RELIABILITY OF DELIVERY, LENGTH OF LIFE, VALUE FOR MONEY.

	Experience		Speed of delivery	Reliability of delivery	Length of life	Value for money
	Yes	No				
Clarkson	☐	☐	___	___	___	___
Cleveland	☐	☐	___	___	___	___
Dormer	☐	☐	___	___	___	___
Firth Brown	☐	☐	___	___	___	___
Presto	☐	☐	___	___	___	___

This method of questioning takes a broad issue and narrows it down to individual questions which the respondent can more easily answer. It also enables the researcher to derive quantitative answers to qualitative questions by simply summing the responses.

Questions which are leading or incriminating

In consumer questionnaire design it is heresy to ask a question which could lead the respondent towards an answer. Industrial market research also avoids leading questions, although there are circumstances where the experienced interviewer can present his question as a challenge (and thereby lead) to stimulate a response.

Asked of the right respondent in a relaxed interviewing situation, the question, 'Would you agree that British Leyland is on the road to recovery?' becomes a debating point and may give the respondent the stimulus to give his point of view. The interviewer is, in this way, guiding a discussion rather than conducting a formal interview.

Leading questions must be avoided where the researcher is building up a database. Two or three new models of power tool may be mentioned to electricians to determine their preferences. Here any tendency to lead in questions establishing preference would dangerously distort the results.

In the same vein, a question may be so worded as to lead the respondent to modify his answer to avoid being seen in a poor light by the interviewer. A buyer may not like to admit to having little say in the buying decision and may intimate that he is the chief decision maker. Similarly, there could be pressures causing him to suggest that his purchases are bigger than they actually are (as an indication of his power) or that he buys top quality products (to avoid being thought a cheap skate) or that he is powerful enough to negotiate very keen prices.

The researcher may feel fearful of designing any questions at all, given the possibility of unintentionally building in leading questions, misinterpretation or difficult to answer words and phrases which seem to him so clear. It is, of course, important that the researcher avoids at all costs the obvious dangers of muddled questioning, but it is more important that he is aware of what could influence the response. With this understanding he is better able to interpret the responses or, it is hoped, test the questionnaire to iron out difficulties.

Nor is there a single right way of asking questions. A question which is correct in one set of circumstances may be wrong in others. Pedantic wording which is essential in some surveys may be less critical in others. Questions can sometimes benefit from a colloquialism or an informal style. The correct choice and design of questions is easier if the researcher has a good feel for his subject, keeps in the front of his mind what information he needs and how he will use it, and if he constantly tries to imagine how he would respond if he were asked the same question.

Types of questions

There are three types of questions which can be used in a questionnaire:

- [ ] questions on behavior, such as purchasing or usage;
- [ ] questions on attitudes which may include measurements;
- [ ] questions to classify the respondent.

Behavioral questions

These are designed to find out what, when, how and which. They largely deal with factual information and so should be easy to answer from memory and clearly understood in order that accuracy can be achieved. Behavioral questions include:

Have you ever? The question may be linked to a time period (In the last year have you ever . . .?) or a number of occasions (How many times have you ever . . .?). The question relies on the memory for recall and this dulls over time.

Do you ever? Similar to 'Have you ever?' but concerned with what is happening now.

How often? This question may be tied to a time period and followed by a scale:

How often do you buy plastic granules?
Never ☐
At least once a month ☐
Over 1 month to 3 months ☐
Over 3 months to 1 year ☐
Over 1 year ☐

When did you last? Again, this question is dependent on memory and it can therefore be better to pin it down to a time period. 'Thinking about the last 12 months, when did you last . . .?'

Who does it? An important question for establishing who makes the buying decision. For example, 'What are the titles of the persons within your company who specify the brand of electric power tools you buy?' To determine the main decision maker as a lead into the questionnaire, the question may be asked, 'Who is the person within your company with most influence on the brand of electric power tools you buy?' There is a real danger with this type of questioning that it will invite the answer 'Me' from a person who has some influence but who is by no means the major decision maker.

How many? This is a most important question in industrial market research, used frequently to determine annual purchases: 'How many tonnes of angle iron have you bought in the last 12 months?' It can also be used to determine the frequency of his behavior: 'How many times did you . . .?'

Do you have/own? This question may be a lead into the questionnaire. A survey of end-users of electro-pneumatic hammers would need the question right at the beginning:

Does your company:
(a) ever rent electro-pneumatic hammers? ☐
(b) own its own electro-pneumatic hammers? ☐
(c) own and ever rent electro-pneumatic hammers? ☐

In what way do you do it? The question covers a wide range of activities
such as:

> When you order steel, which department do you contact?
> How do you service the machines?
> On the last occasion you used an electro-pneumatic hammer was it
> (a) your own; (b) rented?

In the future will you? Whereas the previous questions relate to past
behavior, this question refers to the future and could be asked in a number
of ways:

> Thinking about your purchases of linen hire in the next year do you
> anticipate buying:
> Less ☐
> The same ☐
> or More than last year ☐
>
> If you were to buy a new concrete mixer tomorrow, which make would
> you buy?

Answers to these questions give only half the story and they are normally
associated with a supplementary question such as, 'Why do you say that?'

Attitude questions

In these questions the researcher is establishing views, opinions and attitudes that may or may not be based on experience. It is usually helpful
(at an early stage in the questioning) to establish what experience the
respondent has had and, therefore, the grounds for his opinions.

Open-ended questioning. This type of questioning is frequently used in
unstructured interviews as it allows the interviewer scope to probe deeply
following the response. The questions can cover a wide spectrum such as:

> What do you think of . . .?
> Why do you say that. . .?
> Which company is best for . . .?
> What was the reason for . . .?

Open-ended questioning can result in very woolly responses, so attitude
measurement scales of various kinds are employed.

Verbal rating scales. These use a question followed by a scale of responses
which could be shown to the respondent on a card or read out to him.

> Thinking about the brand of gear box oil you most often buy, would
> you say that it is:

(a)
{
Less expensive than other brands [ ]
More expensive than other brands [ ]
About the same price as other brands [ ]
Don't know [ ]
}

(b)
{
Doesn't last as long as other brands [ ]
Lasts longer than other brands [ ]
Lasts about the same as other brands [ ]
Don't know [ ]
etc.
}

It will be noticed that the negative statement heads the prompted list as this tends to give a more normal distribution of response since it is less leading.

Numerical weighting scale. The respondent is asked to attribute a score to a particular dimension or feature. 'Out of 10 points how many would you give (STATE BRAND) for quality?' It should, of course, be pointed out to the respondent that the poles of the scale referred to assume 10 to be best/highest and 1 worst/lowest. Provision should also be allowed for 'don't know' as, on a 10-point scale, the figure 5 has a rating and cannot be considered neutral. If there is a large grid of brands and features this type of questioning can tax respondents and it may be quicker and simpler to invite them to self-complete, even during a face-to-face interview.

Diagrammatic rating scales. Instead of using descriptive words as in a verbal scale, a diagram is shown which represents a spectrum or a scale.

On balance, do you believe the latest budget will be good or bad for your company's profits this year? Please place an X at the appropriate point of this scale to indicate your view.

Good for my company's profits [_____△_____] Bad for my company's profits

No effect on my company's profits

Scales can be broken into boxes thus taking on the form of a 5-point verbal scale but without the words which are replaced by positive and negative signs:

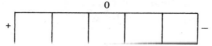

0

+ [| | | |] −

This type of question can be converted to a semantic scale by attributing words to each box.

> How likely is your company to buy a new PABX system in the next 12 months?
> Very likely ☐
> Fairly likely ☐
> Neither likely nor unlikely ☐
> Not very likely ☐
> Not likely at all ☐

It may be appropriate to reverse the order of the scale so that in half the interviews it begins with 'very likely' and in half 'not likely at all', so eliminating the possibility of bias.

Ascription of adjectives. This method of questioning presents the respondent with a list of (say) brands and he is then asked which brand is thought best or worst for price, quality, delivery etc.

Presentation of alternatives. Respondents are given choices, usually diametrically opposed or contentious, and asked to state which they think is true or that they agree with.

> I would now like to read out a list of statements that have been attributed to (STATE COMPANY). After each statement would you tell me whether you agree or disagree?

	Agree	Neither agree nor disagree	Disagree	Don't know
___ is a modern company.	☐	☐	☐	☐
___ is an old fashioned company.	☐	☐	☐	☐
___ is a leader in its field.	☐	☐	☐	☐
___ tends to follow other companies.	☐	☐	☐	☐
Etc.				

Ranking procedures. Ranking is often used in industrial market research to sort out the features which are considered important in the buying decision.

> If you were seeking a new supplier of nails, which of the following factors would have most influence on your choice of supplier (RANK 1) and which would be second in importance (RANK 2), third (RANK 3)?

ROTATE ORDER	RANK
Made to British standard	_____
Most competitive price	_____
Best availability	_____
Supplies other range of fastenings	_____

In ranking questions the tedium is usually reduced by restricting the ranking to the first three choices, irrespective of the length of factors to be considered. The researcher should also pay great attention to the list of factors which he has devised as being important. Unless there has been a pilot survey there is a possibility that the list will not contain all the factors which buyers consider in their decision-making processs.

Classification questions

Special information is normally collected from respondents to classify them into groups which form useful cells of data for comparison at the time of analysis. Typical classification questions include:

- ☐ size of establishment interviewed (number of employees is more readily given than turnover);
- ☐ industry class (this can be based on the Standard Industrial Classification or a self-made one);
- ☐ position of respondent (including his level of responsibility, eg senior buyer, technical manager, draughtsman, etc);
- ☐ location (by standard region).

There is no fixed rule as to whether the classification questions should be at the beginning or end of the questionnaire. More usually they are positioned at the end, as their relevance may not be immediately apparent to the respondent and this could cause mild rancour if asked early on.

Arranging the questionnaire layout

The design of the questionnaire layout depends on:

- ☐ who is to administer the questionnaire;
- ☐ who is to answer it;
- ☐ the nature of the questions which are to be asked.

Some general guidelines follow which will ensure a suitable questionnaire layout for every situation.

1. Have a sensible sequence of questions

If a certain class of respondent is to be interviewed, the first questions should act as a screen to eliminate those who should be passed over. Thereafter questions should move from the broad to the particular in logical order. Thus, questions on a buyer's attitudes to fastening systems will eventually lead to questions on screws and rivets. Questions should also move from the simple to the more difficult if this is possible within the overall framework. Questions which warm the respondent up should be introduced early to gain his enthusiasm and support for those more difficult ones which follow.

2. Group questions on a similar theme

Questions covering specific subjects such as trends, suppliers or purchases should be grouped rather than scattered throughout the questionnaire. Though this is the ideal, a researcher may believe that the grouping makes it too obvious what he is seeking and for this reason he may spread them through the questionnaire.

For example, if the researcher believes that he would not get a true answer to a direct question on purchase volumes, he may ask typical order frequencies, prices and examples of order sizes at intervals during the questioning. At the analysis stage he can draw together the answers to these disparate questions to arrive at a figure for annual purchases.

3. Locate sensitive questions at the end

Sensitive questions should be positioned towards the end of the questionnaire so that all is not lost if the respondent takes offence and closes the interview. Where possible, sensitive questions should follow easy questions so the respondent is conditioned to give an answer.

4. Leave sufficient space for responses

A frequent gripe of interviewers is the small amount of space left for them to write in the answers. Tightly packed questions with one short line for a response can become a frustration in an interview as they hinder the interviewer's flow and continuity. Small response boxes which are not positioned right alongside the question are difficult to line up visually and can result in mistakes in recording answers.

Printing on both sides of the questionnaire creates problems. It takes considerably longer to turn over, as the questionnaire must be removed from the clipboard and turned around.

5. Make interviewers' instructions clear

Interviewers should never be in doubt about what they need to read out to the respondent and what are instructions to them. Convention has it that interviewers' instructions are in capitals and underlined or in parentheses (see diagram 18).

6. Pre-code as much as possible

Analysis and questionnaire completion are much easier if questions have pre-coded answers where the interviewer has only to tick a box.

There will be times when conflict arises between the benefits for analysis of a complex pre-coded matrix and a simple open-ended question which can be coded later. The designer of the questionnaire should always pay deference to that which is easiest for the interviewer.

Questionnaires can be coded in a number of ways. With a small sample which will be analysed by hand, it is simplest to use boxes which the interviewer can tick.

Q5   How often do you order printed circuit boards? Is it

Tick

weekly or more often
(over) one week to monthly → to Q6
(over) monthly to quarterly
(over) quarterly to annually
less than once a year → to Q9
never → to Q15

Large-scale studies with 100 or more interviews or those involving complex cross analyses, are best analysed by computer. Instead of boxes, responses are attributed a number which is circled. The series of numbers is known as a column and each column also has its own number. This makes it convenient when inputting data into the computer as the column number becomes a shorthand for that question (see diagram 19).

Data can be fed into the computer either directly or by transferring data to punched cards which are subsequently read by the computer in batches (see also Chapter 27).

7. Make the questionnaire visually attractive

It was stated on page 205 that the design and layout depend on who is administering and who is answering the questionnaire. Self-completion questionnaires are perhaps the most difficult of all to design. They must be

Q4 PLASTIC BELOW-GROUND DRAINAGE PRODUCTS

Turning now to plastic below-ground drainage products:

(i) Which manufacturers' names or brand names do you know of for plastic below-ground drainage products?
RECORD ALL·NAMES MENTIONED EXACTLY AS STATED:

_____

_____

Do any more names spring to mind? _____

Any more? _____

(ii) I am now going to read out a list of names. Please say which you know of as makes or brands of plastic below-ground drainage products.
READ OUT EACH NAME. ALSO RECORD (SEPARATELY) UNPROMPTED MENTIONS (as per (i))

(iii) ASK FOR EACH KNOWN NAME:
Would you say NAME is above average (+)
average (0)
below average (−)
for: *quality* of below-ground drainage products?
value for money of below-ground drainage products?
breadth of range of below-ground drainage products?
availability of below-ground drainage products?

Name	Prompted recall Q2(ii) Tick	Unprompted recall Q2(i) Tick	Above / Average / Below (+) (0) (−)			
			Quality	Value	Range	Availability
Marley						
Osmadrain						
Terrain						
Wavin Plastics						
Plastidrain						
Paragon						
Key Terrain						
Hepworth Plastics						
Polydrain						
Marscar						
Y I P						
Hunter						
Brett						
Upodrain						

etc.

DIAGRAM 18
Sample page of questionnaire showing interviewer's instructions in capitals and underlined

Fork-lift truck survey
Telephone

	(1)	(2)	(3)

Company _____   Respondent's name _____

Address _____   Position _____

_____   Interviewer _____

Telephone number _____   Date _____

Area	(4)
New England	1
Middle Atlantic	2
Deep South	3
Midwest	4
South West	5
North West	6
West Coast	7
Great Lakes	8
Alaska	9
Hawaii	10

Good morning/afternoon. I am carrying out a survey on fork-lift trucks.

Q1   Do you operate any fork-lift trucks at your establishment?

YES   NO   If NO skip to Q7 [   ]

Q2   (a)   How many fork-lift trucks do you have in your establishment?

	(5)
1	1
2 - 5	2
6 - 10	3
11 - 25	4
26 - 50	5
51+	6

(b)   How many of these trucks are:

front loading?	(6)	side loading?	(7)
0	1	0	1
1 - 5	2	1 - 5	2
6 - 10	3	6 - 10	3
11 - 25	4	11 - 25	4
26 - 50	5	26 - 50	5
51+	6	51+	6

DIAGRAM 19
Sample page of questionnaire showing column numbers
for coding response

immediately clear and easy to fill in by the persons they are aimed at. In industrial market research, respondents are usually managers with considerable experience of clerical work. However, market research questionnaires are viewed by most as just another form and, since there is no compulsion to respond, there is a danger that they will end up in the waste paper basket unless the respondent has an incentive to reply. If the questionnaire is visually attractive it helps. It costs no more to print the questionnaire on coloured paper. Not only can this look appealing, but it also helps it stand out in the sea of white paper which covers most respondents' desks. Cartoons can give visual relief and again add interest.

Every attempt should be made to lay the questionnaire out on one piece of paper. It looks better and avoids stapled pages going adrift. Ideally the questionnaire should be restricted to two sides of A4 (which effectively limits the number of questions to between eight and twelve) or, if longer, A3 folded so that there are four pages in booklet form.

Structured interviews for use in large-scale face-to-face or telephone research studies similarly need careful attention to detail. Layout, interviewers' instructions and question composition can affect the speed of work and its accuracy far more than in an unstructured interview, in which the researcher has the opportunity to feel his way through the discussion and write up separate notes rather than fill in a questionnaire.

Pilot testing the draft questionnaire

The perfect questionnaire has yet to be written at first sitting. When a draft which appears acceptable to the researcher has been prepared, it should be tried on at least two or three colleagues to determine whether any obvious ambiguities have been missed. Next, the questionnaire should be tested for its technical competence in the field. The aim is to determine the clarity of the questions and to a lesser extent its flow and layout. It is always better to test the questions using the interviewing medium which will ultimately be used — postal, telephone or visit. Time and cost may not permit this and so the telephone may be used for expediency. Naturally, it is not possible to test a full visit questionnaire over the telephone and so the researcher would break it down into groups of four or five questions to be tested in isolation among (say) 20 respondents. A thorough test would use experienced interviewers who run through their questions with the respondent and then return to pose further questions designed to establish his thought processes which led to the response. For example:

Parts immediately available

Pays attention to needs of customer

Quality of dealers

Overall quality of manufacture

Modern trucks

DIAGRAM 20
Examples of cartoons used to enliven questioning.
These cartoons are taken from some used in a question which asked
respondents to rate (from 5 for excellent to 1 for unacceptable) each of
several truck makers against each of 11 product or company attributes.
Quite hard work!

Can I return to the first question you answered? You said:
READ OUT RESPONSE.
Would you briefly explain to me how you arrived at that answer?

PROBE IF NOT CLEAR:
There must have been some reason for your saying that. What was
in your mind?

The interviewer records answers to these questions and notes whether
the question was understood or not. Following this interrogation the
interviewers themselves should be questioned by the researcher to establish
if they have a view on how the questions or layout can be improved.

The researcher can now determine whether respondents understood the
precise nature of the wording; whether they made guesses at answers or

if they were based on fact; whether they answered the question freely or with reticence or difficulty. His questionnaire can be redesigned to take these factors into account.

The frequency of testing questionnaires in industrial market research is often quite low. In a small sample of 20 unstructured interviews, it is a nonsense to spend time testing the questionnaire on 10 of them. The researcher, effectively, is testing the questionnaire from the start and modifies it as he proceeds. By starting the interview programme with the smaller or less critical respondents, any changes to the questionnaire can be made with no serious loss of information.

Summary

Questionnaires are used to collect data from respondents. Different types of questionnaire are used in structured, semi-structured and un-structured interviews but in every case they should be designed to obtain an accurate response with the minimum effort. Care must be taken in the formulation of questions to avoid ambiguities, questions which are difficult to answer, or leading. The questionnaire designer must be familiar with the many types of questions he can ask which are recording either behavioral, attitudinal or classification data.

The layout of the questionnaire affects its flow and ease of handling. Questions should be sensibly grouped, in a logical sequence, well spread out with clear instructions and coding frames.

Pre-testing the questionnaire is important for large-scale interview programs and can be carried out by telephone after splitting the questions into small groups of four or five only. The small samples which are typical of many in-depth surveys do not lend themselves to formal testing although modifications are generally made as the fieldwork proceeds.

Chapter 20
Personal Interviewing

The role of the personal interviewer

Primary information in industrial markets is collected mainly by personal visit or telephone interviews and, to a lesser extent, postal surveys and observation. Personal visit interviews are a face-to-face meeting between researcher and respondent for the purpose of collecting behavioural, attitudinal or classification data.

Advantages
Personal interviews have a number of advantages over telephone or self-completion methods of data collection:

Depth. A respondent is quite naturally willing to spend more time in a face-to-face interview than he is over the telephone or filling out a mailed questionnaire. This means that subjects can be discussed in more detail, more probing is possible and, as a consequence, greater depth can be achieved. Cooperation also tends to be better in a personal interview. Respondents find it harder to refuse to answer questions face to face than over the telephone and it is easier to alleviate concern about confidentiality in a personal discussion.

Greater accuracy. In a personal interview the respondent has more time to consider his response. He can if he wishes make phone calls or examine files to obtain the data. The interviewer can make a judgement as to the accuracy of a response and, if needs be, ask if there is any way of substantiating it — possibly by talking to another person.

Better feel. Over the telephone or in a postal questionnaire the interviewer cannot get a feel for the company. At a visit he will be able to see the size and nature of the company and it will be more obvious if the respondent is truly the best person to answer the questions.

Better explanations. Respondents in personal interviews very often sketch out diagrams to clarify a point. They can also use brochures or products to add to their statements. Similarly, the interviewer can draw diagrams, show cards or, size permitting, a sample of the product to explain his questions.

Product placements. With new product research the interviewer may wish to ask the respondent to evaluate a sample product there and then, or to try it over the next few days or weeks. This is much easier to organize in a visit than by post.

Disadvantages

Against the advantages of personal interviews can be set a number of disadvantages compared with other methods of data collection.

Cost. Far fewer visit interviews can be carried out in a day than by telephone, and the number is much more dependent on each respondent's location and status than on the length of the discussion. Indeed, it is not unusual for a researcher to spend several hours travelling to obtain an hour-long interview. Because most industrial market research visits are by appointment, time must be allowed for setting up. Taking into consideration appointment making, fieldwork and writing up notes, three to four interviews per day is a good average when respondent companies are concentrated in a city. Often two interviews per day is the maximum when a subject is covered in depth. Telephone interviewing achieves an average of four or five times as many interviews per day and incurs lower expenses. Structured interviews can be carried out by specialist telephone interviewers who are less expensive than consultancy staff. Taking these factors into consideration, one visit interview costs on average ten times as much as a telephone interview.

Time. Arranging personal interviews, carrying them out and writing them up takes much longer than telephone work. Very often the time-scale cannot be shortened by using more 'legs' on the visits as this would mean too many wasted first and second interviews as interviewers go through the learning curve.

Types of industrial interview

The industrial market researcher recognizes three types of interview classified according to the freedom of the interviewer to stray from the sequence and wording of the layout and questions in the questionnaire.

Structured interview. This uses a questionnaire with a rigid layout and wording which the interviewer must follow precisely. It is used in circumstances where the respondent's answers can, within limits, be pre-empted. Provision can be made for recording information by ticking or filling in boxes. This data collection method is especially suited to postal surveys and telephone or visit interviews carried out in large numbers. Structured questionnaires are also necessary if the interviewer lacks a detailed knowledge of the subject. In a well-designed structured questionnaire there should be no cause for confusion or need for the respondent to seek clarification. The interviewer's role is one of simple administration.

Semi-structured interview. This is made up of a mix of formal questions of a structured nature and others which are less restrained, so allowing open-ended probing. It is probably the most common type of interview used in industrial market research, being favoured because it is flexible enough to accommodate the varied circumstances that exist between companies in different sectors and of different sizes. Information is recorded on a questionnaire consisting of many open-ended questions and other useful information may be attached as a supplement.

Unstructured interview. This is used in in-depth interviewing. The unstructured interview is guided by a checklist of questions which are discussed in an order to suit the respondent. In designing the checklist, the researcher may not be entirely sure of the full range of questions he should be asking. These will be opened up as the discussion gets under way. There is, therefore, a good deal of spontaneous questioning sparked off by the points raised. Recording the information requires its own skills. The researcher must be adept at questioning and maintaining the interest of the respondent while at the same time writing copious notes on his comments. It is important that these are written up afterwards into a visit report which can be used by the researcher (or anyone in his team) as an input for the final report.

Occasionally, unstructured interviews are taped. The decision to tape depends on the office environment and nature of the interview. Recording in open plan offices can make respondents feel conspicuous and therefore constrained; similarly, tape recording a sensitive interview with a competitor of the research sponsor may create unnecessary additional inhibitions and be counter-productive.

Planning the interviewing schedule

Companies which are selected for personal interview are those for which a response is critical to the survey or where the information required is detailed and complicated.

The sample frame should be plotted on a map to identify clusters of respondents which can conveniently be visited. Those companies which are crucial to the success of the survey should be marked and become the first contacts. All other interviews in the area will be built around them.

Prior to making contact, the researcher should estimate the length of an interview and the travelling time between points so that he can plan his ideal timetable with each day broken into hours for visiting specific companies, travelling or eating. Very seldom can a schedule be organized which is exactly suited to the researcher's plan and so a back-up list of companies should be drawn up — assuming, of course, they are available in the locality.

Where a potential respondent lies well out on a limb, the researcher must question the benefit of making a visit as opposed to a telephone interview, as the price is an extra day which could be used to carry out three or four more visits. The temptation to avoid long journeys to isolated firms is great and demands that the researcher draws up a balance sheet of pros and cons of making the trip in order that his decision is as objective as possible.

Obtaining the interview

There are only a handful of people in each company capable of answering market researchers' questions. Their exclusivity places them under constant pressure to help market researchers and salesmen alike and, quite possibly, the roles of these two occupations may not always be distinguishable to the respondent. The market researcher could, by some, be viewed as having nothing positive to offer — worse, he makes demands on the respondent's busy timetable and asks difficult and taxing questions.

To gain the interview the researcher needs qualities of salesmanship. He has no product or service to sell, only himself and the intangible possibility of improvements to future products and services. In the researcher's favour, most people have a high level of interest in their jobs. To be singled out to talk about their work and be under no pressure to buy is an indulgence and ego boost.

It is important that the interviewer has worked out his introduction before picking up the telephone to make the initial contact. A fluent, confident and businesslike introduction is needed. An apologetic or diffident approach invites rejection.

Here are a number of tips to bear in mind in formulating a successful introduction:

1. *Where possible, mention a mutual contact.* If a third party can be named as the person who suggested the contact, the respondent will feel involved, possibly obligated. 'John Davis, marketing director of Davis & Clark mentioned your name and said that you would be likely to help me in a survey I am carrying out into precision ground bar,' or 'I have just been speaking to your project engineer, Terry Knowles, about solenoid valves. He suggested that if I telephone you, you may be able to help with a survey I am carrying out.'

2. *Be brief:* long-winded explanations may exasperate and alienate the respondent.

3. *Justify the visit* by suggesting a benefit to the respondent (a newer, better product, improved service, etc).

4. *Appease the respondent's conscience and concern.* Some respondents cannot imagine that they know enough to help. If the interviewer says that he will be visiting another firm in the area at the same time, the respondent will feel happier agreeing to the meeting as he thinks that, at the worst, some benefit will be obtained from the other visit.

5. *Suggest a time and date which suits you* but be ready with an alternative.

6. *Give assurances.* If you know the respondent is the right man but he claims not to know enough to be able to help, assure him that your need is for a broad appraisal. Where confidentiality is posed as a problem, give assurances, in writing if necessary.

7. *Confirm the arrangements by letter.* When an interview is set up more than a few days in advance, a letter should be sent recapitulating the purpose of the visit, confirming the time and venue and thanking the respondent in anticipation. This reduces the possibility of misunderstandings and provides the respondent with some 'official' statement of who is doing the work.

Unfortunately, life is never simple and problems will arise. Sometimes these are peculiar to the survey or the company, and native wit must be used in overcoming them. Nevertheless there are some common problems which can more easily be countered if prior thought has been given. Some frequently occurring problems and pitfalls are listed below together with suggested solutions:

Never accept as definite a meeting that has been arranged by someone else. You may, for example, speak to a colleague in the same office who says he is sure the respondent will help if you call on a certain date and he promises faithfully to pass on the message. Ten to one the man will be out or in a meeting when you call. Interviews arranged with secretaries are usually acceptable, but make sure you confirm them, preferably in writing.

Don't be put off by people who are too busy. Busy people can always make time if they want to — push for 10 minutes at eight o'clock or five o'clock. Offer him a bite to eat: even busy men must take sustenance.

The respondent is always in a meeting when you phone. Find out from his secretary or a colleague when is the best time to catch him. Often it is first thing in the morning when he is sorting out his mail. This costs more in telephone calls but is better than many fruitless calls at the cheaper rate.

The respondent says the sponsor already knows all there is to know. Explain that you are taking a rather special slant and are looking at a particular aspect of the market that has not been covered before.

The respondent wants to know what sort of questions you will be asking. Never get down to detail on the telephone. This invites the respondent to say, 'I can't tell you that' or 'I don't know'. Talk in broad terms, for example, 'We will be asking general questions on the type of cable you buy'.

The respondent asks you to send a questionnaire through the post and promises faithfully he will complete and return it. Experience shows that this approach seldom works. Explain that the questionnaire has not been designed for self-completion and it just is not possible for the respondent to complete it unless you are there to help.

The respondent is always being pestered by researchers and what will he get out of it? Tell him the interview won't take long, that you think he will find it interesting and that this exercise is, it is hoped, to help a supplier become more efficient in supplying goods to people like himself. Sell the respondent a benefit so that he really does feel he is getting something out of taking part. Only as a last resort offer to pay him or his company. Payment for interviews in the long run works to the dis-advantage of market researchers as it raises the costs of surveys and intro-duces possible bias in attracting mercenary (and possibly untypical) respondents.

With the best will in the world, some of the confirmed visits will be cancelled due to last-minute illness, crises, or plain forgetfulness of the respondent. Some excuses may be hard to swallow but they must be accepted gracefully as it may still be important for the interviewer to try again. Sometimes it is possible to retrieve something from the setback by the interviewer presenting himself early for the next interview on the list or calling speculatively on one of the reserve companies on the sample frame which is close by.

Conducting the interview

The interviewer arrives at the company and makes contact with the respondent. Most respondents prefer to hold the interview in their offices or a conference room. A busy and draughty reception area is not an ideal interviewing environment and, if the respondent appears to want to conduct the discussion there, he should be given every encouragement to find somewhere more convivial.

Interviewers are unquestionably at an initial disadvantage compared with a representative who calls regularly and has established a social rapport. However, the interviewer is not bound by established protocol and therefore need feel no embarrassment or concern at endangering it. He must nevertheless achieve a high level of cooperation immediately and maintain this throughout the interview. Cooperation is created in part by an easy manner but also by obtaining the respondent's sympathy for the goals of the project. This sympathy will be heightened if benefits for the respondent and his company can be presented convincingly. These may have been pointed out during the setting-up telephone call but they are worth re-emphasizing before the interview begins. The respondent should be warmed up on simple questions requiring a generous discourse from him. When a relaxed environment has been established, the interviewer can begin to steer and control using the questionnaire as the guide. If the guards of the respondent remain raised, he may remain reserved and respond with the 'party line' rather than his true feelings.

At the outset the interviewer should position himself with clipboard and questionnaire in readiness to take notes. Reaching for the clipboard at a later stage and drawing attention to it by asking permission to take notes draws undue attention to conduct which the respondent accepts as part and parcel of the interviewer's role anyway.

If a tape recording is required then an explanation becomes necessary and should be given as soon as possible. The first few minutes of play will be somewhat inhibited until the machine is forgotten by the respondent.

Where the interview is not taped, and this includes the majority, the interviewer must rely on his notes to record the answers. Interviewers who can recall respondents' comments without the need for notes are a rarity. It may, however, be justified to stage manage the packing away of clipboard and questionnaire to encourage the respondent to relax fully, having finished the interview. If there are sensitive questions to ask, now could be the time. It will, of course, be necessary to commit the answers to memory for five minutes until back in the car when the questionnaire can be fully completed and checked over.

A problem many respondents face is that, under questioning, they believe they do not know the answer when really they do. They may think

their purchases need to be given exactly whereas rounding is quite acceptable. If a respondent cannot be persuaded to give an estimate, some levels
may be suggested to him: 'Was it less than a million units?' Fine tuning
can take place from here. Once a numerical base for his purchases has
been established, a breakdown by size, shape and class can be obtained in
percentage terms and worked backwards at a later stage.

Communication problems are reduced in personal interviews but they
still exist. Respondents may mishear or misunderstand questions. The
interviewer may misunderstand or not hear the reply. The scope for error
is large and it is most important to check back on major points, especially
those which seem to have received an off-beat response measured against
the benchmark of answers from other interviews (a feel for what seems
right and wrong is very quickly gained).

Often respondents give vague answers. For example, if a respondent
is asked why he thinks his purchases will grow over the next five years he
may reply, 'Because our sales are increasing'. This does not fully answer
the question: supplementary questioning should follow to find out *why*
his sales are increasing — perhaps his company's product is finding new
markets overseas or substitution is taking place in favour of his products
on the home market. Other frequent vague responses are, 'Because it is
best' (why is it best?), 'We always have done' (why have they?), 'It's not
good enough' (why isn't it good enough?). Some respondents wander from
the subject of the questionnaire and use the interviewer as an audience
for their petty gripes. They must tactfully be steered back on course.

On closing the interview, the interviewer should extend the usual
thank-yous and leave the door open for a fellow researcher at some future
date or himself, if the need arises to check back when analysing the
results. It takes very little time to drop a short letter thanking a useful
contact for his help and goes a long way towards ensuring a warm reception on a future call.

The character of the interviewer

Industrial market research interviewing is an art. Instruction will help the
novice but there is no substitute for experience.

A good industrial market research interviewer demands qualities which
are rarely found in many people. In no particular order they are:

- ☐ self-starter
- ☐ ability to work hard
- ☐ tenacity/persistence
- ☐ charm

☐ objectivity
☐ enquiring mind
☐ intelligence
☐ conscientiousness.

Of course, these same qualities are desirable in many occupations, including selling. At face value, therefore, salesmen should theoretically make good *ad hoc* interviewers for an internally organized market research project. Unfortunately, there are too many conflicting pressures which prevent this. The important relationship they have created with buyers and specifiers may be threatened by what may be seen as impertinent questions. Salesmen themselves may find difficulty administering the questionnaire. They may feel that they already know some of the answers and could even be tempted to hide or bend findings to justify their past actions. Finally, it could be argued that a salesman who spends time on market research is taking his mind from his prime objective of selling — one is sure to suffer.

Summary

Personal or face-to-face interviews are one of the most important means of obtaining depth information from buyers, specifiers or others holding a view of the market. The detail that can be collected in such interviews more than compensates for their high cost in expenses and time. Three types of interview are used in industrial market research. *Structured interviews* have a rigid layout with little opportunity for the interviewer to ask additional questions. *Unstructured interviews* are more like discussions, guided by a checklist which the interviewer uses to ensure that all the topics have been covered. Between the two are *semi-structured interviews* which are popular in industrial market research as they contain standard questions and yet allow for the detailed probing of responses.

The first step in an interview campaign is planning the visits by building a framework of respondents around key interviews. Interviews are normally set up over the telephone with the interviewer attempting to slot respondents into his ideal schedule.

The flow of information in a face-to-face interview is greatly helped if the respondent feels relaxed and the interviewer intelligently probes or adjusts questions to suit the respondent's unique circumstances.

There are very few occasions when salesmen should carry out industrial market research interviewing.

Chapter 21
Telephone Interviewing

The role of telephone interviewing

The costs of transport during the 1970s increased out of proportion to telephone charges and as a result, telephone interviewing has become a much more important tool to the industrial market researcher. The telephone is used by him in three ways:-

1. *To set up personal interviews.* The telephone is usually the first means by which an interviewer contacts a company prior to visiting it. Over the telephone the interviewer confirms the respondent's eligibility for interview, identifies and makes contact with the right person, establishes cooperation and agrees a convenient time to call.
2. *Interviewing and collecting data.* This is the principal role of the telephone in industrial market research.
3. *Check backs.* The telephone is a convenient method of back checking — a most important procedure in large surveys where the researcher needs the assurance that the work has been carried out satisfactorily. In small surveys the telephone is used to check back and confirm points or collect additional information which was missed in the interview.

Virtually all industrial establishments are linked to the telephone network so the medium provides universal entry to the researcher. The telephone compels an answer. If an interviewer can get connected to a respondent's phone by the switchboard, and he is at his desk, he is certain to answer it even when busy. A letter can be ignored or passed over, a telephone demands attention. Telephone interviewing, like personal interviewing, can vary from the highly structured to the totally unstructured. Most large scale telephone surveys have to be structured, otherwise analysis would be impossible. However, a single researcher can quickly and efficiently piece together a picture of a market from many sources through numerous unstructured telephone interviews.

243

The pros and cons of telephone interviewing

The telephone has some marked advantages as well as serious limitations as a research technique. These must be fully appreciated as they influence where and when it can be used.

Advantages of the telephone in industrial market research

Cost. Personal interviews generally require an initial telephone contact as well as a visit. They are, therefore, far more costly in both time and expenses. The number of telephone interviews which can be carried out per day depends on the accuracy of the sample frame (a poor sample frame reduces the strike rate and considerably cuts back the number of interviews achieved per day), the length of the questionnaire, the accessibility of respondents, the time of year (holiday seasons are bad) and the day of the week (Fridays can be difficult). A good average is 10 to 12 a day but this can range from four or five or rise to 50 depending on the circumstances. Taking into consideration the saving in expenses, telephone interviews cost only one-tenth of a personal visit.

Speed. Telephone interviewing is fast. There is no wasted travelling time, traffic jams or long waits in receptions. In fact, once the interviewer has been connected to the respondent, the telephone allows chit-chat to be abandoned and questioning can begin immediately. This focusing of attention on the job in hand still further improves the efficiency of the telephone over the visit interview to the extent that 10 minutes over the telephone may be worth 20 minutes or more face to face.

Control. Telephoning can be carried out and organized from one location. Interviewers can easily be briefed and supervised throughout their work. If a researcher meets a technical difficulty in the middle of an interview there is someone available to provide guidance. Visits, on the other hand, are carried out in isolation and the lack of control has an attendant risk of misunderstandings by the field force which may go unnoticed.

Universal access. Geography presents no barriers to the telephone in industrial market research. Interviews with companies in remote areas or even overseas are as easy as those which are local while the cost savings become proportionately greater with distance. Respondents telephoned from a distance (especially overseas) are flattered they have been chosen to give their views and usually prove most cooperative.

Limitations of the telephone in industrial market research

Depth. There is a limit to the time a respondent's attention can be held on the telephone. Structured interviews by telephone seldom take more than 10 minutes. This time barrier limits the number of subjects which can be covered and is therefore an inhibition to depth study. The telephone abhors silences and questions are likely to receive immediate answers. Thus, difficult questions seldom get the lengthy consideration which they deserve and this too adds to the unsuitability of the telephone for depth investigations. In exceptional circumstances the interviews can go on longer and 20 to 30 minutes is possible. However, to achieve such sustained interest on the part of the respondent requires the subject to be of great interest to him and the interview format must be unstructured and flexible.

Visual prompts. Market research interviewing often needs the respondent to look at prompt cards — semantic or diagrammatic scales, lists of companies, pictures of products or a sample product itself. With considerable organizational difficulties, prompt material can be forwarded in advance by post but for most purposes the telephone is best avoided whenever their use is required.

Confusion. The telephone relies entirely on sound for communication. Everything depends, therefore, on the diction of the two speakers, the sharpness of their hearing and the clarity of the line they are using. A crackly line, a strong accent or a weak voice can result in mishearing and misunderstanding without either party realizing what is happening. The chance of confusion is much greater over the telephone and this makes it a dangerous medium to use for complicated interviews.

Applications for telephone interviewing

Bearing in mind the advantages and limitations of telephone interviewing, it is possible to draw up applications for which it is suited.

Screening. The telephone is ideal for simple, quick fact collection which could be used in its own right to feed into a survey or to screen out companies which are worth further study — possibly involving personal interviews.

Market size assessment. Using the telephone to collect simple consumption data which can be grossed up, a quick and inexpensive assessment of market size can be made. Care must be taken in certain cases. For example, a survey to assess the numbers of typewriters purchased in a large company may prove inaccurate if one respondent is relied on as a source of data. Typewriters may be purchased by many heads of department and no single source can possess the total picture. At a visit these complexities may be more easily solved than over the telephone. Market shares can also be assessed over the telephone, but here too difficulties can result from respondents' reluctance to divulge sensitive data on suppliers to a faceless and unknown interviewer.

Advertising effectiveness. Advertising effectiveness studies can be carried out by telephone including measures of awareness or the recall of promotions. As with all telephone research, these studies are best kept simple.

Top-line image studies. Just as the telephone can cope with simple advertising effectiveness studies, so too it can be used to obtain dip-stick measures of image. These could be questions listing companies from which respondents must choose the best (and worst) for quality, delivery, prices, etc.

Identifying sales prospects. Ultimately, it is hoped that all market research will assist sales but, if it is used surreptitiously to obtain information, it is known as sugging and is against all the principles of the profession. If the respondent knows from the outset the true purpose of the research and who it is for, the use of market research is permissible and the telephone is an efficient means of identifying and collecting data on sales prospects.

The telephone, therefore, is ideal for surveys where information requirements are simple. It is less suited to complex studies such as qualitative surveys exploring attitudes and complicated behavioural patterns. Attitude surveys, detailed fact collection, intricate advertisement testing or new product research are all better undertaken by personal interviews.

Selecting and training telephone interviewing staff

The telephone allows only partial communication between the interviewer and respondent. Visible signals are impossible. In a personal interview the interviewer may read meaning from facial expressions and fidgeting. Face to face, the interviewer can more easily put the respondent at ease. In a telephone interview all communication is through the voice which must be clear and functional, warm and charming, strong and assertive. A voice with personality is important for the telephone interviewer as it helps to achieve cooperation, maintain interest and overcome objections. The telephone interviewer must also be blessed with the quality of resilience to overcome the inevitable rebuffs. The ability to concentrate for long periods is necessary because the interviewer must follow and record almost every word of the respondent — a lapse could miss a point or result in a misinterpretation.

Telephone interviewing sounds easy. In practice, good telephone inter-

246

viewers are few and far between. They must have a pleasant and confident telephone manner which can be developed through practice. A newcomer to telephone interviewing can receive help to achieve confidence by training. Constant reviews of the questionnaire until it is known almost by heart will do a good deal to boost confidence. Role playing over internal phones will overcome telephone shyness and familiarize the interviewer with the tools of the business.

Carrying out the interview

The first hurdle the interviewer faces is the achievement of cooperation from the switchboard as the operator must provide the name of the right person and connect the line to his or her office. Many a telephone interviewer has fallen at the reception. Company switchboards are usually too busy for the operators to sort out a vague request to be 'put through to someone who can help with purchasing'. They need instruction they can understand: 'your buyer responsible for adhesives, please,' or 'the technical manager responsible for fastening systems'. The researcher may get the wrong person first time but he can use that name as a reference to help achieve subsequent cooperation: 'Good afternoon, I have just been speaking to your Mr Jones on a survey I am carrying out into fastening systems. He suggested that you might help me with some questions on adhesives.' Secretaries, like switchboard operators, are an obstacle to the telephone interviewer. Unfortunately, there are no simple rules which beat them all. Some respond to being taken into one's confidence and become valuable allies in seeking the best time to catch the boss. Others remain impenetrable and claim on behalf of their manager that he would not wish to help. With a truly awkward secretary and a vital respondent, a private and confidential letter to the manager may be required. This will seldom be necessary if, from the start, the secretary receives the same respect, courtesy and authority that is used for all respondents.

Having identified and got through to the right respondent, the interviewer should launch straight into the questionnaire. An assumptive approach yields a more positive response than one with lengthy descriptions and deferential requests for permission to continue. With a well-designed questionnaire the first question usually hooks the respondent. He becomes interested, involved and committed.

Fluency in administering the questionnaire is critical. Breaks in questioning could allow the respondent's mind to wander — perhaps back to things he feels he should be getting on with. Stumbling and the poor delivery of questions exposes lack of training in the interviewer and will irritate the respondent. The respondent's interest must be kept at all times. He may need encouragement over and beyond the words on the questionnaire. They may seem trite, but encouraging phrases such as 'That's fine', 'We're on the last lap now', 'You're doing very well', can help the respondent through long and difficult questionnaires if they are used at the appropriate time and said in the right manner.

The interviewer has the problem of keeping his mind on three different tasks while interviewing: the asking of questions or listening to responses, making notes, and thinking ahead to the next question. In an unstructured or semi-structured interview, the note taking is most demanding. At least the telephone allows the researcher to write furiously without the respondent being put off by seeing his every word recorded. With structured interviews response categories would need little more than circling numbers or ticking boxes and as a result, more attention can be paid to the control and delivery of the questionnaire.

Summary

Telephone interviewing has the major advantage of being inexpensive, fast, and more controllable than personal visits. The ubiquitous use of telephones in industry makes this approach ideal except where great depth is required in the interviews. Telephone interviewing is, therefore, suited to screening, the assessment of market size and simple attitude and awareness studies.

The best telephone interviewers convey strong personality in their voices. They must have the resilience to withstand rebuffs and ability to concentrate without faltering on the questioning.

The telephone interviewer can only begin when the correct respondent has been identified and contacted. The barriers of obdurate switchboard staff and secretaries are best overcome by a confident and courteous approach. During the course of the questioning the interviewer must maintain the respondent's cooperation and interest by being fluent and responding to signals of impatience with words of encouragement.

Chapter 22
Postal Surveys

Postal surveys as an alternative to telephone or personal interviews

Postal surveys have a poor image, so much so that some industrial market researchers dismiss them as an unsuitable research technique. There are two reasons for this view: most postal questionnaires end up in the waste bin and this implies that whatever response is generated comes from an atypical minority. Second, postal questionnaires do not allow a subject to be discussed in the detail that is possible in a face-to-face interview or even in one held over the telephone.

Both these disadvantages can be overcome. The representativeness of postal response can be assessed by a telephone check on a sample of non-replying companies, while the physical absence of an interviewer can on occasions be beneficial as it allows the respondent to consider his answer in his own good time without the bias of the researcher's presence or questioning technique. Postal surveys are a specialized tool with an important role to play in industrial market research as long as they are used in the right circumstances and with the necessary controls.

The decision to use personal interviews, telephone interviews or a postal survey depends on the answers to two questions:

1. What type of information is required?
2. What is the structure of the industry being researched?

Where the information required is qualitative, unstructured or detailed, there can be no substitute for a personal visit. Although qualitative research can be carried out with postal questionnaires, the response should be restricted to some form of scale, either numerical or semantic. Open-ended questions in a self-completion questionnaire can produce vague and useless answers. For example, the question, 'What made you choose your current supplier?' may well stimulate the response, 'Because they were best.' The same question asked face to face could, however, generate a wealth of information as the interviewer is in a position to probe why the supplier is considered best. Postal surveys are most appropriate where questions are simple, factual and can be answered from simple multiple choices (ie, questions where the respondent merely has to tick a box which indicates his choice of answer).

The structure of the industry that is being researched also has a bearing on whether personal/telephone interviews or a postal questionnaire should be used. Wherever the industry contains a few dominating companies it would be dangerous to use a postal questionnaire, as the failure of just one company to respond could affect the findings. A survey of mainframe computer manufacturers would hardly be representative unless responses were obtained from DEC and IBM who together dominate the market. Furthermore, if the buying decision is split between two, three or even more departments, as is frequently the case with industrial products, a postal questionnaire would fail to pick up the opinions of all the decision makers as it must be addressed to one person only. Unfortunately, this problem cannot be overcome by asking the first respondent to pass it on to another decision maker. To do so would dramatically cut the response rate.

The divided nature of the buying decision need not detract from using a postal questionnaire if the objective is to collect hard facts (the works manager can say how many tonnes of steel he uses just as easily as the buyer), but it does present problems when exploring factors which influence the buying decision. The works manager may believe quality to be the most important factor while the buyer may say it is price.

In general, postal questionnaires are best suited to researching organizations where there is one key decision maker. These are likely to be relatively small and scattered widely across the country. Typical examples include printers, hospitals, plumbers, bakers, garages or merchants.

Postal research may also be the preferred method if, for whatever reason, the company carrying out the survey can offer a sufficiently strong incentive or muscle to generate a high response. Government departments can undertake postal surveys and achieve high response rates using their 'official status'. Similarly, organizations offering a free entry in a directory may pull a high return if the respondents believe that they will benefit from inclusion.

Diagram 21 shows how a decision tree can be used to choose between personal/telephone interview or a postal survey in a research project. The choice of technique depends on the information requirements and the structure of the industry. Cost may well be the deciding influence. Given a limitless research budget, personal interviews are nearly always preferable. Somewhere between postal surveys and personal visits falls tele-

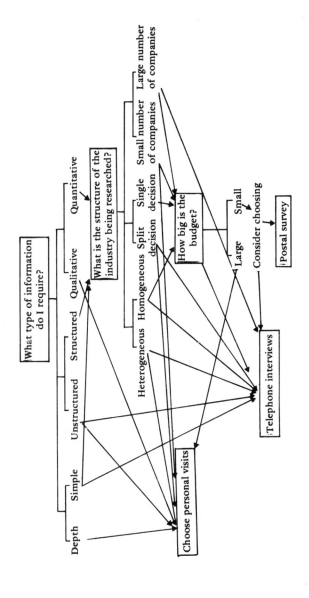

DIAGRAM 21

Decision tree leading to the selection of personal, telephone or postal surveys

phone interviewing — a compromise in cost and information flow between the two extremes.

Postal research, telephone and personal interviewing are not mutually exclusive and can all be used in the same survey.

The 80/20 rule applies to most industrial samples and enables a researcher to divide the list of companies to be contacted into groups according to their size. All the largest companies can be picked off for the personal interview program. A sample of the medium-sized companies can be visited and telephoned while data from the small companies is collected by postal questionnaire and telephone. Such a balanced method of sampling ensures that key companies are covered, all levels of the industry are researched and at the same time the costs are much lower than a survey involving only personal visits.

The costs of postal surveys

A postal survey is made up of a number of different costs of which postal charges themselves are nearly 40 per cent of the total depending, of course, on the response rate achieved. Table 19 illustrates the relative importance of each cost, based on the buying in of all services including typing, folding and inserting the mail shot. Not included in the table is the cost of the mailing list. The use of a directory already available in the office would cost nothing while a special computer listing would run to several hundreds of dollars.

Table 20 shows the comparative costs of postal, telephone and personal interviews expressed as an index and taken from a typical survey. The costs are influenced by the variable expenses incurred by each approach and also the need to employ more expensive staff for semi-structured and structured interviewing. Whereas telephone interviews cost only 25 per cent more than a postal reply, semi-structured interviews cost over 8 times a postal response.

Factors influencing postal response rates

The total cost of a mailing list is not in itself important. What matters is the cost of each returned and completed questionnaire that is valid for analysis and this is dependent on the response rate. Response rates to postal surveys can vary from 5 per cent to over 50 per cent from one mailing. As the objective of every researcher is to achieve the maximum possible response rate it is worth while considering the factors which affect it.

TABLE 19

Breakdown of costs in mailing 1000 postal questionnaires

Cost centre	Percentage of total cost
Outward post	31
Return post (20 per cent response)*	7
Typing/folding/inserting	15
Printed questionnaire (2 sides A4)	13
Printed reply-paid envelope	10
Typesetting of questionnaire	10
Printed cover letter	7
Outward envelopes	7
Total	100

* Using business reply service.
If return envelopes were stamped the cost would be higher but so, too, would be the response, ie 25 to 30 per cent overall.

TABLE 20

Comparative costs per valid response of different interview methods

Type of interview	Index of cost per effective interview
Postal*	100
Telephone	125
Structured visit	425
Semi-structured/unstructured visit	825

*Assuming a 20 per cent response rate.

The accuracy of the list of companies in the sample has a marked effect. A sample frame containing many companies which have gone out of business, moved, or do not buy the product that is being studied, is likely to generate a poor response. Time spent on weeding the sample frame to make it as accurate as possible pays great dividends in raising the response.

Addressing the questionnaire to the right person is similarly important. It is better to address the envelope and letter to a respondent named personally, but as this is frequently not possible, at least the correct title should be used. The title should be specific (eg, the Chief Buyer — Steel Products) rather than vague (eg, the Design Engineer), and if in doubt, the questionnaire should be aimed high in the management hierarchy rather than low. It is surprising how many managing directors pass on a questionnaire to the right person, and of course, when they do so, the chances are that it will be diligently completed and returned.

The interest which a respondent has in the subject also influences the response. A postal survey about trucks will achieve a better response from road hauliers than will a survey on ball point pens among buyers in general.

The length and complexity of the questionnaire can lower the response rate, though the effect of this can be reduced by making it visually appealing with questions designed to maintain interest. The questionnaire should be easy to answer and return. A pre-paid envelope is essential. The effect of a stamp as opposed to a business reply number makes only a marginal difference (compare the accuracy of the sample frame which makes a very significant difference) and can be tedious to organize in a large survey.

The presentation and persuasiveness of the covering letter help to improve the response rate. The day of the week that the questionnaire is received can affect the response rate, with Mondays and Fridays well worth avoiding. For obvious reasons the questionnaire should not be timed to land just before, during or immediately after a holiday.

Asking the respondent to identify himself and his company will reduce the response, as there is the fear that evidence in writing can be used as ammunition at some future date.

Though these factors should all be taken into consideration in the design of the survey, they mostly have a marginal effect on response compared with the key influences which are the accuracy of the list, targeting it to the right person, obtaining the respondent's interest and making the completion and return as easy as possible.

Designing the questionnaire and cover letter

Many of the principles of questionnaire design discussed in Chapter 19 apply to postal questionnaires, only more so. No interviewer is present to answer queries, no probing is possible; the respondent can pre-empt questions by scanning what lies ahead. Ambiguities, complex questions, sophisticated words must all be assiduously avoided. In addition, there are some aspects of postal questionnaire design which require special attention:

The length of the questionnaire. A respondent with a high interest in a subject will tolerate a longer questionnaire than someone who has not. Four to six A4 pages of questions would be considered lengthy; two pages would be a good length to aim at for most surveys.

The layout and design of the questionnaire. The questions must flow naturally and the visual impact must be simple and attractive. A simple routine question at the start of the questionnaire should lead the respondent into the body of the questionnaire. An example might be:

Q1 Has your company purchased any industrial adhesives in the last 12 months?

YES ☐ Please answer question 3 onwards.

NO ☐ Please answer only question 2.

The filing products sketches (overleaf) were used to accompany a questionnaire on various types of filing products. Though the products are in common usage, pilot research showed that terms used to describe them were highly variable — hence the need for visual and verbal definitions.

By structuring the questionnaire from simple questions to those which are more difficult, the researcher is easing the respondent into his work. Once started, he will be motivated to continue and finish. The embarrassing or controversial questions, left until the end, now stand a chance of completion.

Questions should, wherever possible, have pre-coded responses to make completion easy. This has the disadvantage of taking up a good deal of space and so becomes off-putting at first glance. To overcome the problem, questions should be attractively designed and laid out. Typesetting or proportional spaced typing and photo-reduction can give a questionnaire a cleaner and less formidable appearance. Drawings, diagrams and pictures can stimulate and create interest.

Printing the questionnaire on coloured paper can add to its attraction and make it more noticeable on a respondent's desk covered in white paper.

The cover letter. A postal questionnaire must be accompanied by a letter which explains the purpose of the survey and attempts to sell the respondent the idea of completing and returning it.

The cover letter should bond the sender and respondent with the use of the words *you* and *we* or *I*. The writing style must engage the interest of the reader and it should also convey a professionalism which gives the respondent confidence that his reply will be put to good use.

In the first paragraph, an explanation of the objectives of the research is required. No matter how vague it may sound, the respondent must be sold a benefit or incentive for replying. This could be the promise of an improved service, increased efficiency or a more comprehensive range of products. The incentive could also be material — a small gift, inclusion in a draw, or a summary of the findings. Explain to the respondent that his reply is critical to the success of the survey; he should be assured that the completion and response can be carried out quickly and easily. Finally, an offer of complete confidentiality should be given to allay fears that there will be any future embarrassment or sales pressure.

Filing products survey

The sketches below show the filing products which are being researched.

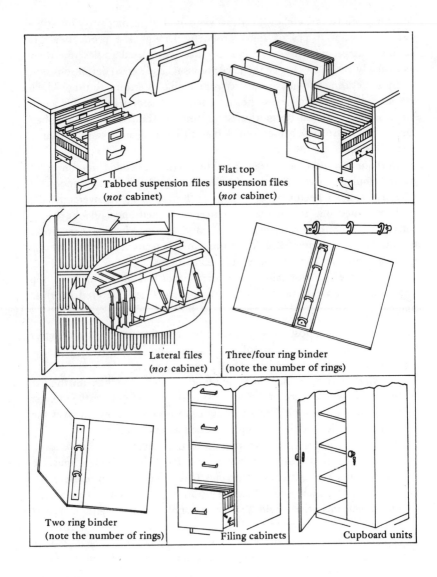

Tabbed suspension files
(*not* cabinet)

Flat top
suspension files
(*not* cabinet)

Lateral files
(*not* cabinet)

Three/four ring binder
(note the number of rings)

Two ring binder
(note the number of rings)

Filing cabinets

Cupboard units

Dear Sir,

We would like to send you a free gift in return for a few minutes of your time!

We are an independent market research company and have been commissioned by a well-known truck manufacturer to obtain the opinions of commercial vehicle fleet operators on some truck makes. The information we obtain in this way will help our client to improve his services to the transport industry. Your own company has been picked as part of a carefully chosen sample and a reply from you would really be appreciated.

You will find with this letter a questionnaire which we would like you to fill in. The questionnaire is designed for self-completion, generally 'ticking' boxes, and because we are interested in opinions, you won't need to spend time looking up records. You will be able to fill in the questionnaire in a few minutes. The completed questionnaires we receive will be analysed by computer and we will then prepare a report of findings for our client. As a result of helping us you won't receive a sales call since our client will not see your questionnaire or even know that you have taken part in the survey.

To ensure we obtain truly unbiased opinions we are not stating now who our client is. When we receive your questionnaire we will, however, send you a small gift, in token of our appreciation for your help, and with this will be a letter naming our client.

We are enclosing a pre-paid envelope to speed (the post office willing) your completed questionnaire to us. If your company does not operate any trucks over 3.5 tons GVW we would still like you to complete the first question and return the questionnaire.

May I thank you in advance for your help in our work.

Yours sincerely

Peter Jackson

The greater the degree of personalization of the letter, the more influence it will have. Letters addressed to a respondent by name, top copy typing, a personal signature and a specific datemark — all will help create impact. These effects can now be built in quite easily using word processors.

Coping with the response

Predicting the response rate of postal questionnaires is almost impossible without previous experience or a pilot test. The response could be from just a few per cent to over 50 per cent. Though the overall response rate cannot be accurately predicted, the rate of response can. A campaign mailed on a Monday will have 20 per cent of all returns in by Friday, nearly half by the following Friday, and at the end of the third week three-quarters or more of the returns will have been received.

The researcher may attempt to boost the response with a second mailing. If the initial mailing yielded a 25 per cent response, a second mailing could draw a further 10 to 15 per cent. The researcher needs, therefore, to consider whether he should send a second mailing to the non-respondents and accept a lower response or draw up an extension of the first sample and achieve a 25 per cent response from the fresh list.

Much depends on the importance of winning a high overall response rate. If a high response is critical then a second mailing is justified and would be timed about two weeks after the first. Time could, of course, be a prohibiting factor, as the second mailing will add another three weeks to the study. Where a high absolute response is required it would be better to mail a fresh sample. A repeat mailing to the sample tends only to be used when the researcher can identify respondents and cross them off the sample frame as their returns come in.

When a second mailing is sent out to the original sample, the researcher could use a different coloured paper for the questionnaire if he needs to be able to identify the two response groups easily. A special cover letter should accompany the second mailing, reiterating the objectives and emphasizing the importance attributed to a response from that particular company. There should also be an apology anticipating the fact that some respondents will have returned their questionnaire which has crossed in the post with the reminder.

The researcher must decide how important or otherwise it is that he knows who has replied. When a respondent is asked to identify his company it can reduce the response rate, but the level of reduction is often over-exaggerated — it is usually less than 5 per cent on a response of 25 per cent. Obtaining the maximum response without asking the respondent to identify himself can be achieved by marking each questionnaire in a unique position and recording the position of the mark on an overlay sheet. The mark on the overlay sheet is given a number corresponding with the same number against the company on the sample frame. When the questionnaire is returned it can be identified by placing the overlay on it, identifying the number which corresponds with the mark and reading the number and company on the sample frame.

Coding can be carried out by any number of ingenious means including clipping the questionnaire and overlay around the edge with scissors or, less subtly, discreetly numbering each questionnaire in a corner. Whether the effort of coding the questionnaires is justified in view of the quite small effect on response of self-identification is for the researcher to decide and will depend on the sensitivity of the questions asked as well as the number of questionnaires mailed.

Checking the validity of postal response

One of the most important weaknesses of postal surveys is the danger that those who respond are in some way different from those who do not. Respondents could be those with the stronger views but not necessarily the deeper purse. They could be those with time on their hands and this could be related to a quieter business. If a material incentive is offered they could simply be people who like give-away pens, key rings or lotteries. If the postal survey is just one part of a wider exercise including telephone interviews and visits, the other interviews can be used to check on the representativeness. Where the postal survey is the sole method of end-user data collection, it is worth carrying out a short telephone interview with non-respondents (if they can be identified separately) to determine any differences between them and postal respondents. Non-respondents may not be identifiable in an anonymous and uncoded questionnaire, in which case a mini-survey of companies selected randomly from the sample frame will be required to produce a result which can be used to weight or at least qualify the postal response.

Variations on postal surveys

There are other applications for self-completion and postal surveys besides the conventional mailings which have been described.

Postal surveys with new products

A self-completion questionnaire (or card) can be included along with a new product to establish a response from new buyers. The incentive to

259

complete the questionnaire could be linked to a guarantee card. This type of 'survey can be useful to build a profile of the type of company which is buying the products. It also provides an opportunity to probe attitudes to the product shortly after it has been used for the first time.

Postal surveys to support telephone interviewing

Postal surveys can be carried out in conjunction with telephone surveys. Sometimes the postal questionnaire can be sent in advance of the telephone interview to allow the respondent time to collect data or consider a question. At the time of telephoning, the respondent could be armed with the questionnaire which he has received through the post. The questionnaire in front of the respondent serves to clarify questions and allows prompt material and visuals to be used.

Postal surveys to support personal interviews

At a personal interview the researcher may wish to leave the respondent with a task which he will carry out and report on, using a postal questionnaire. A new product may be left for him to try out or he could be invited to try using a product in a different way. The interviewer can use the visit to explain any intricacies of the questionnaire and to establish a level of commitment and cooperation which will yield a very high response.

Summary

Postal surveys are a low cost interviewing method which is suitable for collecting simple data from a homogeneous sample.

The chief weakness of postal surveys is the danger that respondents may differ in profile from non-respondents. This is best checked by a small telephone survey of non-respondents. Where a respondent needs to be able to take time over his answers to questions or possibly consult some other source before answering, postal surveys can have an advantage over telephone interviews.

The higher the response rate to a postal survey, the lower the cost per reply and the greater the representativeness. Response rates are influenced most by the accuracy of the sample list, the targeting of the questionnaire to the right person, the level of interest which the respondent has in the subject, and the length and complexity of the questionnaire. Response rates can vary from below 10 per cent to above 50 per cent but most are between 15 and 25 per cent from a single mailing.

1. Take overlay, carbon
   paper and questionnaire

2. Position sheets
   together

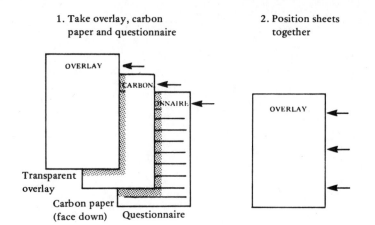

Transparent
overlay

Carbon paper
(face down)   Questionnaire

3. Make a dot on overlay and it
   will transfer through the carbon
   to questionnaire

4. Remove the overlay and
   give the mark a number

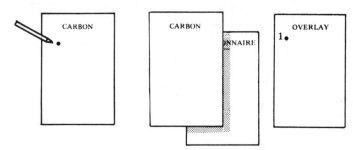

5. Attribute same number
   to a company on
   sample frame

6. On returned questionnaire
   find which dot marries
   with one of overlay marks

7. Locate number on
   sample frame to
   identify company

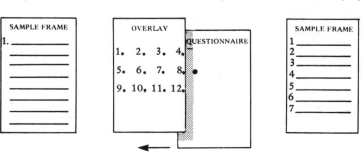

DIAGRAM 22
Steps in placing identification marks on a postal questionnaire

261

Chapter 23
Observation

Observation in industrial market research

There are many circumstances in industrial market research where data can be collected by observation rather than questioning. As the term observation implies, the method leans heavily on visual recording, though listening can be equally important on occasions.

Observation is used when:

1. It is not necessary to ask questions to determine what or why something is happening; and
2. To ask a question may actually produce an incorrect answer.

For example, a conventional survey of transport and distribution managers asked them what information they needed to carry out their work effectively. Even after prompting, respondents claimed that they rarely used information. However, researchers who were placed in transport departments to see and hear what information was actually used, recorded a wide variety of types: legal, the pricing of fuel and parts, route planning data, weather and road conditions, sea and airport timetables etc. Observation uncovered the true use of information which, because it was taken for granted, was not exposed in a conventional interview.

Observation eliminates bias which can occur from the construction or administering of the questions. However, there is always the danger that observation itself is open to misinterpreting or misunderstanding what is seen and heard. In the example of transport information recording, a high level of responsibility lay with the observers who had to decide whether an apparently casual conversation between colleagues in the transport office contained reference which constituted a search for information.

The very presence of the observer may in turn introduce a bias by affecting the actions of people who are being studied — they may unconsciously try to impress, please or even mislead the observer. If the observation is carried out over a long enough period and the subjects become accustomed to it, the effect of bias is reduced. Nevertheless, observers should always assume a low profile where they are recording people's actions. A hidden or inconspicuous position is to be preferred except where ethically in doubt. The vantage point must be chosen with care. Clear visibility of the scene is critical, including possibly the opportunity to view from different angles.

Applications for observation

Observation is little used in industrial market research, often because its application is not obvious. Indeed, the role of observation is usually unique each time it is employed. Some examples of area of use are:

Respondent reactions

An interviewer can sometimes make a judgement, which qualifies an answer to a question, from the facial or verbal expression which accompanies it. Throughout an interview, the interviewer develops a sense of how strongly or otherwise a respondent feels and how knowledgeable or otherwise he is. Interviewers' comments on their assessment of the respondent can help the researcher interpret the questionnaire.

Buying procedures

Most industrial buying is carried out in private using the telephone, a letter or face to face with the salesman. There are situations where the industrial buyer 'shops' in the same way as a consumer and here he can be observed. Cash and carries are an important method of distribution to retail grocers, catering companies, pubs, businesses, automotive accessory retailers, etc. Observers can watch how buyers make their selection and could couple this with a subsequent interview to explore why certain action was (or was not) taken.

Operating procedures

Observation is an excellent method for analysing how something is currently done. It can be used for production processes or transport flows. An interviewer may produce an answer to the question how something should be done; observation will show how it actually is done, including any short cuts or malpractices.

Stocking display

Wholesalers, cash and carries, and distributors, all have a 'retail' face which is exposed to the customer. This face could be a trade counter with a few posters and point of sale material or it could be merchandized displays of stocks. Observation can be used to establish what types of display are used, how effective they are and which companies' products get precedence.

Pricing

Where industrial products are sold over the counter or from a price-list, the prices of competing suppliers can be compared by observation. Very often, however, prices are simply a starting point from which discounts are given and these may not be published.

Sampling

Sometimes a sample can be selected by observation. Lists of commercial vehicle operators with certain makes of machines in their fleet can be built up by observation.

A survey of companies buying cardboard cartons for food packaging can be determined from store checks across the country which record those firms using such packing or producing products which could use it.

Quality checks

The reliability of industrial products can be checked by visiting users and observing levels of wear and performance.

Company size and performance

A researcher may obtain a better feel for a competitor, distributor or customer by looking at their premises. Visual checks will indicate valuable information such as the square footage and nature of the buildings. From observation it may be possible to split out warehousing as opposed to productive space. Land for expansion, recent extensions and current building work are all highly visible.

New products

Prototype products can sometimes be seen on test. To locate a product on test, the researcher needs a tip from a cooperative customer or contact who is evaluating it and is prepared to share the experience. More usually a researcher is dependent on exhibitions which are a frequent showground for observing new products.

Planning the observation

Planning the observation exercise requires answers to four questions:

1. What information is required?

A full listing of the many questions must be prepared and should be realistic within the confines of the observation technique. Observation will show how a product is used — it will not produce data on attitudes. Creating a sample frame by spotting trucks should not be over-ambitious. While the truck may have a full address and telephone number on it, this would be too much to read and write down as it flashes past. The company name and the town where it is located is the key priority — a call to directory enquiries can be used to fill in the gaps.

2. Where will the observer be located?

The positioning of the observer may need permission from a company who will require assurance that their customers or workforce will not be inconvenienced. On many occasions, however, it is unnecessary to obtain permission and observation can take place as if by a member of the public. It may nevertheless be important that the interviewer remains inconspicuous and this should be taken into consideration in planning the siting.

3. When will the observation take place?

The event which is to be observed could occur at different times and the observation programme must be planned to take this into account. More than one observer could be necessary if rapid action has to be noted, while a prolonged observation period would require shifts. It may also be important to avoid certain times which could present a distorted picture — perhaps because of holiday periods or shut downs.

4. How information will be recorded

The observers must be briefed to record the event in exactly the same way. Their own sight and hearing may be sufficient, backed by notes or the completion of a specially designed questionnaire. A permanent visual record on film can sometimes be a valuable aid to analysis and can provide the client with a feel for the subject. Photographs of companies which have been visited can give a dramatic indication of their size and prosperity. Photographs can also record displays, new products and product failures. Thought must be given to the person who will operate the camera. A fairly clear record can be obtained using a simple camera and so avoid the additional complications which will occur if the observers need to be proficient with complex and expensive equipment.

The method of recording the observed event will influence how the analysis is carried out. If the observation record sheet is designed as a questionnaire then the analysis will be quantitative and based on the breakdown of numbers into response categories. At other times the observation must be written up in the same manner as an unstructured interview, in which case the analysis will be more interpretative and in a similar vein to a qualitative report.

Summary

Observation can be used where the collection of information is dependent on sight and sound and does not require interaction with the observer as is the case with interviews. Observation could be used more often in industrial market research for recording and analysing respondent reactions, buying and operating procedures, displays, prices, sample frame construction, quality checks, competitor size and new product launches.

In planning an observation programme the researcher must decide what information he needs, where the observer will stand, when the observation will take place and how the information will be recorded.

Chapter 24
Group Discussions (or Focus Groups)

Qualitative and quantitative research

The measurement of market size and shares in industrial marketing is important for determining where a product or a company stands. It enables management to judge whether a market is worthy of its interest and is a base from which goals can be established. To increase market share, to enter a new market, to launch a new product, require additional information on how and why buyers buy. Such insights can only be obtained by qualitative research.

There are, therefore, two important axioms on the uses of quantitative and qualitative industrial market research:

☐ *Quantitative* market research provides *measurements* which are used as benchmarks and for setting goals.
☐ *Qualitative* market research provides *insights* which can be used to sharpen the marketing process and thereby achieve the goals.

Typical questions which qualitative market researchers may be asked to answer are:

☐ What problems (or needs) does a user face?
☐ How does he solve these problems at present?
☐ Why has he chosen this approach to solving his problems?
☐ How satisfactory is the approach which he uses to solve his problems?
☐ How acceptable would a new approach be to solving his problems?

It is important to recognize that a perceptive comment from only one respondent could be all that is required to identify a need or spot a more effective means of dealing with users' problems. Qualitative market research is concerned with the depth of the information rather than the breadth. Obtaining this depth, analysing it and reporting the findings is only manageable with small samples. The small number of product buyers in many industrial markets means that researchers are conditioned to sample sizes of tens and twenties rather than hundreds or thousands. As a consequence, most industrial market research has a high qualitative content. Nevertheless, researchers have to be prepared to explain to suspicious management that a small sample can be acceptable and provide an accurate reading of the market.

Qualitative research techniques

Two techniques are available to the market researcher in the search for qualitative data — depth interviews and group discussions (also known as focus groups). There is no agreed definition of a depth interview but generally it involves a visit, is unstructured, and can last anything from half an hour to two hours. Group discussions (or groups) are a technique, refined over many years by consumer market researchers who, in turn, borrowed it from the social sciences. They consist of small numbers of carefully selected people who discuss a subject under the guidance of a leader (referred to as a moderator). The occasions when depth interviews are more suited than groups depends very much on the circumstances. In industrial markets researchers are frequently forced to accept that it is logistically too difficult to bring together respondents holding senior positions who are scattered across the country. For this reason depth interviews are and will remain for some time (until multiple verbal/visual link ups become feasible) the most widely used qualitative research technique. There are, however, a number of other factors which favour groups in preference to depth interviews. Sometimes these are the nature of the problem being studied, sometimes they are the result of inherent limitations of one of the techniques (see also page 142).

Group discussions are especially useful techniques for researching new products, testing new concepts or determining 'what would happen if . . .'. They work because of the interaction between group members. Individuals are not under pressure to give spontaneous answers. Each can consider the points raised by other members and, as they digest the implications of the issues raised, ideas may be sparked off which would otherwise remain hidden in a personal interview.

The number and composition of groups

Between six and eight members normally constitute a group though there are no rules as to the ideal number. Ten or twelve must be considered a maximum because anything larger prevents each member making a significant contribution to the discussion. Further, in a large group, there is a greater chance that some participants will treat it as a stage to remonstrate and dramatize rather than be constructive in their arguments. As few as three group members can still be effective since there is, even with these small numbers, sufficient scope for the cross fertilization of ideas.

No standards exist for deciding the number of group discussions which should be held. One may be sufficient though two is the preferred minimum in order to obtain a better feel and expose the possibility of a freak response. Even with two groups, a disparity of views between them would raise doubts as to which was correct. It is, therefore, advisable to carry out three or four groups while the benefit of more than (say) eight is questionable. A large number of groups is only justified if it is thought necessary to hold separate discussions with different classes of respondent (eg, respondents from large companies as opposed to small ones; northern companies in contrast to those from the south; users and lapsed users, etc).

Venues and timing of groups

Whereas consumer groups tend to be held in an interviewer's home, industrial groups are almost always convened in a hotel. A hotel venue is more businesslike and suited to the expectations of a person attending on behalf of his company. However, the standard of the hotel should be selected carefully to accord with the type of respondent. The venue must be easily accessible to all, preferably well-known in the area and with good parking facilities.

The room in which the group is held should be inspected in advance. It needs to be small and intimate rather than large and impersonal. It should also be free from excessive traffic noise.

The time of day at which an industrial group is held cannot please everybody. Lunch times have advantages, but the combination of travelling time to the venue and the duration of the group itself takes no less than two hours and puts pressure on busy schedules. Early evening (say 5.00 pm), straight from work, is an alternative but faces the complication of different finishing times and the infringement on people's own time. Later in the evening at around 8.00 pm can be more acceptable to some respondents though the risk is introduced of their being diverted by domestic arrangements or simply settling into television viewing.

Table 21 classifies the type of industrial respondents against the time of day best suited to their attendance.

TABLE 21
Ideal times for group discussions by class of respondent

Time of group	Class of respondent
Lunch-time	Buyers, transport managers, general managers, local authority officials
Early evening	Tradesmen, works managers, middle managers (marketing/ finance etc)
Late evening	Senior managers, sole proprietors, retailers

Achieving an adequate attendance

Because group discussions rely on such a small number of respondents, it is essential that great care is taken to recruit the right profile. A description of the target respondent must be determined at an early stage and could include any of the following criteria:

☐ have a specific job function
☐ be aware of a product or a company
☐ be a current user or past user of a product or company
☐ represent a company of a certain size (or buying volume)
☐ be of a certain age/gender.

A quota of respondents is set within these criteria, a list is constructed of companies for interview, and recruitment begins by visit or telephone using a specially designed questionnaire. The recruitment questionnaire provides a screen to eliminate respondents who do not meet the criteria and collects advance data on basic questions from those who do. It should not be too long, otherwise respondents will assume that this is only a foretaste of a detailed grilling.

The success of a group discussion is largely dependent on meeting the target figure for attendance. To achieve this the prospect of the group should sound inviting, while barriers which could reduce attendance must be removed. Techniques which can be used to achieve the maximum attendance level are:

Creating positive reasons for attendance

☐ Refer to the group as 'a meeting of people like yourself from other companies'. The term 'group' is meaningless jargon to a respondent — he must understand what he is being asked to do and be able to identify with others who will attend.

☐ Sound enthusiastic. Whip up the respondent's own enthusiasm so that he feels important. Make the group sound exciting — make him want to attend.

☐ Tantalize the respondent. Give him a hook calculated to draw him in. To a transport manager this could be, 'We will be asking you to comment on a new truck.' To a retailer it could be, 'We will be discussing the way other people draw their customers in.' (Of course, the hook must be realistic, otherwise dissonance will occur if the group fails to live up to expectations.)

☐ Provide a material incentive. Drinks, a buffet, and a bottle of spirits or some other gift as a token for the respondents' trouble is usually sufficient.

Removing barriers which could prevent attendance

☐ Fix the time and date to suit him. If groups are being held on different dates and times of the day, slot the respondent into one which he can most easily attend.

☐ Arrange to pick him up. If transport to and from the group is difficult, arrange a taxi or pick-up service. It makes the respondent feel important and the cost is small by comparison.

☐ Reassure him. A respondent may believe that the exercise is a ploy to sell him something, or he may fear his ignorance will be exposed and he could be made to look foolish.

After the initial approach has been made to the respondent and a promise has been obtained from him that he will attend, a letter should be sent confirming the arrangements. The letter acts as a formal reminder to the respondent of the date, the time and the venue, and verifies the purpose of the project. The content and construction of the letter must be business-like, fully descriptive and emphasize how important it is that he attends. A map showing the location of the venue should be enclosed with the letter to ensure no one gets lost.

One or two days before the group, respondents should be telephoned to remind them of the event and also to provide the researchers with a last-minute feel for any likely changes in the attendance level. Even with all these precautions, only around half to two-thirds of respondents who promised to attend will actually do so. This presents a nightmare for the researcher as he does not know until the time of the group whether he will have achieved overkill with too many respondents or have too few to generate a good discussion. The weather, sports events and TV programs cannot always be foreseen and play havoc with response rates.

In the event of a very high turnout the researcher must decide whether he can cope with a group of 14 or 15 respondents or if he should apologize to some and send them straight home with their bottle of whisky. It may be worth while pre-empting the possibility of a high response and arranging for two researchers to be present so that the group can be split into two, accommodation permitting.

Hosting the group

The hotel staff should be fully briefed to direct respondents to the room where the group is being held. A notice of welcome in the foyer and signs to guide respondents to the room should be arranged.

Some respondents always arrive early and others late. The researcher may be advised to keep away from the group during this period of assembly as natural curiosity on the part of those respondents who have arrived may draw a premature discussion. An assistant or hostess should be available to welcome respondents, explain the procedure, serve food and drink and engage in small talk.

The assistant will also prove useful during the course of the group, helping with changing tapes, passing round sample products, or working visual display equipment. After the group the assistant can give out the incentive (for which respondents should sign) and encourage those who appear to want to chat to retire to the bar rather than sit talking all night in the room.

Administering the group

Groups are led by a researcher whose role differs greatly from that of an interviewer. The group leader exists:

- ☐ To steer the discussion through a range of subjects which are relevant to the problem. The order of these topics is equally determined by spontaneity within the group itself.
- ☐ As a catalyst to provoke responses or introduce ideas. Sometimes the researcher should play devil's advocate or feign ignorance.
- ☐ To draw a response from those who are quiet and curb those who attempt to monopolize the discussion.

A group leader does not question individuals as in a conventional interview.

His personality is important from the outset in creating empathy with the members, relaxing them and encouraging a lively discussion. A brief introduction should be followed by an explanation that a tape recording will be made in view of the difficulties of note taking. It is then necessary to break the ice by asking each member to introduce himself and his company.

Working from the list of topics he wishes to cover, the researcher aims to move the discussion from the general to the particular. Thus, if the objective of the group is to establish the opportunities for a new design of screw, he may begin by stimulating a discussion of fastening problems followed by an exploration of attitudes to screws and finally homing in on the new screw itself. Diagram 23 shows one page of a checklist used by a discussion leader in a survey on low cost daisywheel printers.

Controlling the group can be a problem for the moderator. Within a small number of respondents there is invariably a dominant respondent who attempts to run the group himself or whose forcibly expressed views colour those of the other members. He must also deal diplomatically with slow thinkers, introverts, extroverts, wits, drunks, compulsive talkers and the indifferent. The ability to be able to bring out the best from each without insult or embarrassment requires the leader to be both authoritative and tactful.

Groups generally take between one and one and a half hours to administer depending on the complexity of the subject and interruptions from films or product presentations.

Summary

Groups are an assembly of six to eight specially recruited people who, with the guidance of a moderator, discuss a subject. The interaction of ideas in the group produces a fertile environment for raising qualitative insights which may be missed in a face-to-face interview.

Group discussions are particularly suited to exploring new concepts.

Industrial group' discussions are normally held in a hotel at lunchtime, early or late evening, as is best suited to the job function of the respondent.

A critical task in the organization of the group is the achievement of an acceptable attendance level. The recruiters need to be skilled in creating positive reasons to draw respondents out and be capable of removing any barriers which could prevent attendance.

During the group the moderator's role is to steer the discussion rather than act as an interviewer.

3. *Printers: General*

3.1 What type of printers are owned, if any?
   PROBE: make
            type: thermal, dot matrix, daisywheel
   What are existing printers used for?

3.2 Are you familiar with the sort of printers you can use with a home computer?
      PROBE: type awareness — thermal, dot matrix, daisywheel
              benefits/disadvantages of each type:
                  thermal — paper cost/format
                  dot matrix — limited letter quality
                  daisywheel — limited graphics

3.3 How much do printers cost?

3.4 If you don't use a printer, do you feel your system is limited for this reason?
   Why?

3.5 What advantages would a printer offer?
   Could you extend the application of your computer if you had a printer?
   How?

3.6 What could a home computer printer be used for?
   PROBE: program records, letters, etc.

3.7 What would be important characteristics of such a printer?
   PROBE: speed, plain paper, quality of print
            Would quality of print be particularly important?

3.8 Any disadvantages of a printer?
   What about cost?
   Has cost been a barrier to acquiring a printer?

3.9 Printers are fairly noisy — would this be a problem in the home?

4. *The new printer*

   Present printer using concept sheets. Then show demonstration printer
   explaining this is not the new printer but does work on the same principle.
   Price of printer NOT to be stated.

4.1 Initial impressions of the printer

4.2 Would such a printer be useful?
   For what?

4.3 The printer produces *quality* print. Is there a real need for such quality?

4.4 While the printer can produce quality print it does have graphic limitations
   (vertical and horizontal lines). Do the graphic limitations affect interest in
   the printer?

4.5 Attitudes to specific features of the design.
   PROBE: size
            weight
            print speed
            paper format (A4 and not landscape)
            plain paper (could be 'headed' paper).

DIAGRAM 23
*Sample page from discussion group checklist on low cost
daisywheel printers*

Chapter 25
Clinics

The application of clinics in industrial market research

There are occasions in industrial market research where a face-to-face interview is not good enough. For example, a company with a prototype compressor may need to obtain a reaction from potential customers prior to its launch. It could be hauled around to each company for respondents to comment on but this would present all sorts of problems: where at the respondent's premises can the demonstration take place (difficult in a city location)? How many interviews can be carried out (10 to 20 would take a long time)? How can comparisons be made with competitors' products (it would be necessary to drag these around as well and this is impractical)? A more practical proposition is for respondents to travel to see the product — a market research clinic.

A clinic differs from a group discussion because respondents are interviewed individually. However, it is quite common to invite a respondent to stay on and join small discussion groups after the clinic, thus exploiting to the full the rare occasion of an assembly of buyers or specifiers.

Clinics are ideal where the nature of the study makes it easier to move respondents rather than the product. The product may be inconvenient to move because it is large, heavy, dangerous, prone to damage in transit or possibly it needs to be viewed in special circumstances, such as alongside competitive equipment or in a certain setting. The principal advantage of the clinic is, therefore, that it gives the researcher control over the environment in which the interview is to take place. New product research or competitive product studies are both suited to clinics but there may be circumstances where products do not feature at all. The clinic may, for example, be used to display promotional material, show a film or operate a computer: all easier to organize at a central venue.

Respondents attending a clinic will nearly always be required to answer rating questions: What do you think of . . .? What score would you attribute to . . .? What do you like; what do you dislike; how could improvements be made? Clinics are not a technique for assessing market size, market shares or market structure. Such data can more effectively be established by conventional interviewing or desk research. Rather, clinics provide qualitative findings. These may, nevertheless, be based on a substantial number of interviews. If the product being studied faces at best only a couple of dozen buyers who are spread geographically (and this is the case in many industrial markets), then an attendance by 10 or 12 respondents could be considered good. A potential universe of thousands of buyers, as for example with power tools or office equipment, could in contrast have a target throughput of 200 respondents over four or five days.

The stages in organizing a clinic

The respondent who attends a clinic will pass through a number of stages as information is collected from him. Typically these could be:

Recruitment

This involves first contact with the respondent and he is asked simple questions to determine whether he qualifies for invitation. The questions should be confined to the bare essentials such as, 'Do you ever buy . . .? and 'How many do you operate?' Recruitment is usually carried out over the telephone and the time for questioning is limited. Moreover, the respondent may feel intimated by a lengthy inquisition. The respondent's eligibility having been established, he is now invited to attend. The word clinic should be avoided when making the invitation. It is jargon which the respondent will not understand and to a layman raises connotations of worrying medical investigations. Far better to refer to it as 'a market research exercise in which we wish to show you . . .'. The researcher should never be under the illusion that the respondent is eager to attend, however enthusiastic his affirmations.

The passage of two or three days may bring new priorities which could result in the dropping of good intentions to visit the clinic. For this reason it is important to sell hard the benefits of the clinic. A respondent must be told that his view is important — that is why he was selected; he will find it interesting; there will be refreshments while he is there and (say) a bottle of whisky to take away. A time and date for his visit should be agreed with him and his cooperation should be re-established before the recruiter puts down the phone. It is most important to confirm the arrangements in writing with perhaps an invitation card and a map showing how to get there. Still the recruitment is not finished. One or two days before the clinic the respondent should be telephoned once more to remind him that he is expected. If the attendance of any individual is absolutely vital, it may be worth while arranging a car to pick him up or sending him a train ticket.

Pre-clinic fact collection

When the respondent arrives at the clinic he will be met by a receptionist who registers his attendance on a control sheet, provides a name tag and hands him any other equipment that will be required. The respondent will be feeling apprehensive about what he has let himself in for. He must straight away be made to feel welcome and a cup of coffee and brief explanation of the program will go a long way to reduce any tension. Prior to the respondent being shown a new product or asked to view a display, he must be questioned about his current attitudes and buying practices, as exposure to a new product could create a reaction which changes an established view. The pre-clinic fact collection is best carried out in a separate or screened part of the hall so that the new product is out of sight. The questions should be straightforward to ease the respondent into the more complex ratings which are yet to come. Typically the pre-clinic fact collection will cover the following ground:

- [ ] how much is bought and how often
- [ ] what range of product types is bought
- [ ] what brands of products are bought
- [ ] why these products and brands are bought
- [ ] what is the satisfaction with the suppliers and the products
- [ ] what modifications or improvements could be made
- [ ] what will be bought in the future.

Clinic ratings

After the pre-clinic fact collection the respondent will be eager and curious to view the product. An interviewer must explain what is required of him. An examination and trial of the product could be followed by questions to establish his views. The product examination must be structured to ensure all features are noted. The respondent must view the product from all points of the compass and comment on styling. He may have to open hatches to assess access, attempt manoeuvres and give opinions on ease of operation. Questioning may be administered by an interviewer, by self-completion or a mixture of both, depending on its complexity. Rating scales could be verbal (ie, very good, quite good, etc), numerical (ie, a score out of five) or pictorial (ie, with + and − at each end; see example on page 228). Ratings are well suited to self-competition but additional probing such as, 'Why do you say that?' or 'How could this be improved?' would generally require the assistance of an interviewer.

Clinic debriefing

The respondent's activity at the clinic may end with the ratings but, depending on the circumstances, there could be value in a debriefing session to cover the points which inevitably were not formalized in the questionnaires. Debriefings are well suited to a relaxed, free-ranging discussion and for this reason the researcher must be experienced in unstructured interviewing; they can be carried out one to one or as a group and, with the respondent's permission, could be taped to facilitate analysis. It may be at the debriefing stage, or at the end of the clinic ratings, that the interviewer introduces probes to find out if the views and buying practices of the respondent have changed following exposure to the new product.

Planning and running the clinic

Setting up a clinic requires meticulous planning. Deciding where to hold it is the first step. If an excavator is to be demonstrated, a different type of venue is required from a machine tool clinic. Exhibition halls, theatres and hotels make the best venues as they are neutral ground and have suitable facilities. Company offices and factory sites may be cheaper but they could bias respondents' answers and even dissuade attendance. The clinic organizer should draw up a shortlist of venues and, after visiting them, give each a score for how easy it is for a respondent to find, parking facilities, size, amenities and the overall location relative to the respondents who it is hoped will attend. Of course some features may be critical, depending on the use to which it will be put. If a cement mixer is to be tried out there must be hard standing, preferably under open-sided cover to keep materials dry and let the noise and fumes escape. If a venue cannot provide these features then it must be eliminated, irrespective of the desirability of other factors.

Once the venue is booked, the date for the clinic can be finalized and the rest of the arrangements tailored to suit. Diagram 24 summarizes the multitudinous tasks which are necessary over a four-week period from booking a hall to the end of the clinic. The analysis of data and report preparation is likely to add a further two weeks to the time-scale so an overall period of no less than six weeks should be allowed.

The number of respondents who actually turn up for a clinic compared with those who said they would at the recruitment stage, create a major headache for the researcher who needs to know in advance how many to cater for in his supply of interviewers, refreshments and incentives. The two most important factors influencing the response rates are the skills of the recruiters and the lure of an interesting subject. A charming female

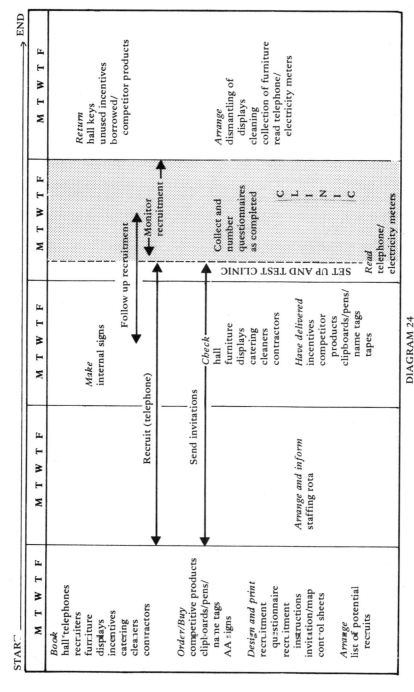

DIAGRAM 24

Organizational chart for industrial clinic

281

voice recruiting male respondents can produce a high promise of attendance but its allure may be forgotten in the period prior to the date of attendance. This emphasizes the importance of follow-up letters and reminder telephone calls. The promise of the sight of a new product in which the respondent is interested is perhaps of greater weight. Buyers of office copiers who are invited to view and comment on a new product will have a lower attendance rate than transport managers asked to look at a new truck. Trucks have a higher emotional appeal to transport managers than copiers have to office managers. A good recruitment response rate at a clinic is one attendance to every three promises. An average response might be one in six or seven while a low interest product could yield only one in fifteen. Holiday periods, sports events and the weather can superimpose an additional curb on attendance. If the buyer believes that he will spend an hour or two looking at a product which interests him, he will attend irrespective of the gift he is offered. Incentives do have a role to play. They tip the balance with some respondents and act as a thank-you to the majority for giving their time and opinions.

Summary

Clinics are used in industrial market research when it is easier to move respondents to see a product or display than to take the product to each respondent. They are particularly useful for testing reactions to new products. Recruiting respondents for a clinic is usually carried out by telephone and supported by a letter of confirmation.

Attendance rates at the clinic are vital and are influenced by the location of the venue, the level of interest which the respondent has in the subject and the powers of persuasion of the recruiter.

At the clinic the respondent passes through three stages. Prior to seeing the new product questioning takes place to establish current buying practices and attitudes. This is followed by his evaluation of the new product. Finally, if time allows, the respondent is debriefed to find out how his views and practices could change after having considered the new product.

Chapter 26
Forecasting

Types of forecast

The purpose of forecasting is to allow management to plan ahead. Without a view of the future, opportunities could be missed or investments made with no chance of a financial return. Four different types of forecast are relevant to the industrial market researcher:

Economic forecasts

These paint a picture of the broad environment in which a company will be operating. They include a prediction of Gross Domestic Product (GDP)*, inflation, unemployment, balance of payments plus a number of other parameters such as money supply, consumer spending, public sector borrowing and so on. The market researcher is interested in economic forecasts for the effect they have on the markets his company supplies. They are, therefore, a backcloth. The market researcher would be unlikely to involve himself in the raw preparation of economic forecasts as this is a specialized activity of econometricians. In any case, he has little need to do so as the financial press regularly publish economic forecasts from specialist forecasting organizations and the merchant banks.

Environmental forecasts

The economic forecast covers the financial environment in which the company operates. There is, however, a wider environment which encompasses the social, political and legal scene. The relevance of these will differ according to the business of the company. All companies are affected by major wars and the depletion of basic resources such as oil, gas and coal. Others will be affected, to a greater or lesser extent,

---

* GDP is the value of all the output of goods and services produced by a country's economy in a period – usually a year.

283

by changes in fashion, climate, social attitudes, politics and specific legislation. Environmental forecasts are generally prepared by social scientists and published as long-term predictions.

Market and product forecasts

These are fundamental to the industrial market researcher as they are concerned with specific sectors. The term is generally applied to forecasts of the end-user markets into which products are sold and forecasts for the product itself. The forecast of end-user demand is an important input in the product forecast.

Sales forecasts

These are a combination of what will happen to a company's sales as a result of the market environment and what will happen if the company introduces a new level of sales and promotional effort. It is, therefore, partly a statement of intent — a target — and partly a true forecast.

All forecasts must have a horizon, whether weeks or years. Conventionally, researchers use three important breaks:

☐ *Short-term* forecasts concerned with periods up to a year;
☐ *Medium-term* forecasts which look beyond a year as far as three years;
☐ *Long-term* forecasts which are predictions beyond three years.

The time periods attributed to short-, medium- and long-term forecasting are entirely arbitrary and have changed through the 1970s. In the late 1960s and early 1970s economies and markets had greater stability and company plans stretched to five years. The shock waves created by the Yom Kippur War of 1973 have shortened the medium term to two to three years, as anything longer is beyond the realms of reasonable accuracy. Even these periods are changeable within the specific context of companies and their markets. In the fast-moving world of computers, long term may be one to two years whereas a manufacturer of coffins can push his long-term predictions out to ten years and still maintain acceptable levels of accuracy.

The role of forecasts inside a company

Market and sales forecasting play a role in a number of areas of company planning.

Corporate planning

The forecasts of the economic environment and the market enable the corporate planners to steer the future course of the company. They highlight general opportunities and, just as important, pinpoint the blind alleys and areas of decline.

Product and market planning

The product and market plans are used to set company objectives and establish budgets for promotion and selling which are needed to achieve the goals.

The product and market forecasts are action oriented. It is from these that companies plan their entry into new markets, or their withdrawal from those with limited opportunities. The more detailed the forecast, the more precise the action can be. A forecast of regional growth prospects allows a company to concentrate its efforts where they will pay greatest dividends. Forecasts for sub-groups of products similarly allow detailed planning for each sector.

Sales planning

The sales plan is based on the forecast of sales which the company believes it can achieve. The sales forecast cannot be viewed in isolation. It represents a share of the total market which can realistically be attained and this, in turn, depends on the strengths and weaknesses of every competing supplier and the level of resources each commits in support of its own sales.

Production planning

Once agreed and accepted the sales plan becomes the master document on which all other internal company plans depend. The first of these is the production plan which is designed to ensure that productive resources are available to manufacture the product mix. Careful production planning is necessary to ensure good deliveries and productive efficiencies. The production manager may face the difficult choice of whether to produce large quantities in bulk, store them and live with expensive financing and warehousing costs, or to remain flexible, manufacturing to meet orders but paying the penalty of lost economies of scale.

Financial planning

The production schedule will incur costs, the most important of which are stocks, tooling, machinery and plant. The sales and marketing plan will require money to be spent on promotion, selling, delivery and the clerical processing of orders. The sales forecast affects the flow of cash into the company and if the predicted cash flow cannot be reconciled with predicted costs in the months ahead, loan options must be agreed with banks well in advance to ensure the lowest possible interest charges. Thus, the financial plan is drawn up using the sales and production budgets and adding to them the overhead burden necessary to run the business.

Selecting the forecasting method

The purpose of a forecast is to predict the future. It is necessary, therefore, that the forecast is expressed in appropriate values and in time periods which are conducive to the exercise. Values should ideally be inflation free, such as numbers, tonnes or gallons. Monetary values can be used but they should be readjusted for inflation and expressed at current prices. Alternatively, the figures could be corrected to an index. The steps of time over which the forecast is made can be as short as days, weeks or months (in a sales plan) but more often they are in quarters or years.

A forecast can never be absolutely correct, except by coincidence. It is after all a method of estimating likely future events and these are always uncertain. It is usual, therefore, to qualify a forecast. Different predictions could be given based on different assumptions or there could simply be an upper and lower limit either side of the best estimate.

The finished forecast should be supported by a description of the underpinning assumptions and their effect. The method of preparing the forecast should also be described, as readers will react more favourably to one they understand. A simple approach is better than a sophisticated but complex method where the user needs to wrestle with the concepts.

Forecasting methods can be divided into two major types: *objective* methods comprising various statistical approaches and *subjective* methods based on surveys of opinion. Table 22 shows the most commonly used forecasting methods and how they are suited to different forecasting periods and applications.

Historical analogy

History often repeats itself. If the researcher believes that a product will follow a similar pattern to one which is already established and well-documented, the earlier analogous trend becomes a base for predicting the future.

TABLE 22
Classification of forecasting methods by application

Classification of forecasting method	Period	Application
OBJECTIVE METHODS *Trend projection* Historical analogy	Medium to long term	New products; products susceptible to change
Moving averages	Short to medium term	Established products with a recognizable cycle
Exponential smoothing	Short term	Products which are changing and entering uncharted areas
Models Correlation	Short to medium term	Where products are influenced by factors on which data is available historically and for the forecast period
SUBJECTIVE METHODS User opinion	Short to medium term	Sales forecasts; new products
Expert opinion	Medium to long term	Market and industry forecasts

This philosophy lies behind the 'product life cycle' described in the Introduction. All products are believed to have a life which has recognizable stages of youth, maturity and old age. Identifying the position of a product at any one point in time in its life is critical, as it enables the researcher to predict future sales and, if necessary, rejuvenate it or introduce a replacement. The time-span from youth to old age could cover 20 or more years and within that period, product modifications distort the smooth lines of the curve. Interference with the curve is created by economic cycles, legislation and social changes so that in industrial marketing it is sometimes difficult to make practical use of the product life cycle, even though theoretically it is a useful concept (see page 9).

Nevertheless, while it may be difficult to plot an entire life cycle for a product, it may be possible to recognize short sections of it. A product launched in America or continental Europe may have followed a pattern which can be expected in the UK a short while later. Allowance must be made for cultural and economic differences. Product launches which proved successful in Europe cannot be expected to be repeated in developing nations.

Moving averages

One of the simplest methods of obtaining a view of the future is to plot an historical series of data and allow the eye to project the trend forward. Moving averages perform this feat mathematically and, therefore, accurately and objectively. The projection by eye may be close to reality over the short term but mathematical prediction will provide a good forecast for up to two years ahead. Moving averages smooth the peaks and troughs in the data, creating a trend line which cuts the centre of the figures.

Moving averages are a suitable method for predicting from a series of data which has shown regular historical patterns and where there is a long series. Thus they are a suitable means of predicting seasonal sales and those with an evident cycle. They are not suitable for predicting events in rapidly changing markets, where there is a short time series of data or where account has to be taken of a recent major event (such as a new government imposing strong fiscal measures).

Exponential smoothing

Predictions using moving averages assume that history, no matter how distant, has an effect on the future equal to that of the most recent past. Often, however, it is recent events which provide the greatest clue to future activity. Exponential smoothing is a mathematical approach which applies such weights. Like all methods of trend projection, it relies on a long series of data but here, five years is probably sufficient, compared with the ten or more years necessary in moving averages. Where such lengthy historical series are not available, the forecast may have to be calculated on quarterly figures, accepting the fact that the forecasting horizon will be that much shorter.

Exponential smoothing is most suited to series of data where there have been no wild fluctuations but a steady growth or decline which is accelerating or decelerating.

Correlation

Correlation is a statistical technique for demonstrating the relationship between two series of data. One set of data is known as the dependent variable and is the item which is to be forecast; the other is known as the independent variable and is the factor which explains the movement in the dependent variable.

The influence of one factor on another is very often obvious:

288

welding rods and CO_2
vehicle servicing and the size of the truck parc
leak sealing services and power generation
the capacity of oil refineries and oil production
steel consumption and car production.

The first test of the existence of any relationship is to plot the two sets of data on a graph to establish visually if the fluctuations appear sympathetic. That they may prove to do so is not, of course, proof of a direct causal relationship. Steel consumption and car production may rise and fall in sympathy — not because cars are the major outlet for steel but because car production is a fair barometer of the country's economic prosperity and it is in this connection that a relationship is apparent. Similarly, historical relationships can change. Commercial vehicles have become increasingly sophisticated in recent years so that garage servicing has increased faster than the size of the truck parc. The extra impetus has been won from the swing away from in-house servicing.

Establishing the strong relationship between two sets of data is the first step. To make use of that relationship and predict the future depends on the availability of a forecast for the independent variable. The accuracy of the forecast of the dependent variable is not only affected by the level of correlation but also by the accuracy of the forecast of the independent variable. Thus there is no point demonstrating a relationship between welding rod sales and CO_2 consumption unless an apparently reliable forecast of CO_2 consumption is readily available over the period of the forecast.

Sometimes an independent variable can be identified which leads the dependent variable. Flat roofs being constructed today can be used to predict sales of the replacement roofing felts market in 10 years' time — the length of life of the original felt. Bad winters influence the sales of road-making machinery six months later when it is needed to repair the ravages of the weather.

For many products, no single independent variable explains the relationship. Fork-lift truck demand is not only influenced by GDP, but also by interest rates (which affect the propensity to buy equipment). When more than one independent variable is built into a formula to establish the coefficient of correlation, the statistical technique is known as multiple regression.

The validity of a forecast based on correlation depends on the accuracy of the forecast of the independent variable and the maintenance of the proven relationship into the future. A relationship which has held good for the past ten years may well change over the next five. This means that regression forecasting is best restricted to short- to medium-term horizons.

Surveys of user opinions

A traditional approach used by market researchers to determine future trends is to ask users how they foresee their consumption of a product or service changing.

In the 1950s and 60s this proved a reliable approach, as users were able to extrapolate their purchases of the last few years with a high level of confidence. In the uncertain years since 1973 it has proved difficult for users to look even 12 months ahead.

Producing *market forecasts* from buyers' claimed intentions is notoriously unreliable for two important reasons. First, buyers are the wrong people to predict the future prospects within a company. They react to demands from production who in turn respond to orders generated by sales. It is the sales and marketing departments who have a better feel for the future though they, in turn, are not without a bias. Second, buyers, like most other employees of a company, tend towards optimism rather than pessimism. It is reasonable that most respondents, if unsure of the future for their company, will incline towards a favourable view out of wishful thinking. It is almost an admission of failure for a respondent to admit that his future purchases will be anything less than their present level.

In constructing the *sales forecast* it becomes necessary to take account of user opinion, especially that of current customers, though this may be subsequently modified by the researcher adding his own interpretation. Obtaining a prediction of likely purchases from a buyer at a company provides one important input for the sales forecast and it also acts as a tacit business commitment.

End users are noted for seeing the future in isolation. They are dismissive of competitors and highly reactive to recent events. A few good weeks' sales and a bullish report on the economy can persuade a respondent that the next two years' prospects are rosy. Similarly, media reports of doom and gloom can talk respondents into a recession. Researchers must not be afraid of tempering end users' opinions. Indeed, it can be better for the researcher to explore the environment which influences a company and then arrive at his own prediction rather than ask the company outright. The researcher could, for example, lead the respondent through a series of background questions which are factual:

☐ What were the trends in purchases over the past year/two years/three years?

☐ To what extent were those increases or decreases in purchases due to changes in demand for the products made by the company as opposed to technological changes?

☐ What changes will be made to the company's products or the method of manufacture over the next year?

This data, backed by the researcher's knowledge of trends in his customers' end-user markets and changing competition, could put him in a more informed position to make his own prediction of each respondent's future demand than the respondents themselves. It should be remembered that a subjective forecast is an expression of individual opinion that cannot be regarded as holy writ.

Surveys of expert opinion

In industrial markets there very often are no statistical series to develop a trend forecast, or a rapid change in the business environment may make such an approach doubtful in any case. The industrial company may be in a business which is concerned with the tendering for and, therefore, the forecast sale of, high-cost single items of plant. The lumpy nature of such demand can lead to large fluctuations in demand depending on when and how the contracts fall.

Very often in industrial markets the researcher cannot rely on statistical series or the narrow perspective held by buyers. He has, therefore, to turn to experts. The experts may be from a variety of sources and all should be tapped. The researcher working in-house often has personnel available to him with considerable experience of a market, who can be drawn upon for their long-term views on trends. Research and development, production management, purchasing, market researchers, promotional staff and sales management can be interviewed separately or as a group by the marketing staff to arrive at a distillation of opinion. There is no single right way to collect the information, as all the methods have their own advantages and disadvantages. Brainstorming sessions are useful in stimulating ideas but the inarticulate suffer while the outspoken may dominate. The Delphi approach, in which individuals' views are collected separately and the findings circulated for modified comment, can provide longer term trends but, through exposing the thoughts of others, it may cause some of the less confident contributors to be unduly influenced — possibly incorrectly.

Depth interviews with experts are a traditional and safe method of collecting data. There are, however, a number of wrinkles which should be borne in mind. Before a respondent is asked to arrive at his predictions of the future, his mind should be turned to the past. Questions should be introduced to stimulate comment on those factors which have influenced the market historically.

These could include technological, distribution, promotional and cultural changes. With the respondent's mind now focused on the causes of the historical trend, the interviewer can probe for views on absolute changes in the market size over the past five years (say). If the market size is unknown to the respondent, he could be asked to make his estimate as an index in which the current year is assumed to be 100. (Never should this question be framed to determine the percentage change in market size, as respondents latch on to rounded rates of 5 or 10 per cent per year which, when compounded, have a dramatic effect on market size that may not be intended if the implications were thought through.) After the historical perspective, the respondent's views on the future can be probed, covering topics such as technology, changes in product use, fashion, substitution, etc. Only now can specific questions be introduced to find out views on the market size over the *next* few years.

Expert opinion can be obtained from a variety of sources besides one's own company. Competitors may be prepared to talk in broad terms about the future of the total market, and it would be very difficult for them to 'cook' their answers if they were asked to justify their statements at every point in the discussion. Also, the interviewer, with the benefit of other persons' views already collected, will be quickly able to spot the deviant. Journalists, university researchers, government officials, suppliers, customers' customers: all may be worth canvassing for their forecasts.

In this way the marketer can build up a picture of the long-term future which is based on more than his own intuition. He is in a position to draw together the points of conflict and arrive at a balanced judgement.

Composite forecasts

A forecast should not necessarily be derived from a single approach. It can be enlightening to compare forecasts arrived at by different techniques. Forecasts should be justifiable and so, where they do not agree, the rationalization process may uncover flaws which help towards a deeper understanding of market trends.

Long-term forecasting is more difficult now than it has ever been. Uncertainty surrounds the supply of many raw materials as well as oil, and for the first time a practical awareness is growing of the problems of robbing the world of resources which cannot be replaced. Second, nations are faced with economic pressures which they do not know how to control. Inflation, recession, interest rates and unemployment affect every supplier of industrial goods and, because their interaction is not fully understood, it is not possible to know how deeply recessions will bite or how long they will last. Third, the world is moving into a period of increasing political tension which has prompted many people to condition themselves mentally to the possibility of a third world war. If such an event is thought possible or even likely, should it be built into a forecast, and realistically, how could this be done?

The difficulties which beset long-term forecasting pose an important problem to the industrial market researcher. He still has to advise his board on the feasibility of laying down new plant, employing labour, entering new markets or developing new products. Without a long-term forecast it is not possible to make provision for resources, since the lead time on commissioning a new plant and tooling might be between two and four years.

Unfortunately, there is no simple answer – indeed the best solution is to use as many forecasting approaches as possible to cross check the findings.

Summary

The industrial market researcher is mainly occupied preparing market and sales forecasts rather than economic or environmental forecasts, the latter two forecasts being widely available in published form and useful as background. All other budgets and plans within a company are dependent on the sales and market forecast.

There are a number of forecasting methods available to researchers which can be classified as objective (statistically based) or subjective (opinion based). The most commonly used objective methods are techniques for trend projection or models based on regression. Subjective methods utilize information and views collected from end users and experts. All methods have their strengths and weaknesses and it is helpful to use more than one approach in order to obtain a best estimate.

Part Five:
Processing and presenting the data

Chapter 27
Analysing the Data

Drawing together sources of data

The consumer market researcher spends much of his time interpreting group discussions or analysing hundreds of questionnaires generated by large fieldwork programs. Industrial market researchers, on the other hand, are more often occupied on a wider range of analysis tasks:

- ☐ findings from desk research
- ☐ end-user interviews (structured, semi-structured or unstructured)
- ☐ overview interviews (nearly always unstructured)
- ☐ group discussions
- ☐ observation.

Most industrial market research reports draw upon a variety of sources of information. Desk research and fieldwork may be merged within sections of the report to describe a point more fully. The industrial market researcher is more often involved in judgements and interpretations based on limited and pieced-together information than the consumer researcher whose fieldwork program has been designed, it is hoped, to supply all the answers.

The industrial market researcher is, therefore, faced with analysing data generated from particular research techniques and pulling together the different data into a report which meets the survey objectives.

Analysing desk research

Desk research generally uncovers volumes of data only some of which is relevant. The researcher must first take his many statistics, articles, brochures, etc and classify them into headings appropriate to their possible positioning in the report. Thus background sales statistics on the research sponsor may be classified to the 'Introduction'; industry sales figures to

'Market Size'; import and export data to 'International Trade' and financial profiles to 'The Competition'. If a problem exists in slotting data into a suitable heading, it is probably redundant within the scope of the survey objectives and should be set aside for reference should it be needed later. Data which spans chapters of the report should be cut and pasted into the appropriate sections.

The judgements that must be made in this classification and sorting are difficult to delegate. This is, therefore, a job for the researcher who must decide the extent to which each piece of information is relevant to his objectives.

End-user interviews

The nature of the interviews will have been determined at the time the research program was designed. The larger the survey, the greater the benefits from a structured questionnaire using pre-coded answers to questions. In theory all answers can be pre-empted. In practice this is most difficult. Pre-coded answers are easier to lay down for the question, 'What did you like?' than for 'Why did you say that?' The researcher must be sure, if he leaves a question open-ended, that it is to allow for genuine freedom of expression rather than laziness on his part.

At the end of the analysis the researcher seeks groups of answers which enable him to describe attitudes or patterns of behaviour. With the analysis in mind, the researcher can achieve this grouping in a number of ways at the questionnaire design stage:

1. The respondent is presented with a range of alternatives and selects accordingly. This forcing of response reduces coding to a minimum but it could falsely restrict answers. It should, therefore, be limited to questions with clear-cut answers such as:

   How many employees work at this establishment? Is it:
   Less than 25   ☐
   26 - 100   ☐
   101 - 250   ☐
   Over 250   ☐

2. The respondent is asked a question without prompting the answers, but the interviewer classifies it into a pre-coded list of possible replies. Here the responsibility for classification rests entirely on the interviewer's shoulders and, because of the need to respond fast to keep the flow of the interview going, the listing should be clear and simple. For example:

298

Q5   What did you do with your old machine tool?
　　　DO NOT PROMPT: CODE BELOW　　　ASK:

Scrapped it	⟶ Was it removed	YES
	from the premises?	NO
Used it for spares		
Have kept it	⟶ Is it ever used?	YES
		NO
Sold it		
Other (specify) _____		

3. The interviewee is asked an open-ended question and the response
is written down verbatim. For example:

Why did you buy a new machine tool from ABC?_____
PROBE:
Was there any other reason?_____

Classifying open-ended responses is a major analysis task and becomes
necessary whenever the number of interviews is sufficiently large to produce a group of respondents with a commercially significant figure.
A number of steps help to ensure that the labour intensive coding is
carried out reliably.

1. *Briefing the coders*
   Coders must be selected for their thoroughness, patience and initiative. They must be carefully briefed on their role before they
   begin work. The briefing should give clear instructions on how to
   devise coding frames (see 3 below), how many codes to create, what
   type of codes should be created and when to seek further advice.

2. *Checking the questionnaires*
   Completed questionnaires must be checked to ensure all relevant
   response categories have been completed. The company name and
   address, the don't know responses, the handwriting may all need
   clarification. Sometimes the responses are obvious and can be edited,
   sometimes the respondent must be re-contacted or the question
   discarded.

3. *Establishing coding frames*
   A coding frame is a listing of useful and sensible response categories
   and is usually set up by sampling a number of questionnaires until
   the coder recognizes a clear pattern. This is relatively easy when
   grouping companies, say in response to the question, 'Which make
   did you buy?' The major companies emerge very quickly and a
   dustbin category can be opened for the also-rans. It is much harder

to establish a coding frame when the answers are to a qualitative question. For example, in one respect the following responses say the same thing and yet in their own way each is subtly different. The coders must, in conjunction with the researcher, decide if they are all to be lumped within one code or separated out.

Question: Why did you go to the exhibition?
Responses: 1. To keep myself up to date.
2. To see new products.
3. To get new ideas.
4. To meet new suppliers.

The design of the coding frame is a vital part of the analysis and determines the extent to which true patterns will emerge. The researcher should either design it himself or closely supervise its design by checking over the first few questionnaires to see that they have been correctly coded.

The coding is most usually marked on to the questionnaire itself. Where the questionnaire has not been laid out with column numbers it may be easier to print coding sheets and transfer the data to these in numerical form.

Many industrial market research surveys are qualitative studies based on a small number of face-to-face interviews. Here the analysis is not so much to establish groupings; rather it is to relate particular responses to companies or simply to add up purchases broken down by supplier to form a picture of market size and shares. With less than 50 respondents this can easily be undertaken by transferring each questionnaire on to one line of analysis paper with vertical columns for the responses. This tabulation provides a complete visual picture of the sample and enables the researcher to achieve a broad view in which the importance of certain respondents becomes clear. The broader view may well highlight data which appears out of line and needs checking. Tabulation is laborious as all responses must be recorded, sometimes with calculations to convert percentages obtained in the interview to absolute figures. However, once complete, all that remains is to sum the columns or read off the responses and the database is ready for writing up. Tabulating quantitative data and limited verbal responses is ideally suited to a personal computer where simple spreadsheet analysis packages enable the researcher to add across and down the columns and manipulate responses to test their sensitivity.

Overview interviews

Interviews with respondents who have an overall view of a market are almost always unstructured, having been guided by a checklist of open-ended questions. The interview is written up in note form rather than completed as a formal questionnaire. Fortunately, there are seldom more than a few overview interviews to analyse (20 would be a lot). Because the overview interviews cover a wide range of subjects, it is not always possible to classify data under the chapter headings of the report. The researcher must, therefore, take one subject at a time, extracting bits from each interview to build up the total picture.

Group discussions

Group discussions present the researcher with difficulties of both analysis and interpretation which are best approached by two steps:

1. listening to and transcribing the data
2. classifying and interpreting data within subject headings.

Listening to and transcribing the data

This is a lengthy chore and is likely to take no less than half a day per tape. Where there is a large number of tapes it is useful to have assistance in the transcription from someone who has been well briefed. With only one or two tapes it is probably as quick (and certainly results in a better 'feel') if the researcher carries out his own transcription. The transcription should be laid out in double spaced typing with the group leader's words boldly identified by underlining.

Classifying and interpreting the data

The final written report should, like all other market research reports, contain a statement of the objectives, the research method, the findings and conclusions. It is the findings which require different treatment from the more usual presentation of statistical or factual data. Under each heading within the findings there should be a statement of the points which emerged from the study and the level of consensus or otherwise which existed. These points should then be supported by direct quotes, wherever possible, identifying the occupation and role (but not name) of the respondent. Clearly a heavy onus lies on the researcher to balance the quotes to the issues he is raising. An isolated response may be extremely valuable and justify a heavy emphasis. However, many throw-away remarks are made in groups which, if reported, become red herrings and are, therefore, best left out. The findings should be restricted to the straight recording of data which has been gleaned while interpretations and recommendations are separated in the conclusions. A short edited tape containing key quotes can prove very effective when presenting the findings to management.

The interpretation of group discussions is, sadly, questioned by some as inevitably it contains the researcher's value judgements. This ought not to detract from the credibility of the work as these judgements are based on a synthesis of all the views and statements thrown at him. It is impossible to develop an objective model which eliminates the judgement of the researcher when analysing and interpreting qualitative data. Indeed, if the research is to have any value, every confidence should be placed in the researcher, and his insights, understandings and judgements should be encouraged.

Methods of quantitative analysis

Manual
There are many occasions in industrial market research when the number of interviews do not warrant analysis by computer. There are no fixed guidelines. Much depends on the complexity of the answers and the need to cross analyse data. Cross analysis is usually spurious if there are fewer than 20 responses per analysis cell. Where there are more it is almost always beneficial to use a computer to carry out the cross analysis. With fewer than 40 or 50 interviews and no cross analysis it can sometimes be quicker and simpler to carry out a count of responses to each question. A recognized method of recording responses is to count in 'five-barred gates' making a vertical mark for each respondent and cancelling the fifth one with a horizontal line across, ie 卌.

Computer processing
The researcher has an option to enter data directly into the computer through the keyboard or to load the information by punched tape or cards. Direct entry is the norm for a small number of interviews (50 to 1000) and allows the researcher the facility of sitting at the terminal and calling up tables which seem interesting or appropriate. With larger samples (1000 upwards) the researcher may opt for batch processing by using a punch card operator to transfer responses from the questionnaire to tape or card and feed these into the computer. It is usual in the batch processing of data for the researcher to prepare an analysis specification which instructs the computer room or bureau what tables are required.

The specification can be written with reference to questions:

☐ analyse Q3 by Q4;
☐ provide a hole count of Q6;*
☐ treat Q2 as an analysis factor and analyse all questions by this factor.

Usually, the instructions are given by column numbers rather than question numbers, so instead of the instruction 'analyse Q3 by Q4' it may say 'analyse column 6 by column 7'. If the computer bureau has a copy of the questionnaire it will be able to provide semantic descriptions (as opposed to column numbers) on the printout. The discipline of preparing the analysis specification forces the researcher to consider what data he needs to meet the objectives. There is no point preparing tables which are interesting but have no bearing on the study.

Laying out the questionnaire for batch computer processing

In order to feed data into a computer it is advantageous to give each answer a numerical code. Instead of ticking boxes, interviewers circle numbers. Up to 12 numbers are contained within a column, so if more response entries are needed, a new column is opened as illustrated in diagram 25.

Open-ended responses should have column numbers left against them so that coders can attribute an entry number when they group the responses received.

Every questionnaire needs a questionnaire number so that it can subsequently be identified and, if necessary, modified or withdrawn. If there are more than 99 interviews, three columns must be allocated to the questionnaire number, eg:

	Col 1	Col 2	Col 3
Questionnaire number	9	8	2

Recording precise numbers uses many columns and is cumbersome. Thus, within the questionnaire itself, questions should be designed which classify numerical responses into easily managed pre-defined groupings. Response categories are therefore closed, for example:

---

* A hole count is a straight count with no cross analysis.

Q6   How many bellows sealed valves did you buy in 1984?

	Col 12
None	1
1 - 5	2
6 - 15	3
16 - 30	4
Over 30	5
Don't know	6

Summary

The industrial market researcher has to cope with data from a variety of sources. Desk research generates a mixture of statistics and comment which must be classified under the subject headings of the report.

End-user interviews may be structured or unstructured. Classifying open-ended questions is an important job, as the coder's interpretation influences the validity of the response. Reliable coding is achieved by a thorough briefing and checking of the coder's work and special care in the design of the coding frame. Many industrial market research surveys provide a quantitative response which is best analysed by tabulation. Group discussions are taped and analysed from notes or transcriptions taken from these tapes.

With small numbers of questionnaires (say 50 or less) it is often quicker to carry out a manual count of responses. With larger samples and where cross analyses are required, computer processing is necessary. Large samples (say 500 plus) are best analysed by transferring data to punched card or tape for entry into the computer.

Q3 (a) Which makes of fork-lift trucks did you buy in 1981?
CIRCLE APPROPRIATE NUMBERS

Makes	Make bought in 1981
Bonser Engineering	1 (44)
Caterpillar Trucks Ltd	2
Clark Equipment Ltd	3
Coventry Climax Ltd	4
Conveyancer Ltd	5
Datsun	6
Eaton Corporation Ltd (Yale Trucks)	7
Fenwick	8
Fiat	9
Henley Ltd (Lansing Henley)	10
Hyster Ltd	11
Jungheinrich	12
Komatsu	1 (45)
Lancer Boss Ltd	2
Lansing Bagnall Ltd	3
Linde	4
PEG	5
Still	6
Toyota	7
Others (name)	8

Note: Column numbers are designated by number in brackets.

DIAGRAM 25

*Sample question from fork-lift truck personal visit survey
showing response codes using column numbers*

Chapter 28
Writing the Report

The purpose of market research reports

Market research reports contain the findings and also, usually, the conclusions of a study project. Every report has a purpose and an audience and must be written with these two factors very firmly in mind.

All market research reports aim to communicate data, though some may also hope to persuade and advise. A report is the compilation of the many findings which answer the objectives set out in the original proposal. A report, is, therefore, the final product of the researcher's work. It is the physical embodiment of the service he has carried out and becomes a lasting reminder of his work. It is rare for a researcher to communicate the results to a sponsor verbally without the back-up of the written word.

Market researchers are, therefore, occupied in seeking information to meet objectives and assembling the findings into reports. In a sense, their role in business is to produce reports which are principally judged by their quality, their format and contents.

Report writing is much more important in industrial market research than consumer research. A quantitative consumer market research report may comprise mainly tables with very little narrative. An industrial market research report contains a good deal of narrative with comparatively few supporting tables.

It is clear that every successful industrial market researcher must learn to write high quality reports.

The structure of a market research report

Every industrial market researcher develops his own report writing style and adopts a structure which enables him to write to a proven formula. A structure which is widely used and has been determined by logic and convention is:

- ☐ Title page
- ☐ Table of Contents
- ☐ Summary
- ☐ Introduction (including objectives and methods)
- ☐ Findings
- ☐ Conclusions (and recommendations)
- ☐ Appendices

Title page

This may also be the front cover of the report. It is, therefore, the shop window and needs to proclaim the professional approach which will follow. It states the title, which must be short and to the point. If the report is confidential, this fact also should be boldly displayed. The report may be subject to restricted circulation, in which case the report number and its reader may be indicated.

Other information which is usefully displayed on a title page is the person or company who has carried out the work and the name of the research sponsor. Finally, the date of issue should be shown.

Table of Contents

The table of contents of a report is a full listing of all the section headings and sub-headings together with their page numbers. In a report with a large number of tables it is probably also appropriate to provide a listing of these.

Summary

Reports of 10 pages or more need a summary which should contain all the salient points from the body of the document including the introduction, findings and conclusions. The Summary is possibly the most important section of the report. It is positioned in pride of place at the beginning of the report and will be read by everyone, including some readers who will find the time to study this section only. The importance of the Summary means it should not be thrown together at the last minute when the researcher has completed all other sections and is tired of the project. A good occasion to write the Summary is after the findings as this will bring together the important points and prepare the researcher for tackling the Conclusions. However, the Summary should also contain a precis of the Conclusions, so the researcher will have to complete that part last of all.

The style and layout of the Summary requires careful attention.

Summaries are generally in words but, depending on the objectives and findings, tables, charts or diagrams may add drama and impact. The Report can probably be broken down into 20 or so key points. The Summary should consist of as many paragraphs as points, each containing a maximum of two or three sentences. Even though it is a summary, sentences should not be abbreviated.

The length of the Summary will be in rough proportion to that of the report. A 20-page report should aim for a single page summary while a 100-page report may require five pages. Of course, summaries can be shortened to half a page irrespective of the report length but brevity should not be at the expense of sense.

Introduction

The Introduction to a report informs the reader why the research is being carried out, what the researcher has set out to do and how he has done it. These topics can be covered under three sub-headings: Background, Objectives and Methods.

Under *Background* the scene is set describing the lead up to the commissioning of the study. This may include a short account of the problem faced by the research sponsor, for example:

> Acme Manufacturing are considering entering the market for die head cleaning plant. An investment of $1 million would be required in production and marketing resources. In order to evaluate the viability of the project Acme Manufacturing require a full understanding of the die head cleaning plant market. John Smith was commissioned to study the market against objectives agreed in a proposal dated 5 December 1987.

Objectives are a statement of the overall objectives of the study and are usually quoted or summarized from the proposal. For example:

> The broad objectives of the study were agreed in advance to be:

> > To analyse the market for die head cleaning plant and to indicate the opportunities for Acme Manufacturing.

> A number of detailed objectives needed to be fulfilled in order to achieve this broad aim and these were as follows:

> > ☐ to assess market size and segments over the last three years;
> > ☐ to assess market shares and provide a profile of the competing suppliers;
> > ☐ to predict future trends over the next three years;
> > ☐ to show what motivates buyers of die head cleaning plant to specify certain suppliers;

☐ to recommend a suitable product range for Acme;

☐ to recommend sales targets for each of the next three years and show the marketing strategies which will enable these to be achieved.

The section of the Introduction entitled *Research Methods* describes how data was obtained, highlighting any deviations from the approach given in the original proposal.

Desk research. The range of sources should be mentioned but nothing over-specific, as a detailed bibliography should be provided in an appendix.

Primary research. This could include telephone, postal or personal interviews, group discussions or observation. The number and type of interviews/groups carried out must be stated, plus additional background such as the position of the respondent or the broad spread of location of the sample. Noteworthy respondents may be mentioned at this stage but again, they are usually relegated to an appendix. The questionnaire should be referred to as being available for reference in an appendix. Finally, it may be significant to describe how the analysis was carried out, when the fieldwork was undertaken and, if changes were made to the original research plan, why this was so.

Findings

The Findings are the body of the report. They present all relevant facts and opinions collected by the researcher but make no attempt to show the implications for the research sponsor's plans. This is the role of the Conclusions. It may be necessary to qualify certain findings, such as a conflict in views between groups of respondents or possible unreliability in some areas.

The subjects which are discussed in the Findings will vary between projects. Sometimes they will include market size, market share, market trends; at other times they may be confined to image or attitudinal data. Whatever the content, the sequence should be logical. For example, buyers' attitudes to suppliers should not be disclosed before naming the companies and describing their position in the market.

Findings should be a generalized statement of the market as a whole, although this does not preclude comments on individual companies. Specific quotes add authenticity to a report and provide a reference which the reader can understand. Individual company comment is important when a respondent is of particular significance (eg, he buys 20 per cent of all the product under study) or illustrative of a general view (eg Richardson's pumps are the most reliable on the market – Plant Engineer, Power Station).

Quoted comments are especially useful for enlivening and adding personality to a report. They forcibly remind the reader that the views which are being expressed are those of respondents and not the researcher. However, the researcher must be careful not to break confidences where this has been promised or requested.

Conclusions

Most industrial market research reports require a Conclusions section which relates findings to the research sponsor's interest and often advises on solutions to specific problems. Conclusions are, therefore, evaluative; they use facts but inevitably contain value judgements.

Conclusions are the showcase of a research report. They provide an opportunity for the researcher to sparkle over and beyond his descriptive powers made evident in the findings. The researcher should always offer to provide conclusions and invariably his objective and expert views will be welcomed.

The industrial market researcher is involved in the preparation of two types of research project and they need different approaches within the Conclusions.

RESEARCH TO IMPROVE A CLIENT'S KNOWLEDGE OF A MARKET

The researcher is not required to solve a business problem; instead he is providing a detailed briefing to help the research sponsor make decisions now or in the future.

The Conclusions, though drawing heavily on the Findings, should not be a mere summary. The researcher can opt for one of two approaches. He can select elements of findings which appear of particular relevance to the client's business or he can re-state important findings but, more importantly, pick out main trends as he sees them. Both approaches involve the selection (and omission) of facts and depend on value judgements. To that extent they are creative.

RESEARCH TO SOLVE A SPECIFIC RESEARCH PROBLEM

Conventional problem solving in business follows a number of steps. The facts on the company and the market lead to a decision followed by an action plan (diagram 26). The facts are, of course, highly relevant to arriving at the optimum decision but the decision and plan may follow a path influenced by emotive or internal political pressures.

Researchers, especially those working outside a company, may not have open access to all the facts on the company's limitations, resources and objectives. The researcher should, in this case, concentrate on the facts about the company as he understands them while paying more regard to facts on the market. His conclusions are, as a result, more objective and he has avoided the political problems of in-company wrangling (diagram 27).

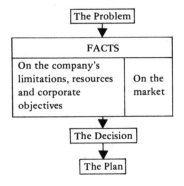

DIAGRAM 26

Steps in conventional problem solving in business

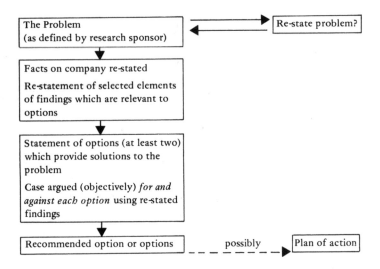

DIAGRAM 27

Steps in the formulation of conclusions for a market research report

Appendices

Appendices are used to contain data which, while of possible value or interest to the research sponsor, is not essential to the presentation of the Findings or Conclusions. They could include:

Questionnaires. It is important that the reader can refer to how questions were asked.

Sources of information. These provide the study with credibility and may be useful to a future researcher who has to follow up the work. They may be divided into sections such as bibliography, telephone respondents, visit respondents, or the sample may be classified by industrial sectors. It is usually sufficient to quote the respondent companies' names and addresses, though sometimes the contacts themselves should be given. If respondents have been promised anonymity then, of course, they must be excluded from the list of contributors.

Statistical methods. These are notes on how data has been calculated, for example significance tests or methods of weighting image factors. If the report contains a statistical forecast, the detailed working should be described in the appendix.

Detailed statistical tables. Lengthy statistical tables may be better in the appendix although key data should be in the Findings.

Financial profiles. As with the statistical data, financial profiles on companies should be given in the appendix.

Descriptions and definitions. Lengthy descriptions of processes should be in the appendix.

Product literature. Sometimes it is relevant to include product literature in a report but the researcher should be highly selective to avoid any accusation of padding.

Appendices should not exist in isolation. They should be referred to in the text and only be included if they supplement the findings. Appendices should be short rather than long and, except in unusual circumstances, should not exceed a fifth of the pages of the body of the report.

The logic of preparing a report

A good report is a planned report. The more detailed the planning, the better will be the finished document and the easier it will be to write. With the proposal and questionnaire as a guide, the researcher should write all the report's main headings and then the sub-headings. Under each sub-heading a summary of the content of the section will speed the writing.

If the report is heavily statistical the tables should be prepared first and assembled into the order they will appear in the report. The report is now hung around the tables.

When the manuscript is completed it should be read and corrected. Once typed it should be read by the author and by some other person who may be more able to spot errors. A reader finds it easiest to pass judgement on the detail in a report. No matter how unfair, an assumption is often made that a report with spelling, typing and grammatical errors has not been carried out carefully.

Presenting the data

Reports contain tables and text and possibly charts or diagrams. Careful attention to the presentation of the data will impress the reader and help the findings achieve greater conviction.

Presenting tables

Tables provide a shorthand means of communicating figures. They should be used to show patterns and exceptions. The researcher should use tables wherever possible, bearing in mind a number of rules:

☐ *Keep it simple.* Two or three simple tables are better than one which is complicated.

☐ *Refer to tables in the text.* A table should be preceded by a verbal description so that when the reader looks at it he gains a quick understanding of the important issue and can easily pick out as much detail as he needs.

☐ *Label all tables.* Tables should have headings stating what they show. The headings should also give the year or the location of the data if relevant. Columns within the tables should have headings which show whether they are tonnes, numbers, monetary values, etc. Sources of information or the base number of interviews should be shown below the tables.

☐ *Use rounded figures.* Most industrial market research data must be commercially and not statistically significant. Estimates of market size, market shares, etc may, in the final analysis, be derived by calculation, but it is spurious accuracy to show decimal places. Two digits are easily remembered and assimilated and are almost always sufficiently accurate. Round off figures but provide a note to tell the reader.

☐ *Order rows and columns by size.* A table with data in decreasing order of importance is easier to absorb than one which is presented in random fashion.

314

☐ *Draw lines to separate data.* A large table with a number of vertical columns may be made easier to read if the columns are distinguished by ruled lines.

Presenting text

Researchers should develop a succinct, punchy style of writing. Their audiences need to assimilate data easily and quickly. Straightforward language and short sentences may not be elegant but they are appreciated by the reader.

The researcher is all the time describing, emphasizing and qualifying data. This can be made more dramatic by the frequent use of paragraphs, solid dots, open boxes or asterisks which pick out important statements.

Presenting charts

Charts and diagrams should be used to simplify complex data or amplify a point. Besides their functional use, charts and diagrams break up the report and add interest. As with tables, it is better to keep a chart simple and powerful than to lose its meaning through over-complicating it.

Charts should be fully labelled and referred to in the preceding text. Table 23 shows seven areas where charts can be used to animate the report.

Summary

Reports are the embodiment of the researcher's work and he is judged on their quality. A researcher can only be acclaimed successful when he develops good report writing skills.

A standard report layout which has proved successful for industrial market research reports is:

☐ Title page
☐ Table of Contents
☐ Summary
☐ Introduction
☐ Findings
☐ Conclusions
☐ Appendices.

Before starting to write a report, the researcher should plan the headings and sub-headings and prepare the statistical tables.

To help the reader assimilate data quickly there is a need to keep tables and text simple. Charts and diagrams help to clarify and enliven a report.

TABLE 23

The application of charts and diagrams in market research reports

To display ...	And describe ...	Use ...
Parts of a whole	Market size Market shares	Pie diagrams Bar charts
Rankings	Measures of image, attitude, behaviour	Bar charts
Data over time	Company sales Market sizes Prices	Graphs Columns
Frequence distribution	Price/volume Customer size/ number of customers	Columns Graphs
Correlation	Sales/market size Market size/ independent variable Price/raw material cost	Scatter diagrams Graphs
Spatial distribution	Location of demand Territorial divisions	Maps
Steps	Timetables Action plans Processes	Sequence charts Critical path charts

Chapter 29
Presenting the Findings

The importance of presentation

Market researchers live so close to the data they collect and interpret that they do not always recognize that others may face digestive problems with it. The researcher's effort is wasted if he fails to communicate his findings effectively. At worst, the research could be misunderstood, mistrusted or fly over the heads of the audience. The presentation of the written report plays an important part in ensuring that the findings have impact. Besides attention to the structure and content of the report, the researcher must window dress its appearance. This should not be regarded as frippery; if it improves the reception of the report it is entirely justified. Attractive layout, wide borders around the text, high quality typing and reproduction and a smart cover and binding are easy to organize and contribute enormously to the report's acceptance. The communication of the data is seldom restricted to the written word alone. The researcher has to present the findings to the research sponsor verbally whether at a formal assembly or at an informal discussion. A researcher should welcome the opportunity which a presentation provides to 'sell' his findings to the sponsor. Good researchers are not always the best salesmen, as the qualities of objectivity and persuasion are rare bedfellows. However, the art of presenting can be learned and used to advantage in improving the understanding of the findings as well as furthering the researcher's career prospects.

What is a presentation?

Within the context of the industrial market researcher's work, a presentation is the verbal communication of his research findings and conclusions. The heavy content of factual and statistical data in the findings raises the danger of the presentation becoming a lecture and this should not be. A lecture places the lecturer in a position of superiority. His audience have chosen to attend in order to acquire knowledge. The lecturer has no need to persuade them that his information is valid or that a course of action should be taken. The researcher addresses an invited audience who may be curious and suspicious to a greater degree than they are eager to learn. When the lecturer has dry material to impart he can be indifferent to his class's boredom or lack of interest. The researcher cannot afford his audience's attention to wander; he must earn their interest and hold it.

Presentations should, therefore, stimulate as well as educate. They provide an opportunity for controversial debate which is not in the report. The audience should be left feeling that they are wiser and ready for action — to go ahead with a project, to look further into the subject or perhaps to seek an opportunity elsewhere. As people leave the presentation they should feel that they have benefited from attending.

Planning the presentation

The researcher is used to working to objectives in his projects. So, too, he should establish objectives for his presentations. Each presentation needs its own objective, not so general as to be meaningless (such as 'to describe the market for daisywheel printers') but specific, even to the point of excluding much of the background data included in the report (for example, 'to show the opportunities over the next 12 months for a daisywheel printer with a retail price of $99 and to provoke consideration of entering the market').

With the objective firmly in mind the researcher can plan the presentation based on:

☐ the material which is to be communicated
☐ the length of time allocated for the presentation
☐ the size of the audience
☐ the composition of the audience
☐ the persons who will be giving the presentation.

The first rule of effective presentation is *keep it simple*. The researcher must consider the data available to him and decide what is essential and what is not. Great care and attention may have been put into the sampling method to ensure good coverage and representativeness. The audience will no doubt take this for granted and will want only the briefest background on methodology. Some of the facts and figures of the market will need to be presented but only the bare bones. The researcher can afford to be general at a presentation as the detail is included in the report or can be

318

provided in response to a question. He should concentrate on giving the audience a feel for the market and his material should be selected to be interesting and have impact. Audiences find it difficult to concentrate for more than a half to three-quarters of an hour at a stretch. This is a further reason for cutting back on much of the data that could be presented and concentrating on the key issues.

The structure of the presentation will in most cases follow that of the report except there will be no summary or appendices. A short introduction is necessary to set the scene, state the objectives and describe the research methods. The findings, which in the written report occupy the bulk, may in the verbal presentation be cut back, with an equal amount of time devoted to the conclusions.

The size of the audience affects how the data will be displayed and the formality of the presentation. Flip charts and spontaneous questions are acceptable when there is only a handful of people, whereas large audiences may impose the need for data to be blown up on to a screen with a question time which follows the discourse.

An audience of senior managers should be given different treatment from operational managers. Senior management are responsible for the direction of the company and have an interest in strategies while operational management need more detail and want to know how the research can help them tactically.

The attention of the assembly needs to be maintained with careful stage management. Different speakers will break the fall off in concentration and revitalize interest. Taped comments taken from interviews with respondents, the unveiling of competitors' products, the switching between a flip chart and screened projection of data similarly arouse attention.

The delivery of the presentation should be unscripted to ensure it is lively, natural and sincere. For most speakers this creates a problem of fluency and overcoming the fear of forgetting important points. Spoken grammar differs considerably from that which is written and sounds better for it. The repetition of words and stumbling in mid-sentence is often unnoticed when it occurs in normal speech, whereas it is nearly impossible to read a script and sound anything but wooden.

The researcher can help himself by using visual aids to form a framework around which the presentation can hang. The aids serve the dual function of interesting the audience and reminding the researcher of what he has to say.

More often than not, the time available for preparing the presentation is severely squeezed and charts have to be prepared in just a few hours. Overhead transparencies are an excellent visual aid for the researcher, being easy to produce on photocopiers and blow up large enough for audiences of up to a couple of dozen; 35mm slides are impressive when they are professionally produced but the cost and time may not allow for them.

Finally, the researcher must rehearse. This smooths the rough edges and gives him the extra confidence that comes from being on top of the job. In practice, researchers do not usually have the time for a dress rehearsal but at some stage beforehand, the presenter should run through the data he will be using.

Giving the presentation

The first few presentations the researcher makes will be nerve-racking. He has a lot to remember, is conscious of the need to appear confident while himself recognizing inadequacies in his data, and faces an audience which is probably more experienced and senior than himself.

The start of his presentation is most critical. He needs to be able to connect with the group and win them over to his side. Nervousness and embarrassment are counter-productive as they transmit tensions to the listeners. A skilled presenter can use a joke to endear himself to the audience, but after a joke that falls flat (and it so easily can with a small assembly and nervous tension) he may never recover. The researcher cannot afford to try clever tricks; he is better promoting himself as serious but relaxed. An anecdote or subtle participation with the audience are the best methods of developing a good initial effect.

Throughout the presentation the researcher should continue to relate to the audience and achieve their participation. Their involvement raises their interest, wins them on to the researcher's side and allows him time to collect his thoughts before moving on.

Some *do's* and *don't's* should help make the presentation a success:

DO
- face the audience.
- stand up if there are more than four people in the audience.
- speak clearly, with confidence and authority, especially about those issues on which you feel most vulnerable.
- invite and encourage participation.
- modulate the voice and sound enthusiastic.

DON'T
- stand in front of the screen (arrange it across a corner of the room so you can stand sideways on).
- address yourself to one person only.
- use humour unless very accomplished (research is a serious business).
- apologize for the methods, the slide quality or yourself.

— argue disagreeably but do stand your ground if you think you are right.

— fidget with the slides or your papers — it is highly distractive.

— hand the report out in advance; again it is distractive.

Summary

A presentation aims to sell the research findings and conclusions verbally to the research sponsor and his management. It provides the researcher with an opportunity to emphasize points and even be controversial.

The key ingredients of a successful presentation are simplicity and rehearsal. Planning is important and consideration needs to be given to the size and composition of the audience, the material and the time available.

Relatively more time should be spent on the conclusions than is the case in the written report.

Visual aids are important to keep the attention of the audience, to communicate findings and, not least, to act as a prompt to the researcher.

During the presentation the researcher should connect with and relate to the audience through participation.

Appendices

Appendix 1: Statistical Methods

Introduction

Statistical methods are important to consumer researchers who, in the quantitative part of their work, are occupied in 'number crunching'. The industrial market researcher spends most of his life on qualitative subjects using small samples measured in tens rather than hundreds and selected by judgement rather than at random. He fights shy of statistics and yet they have a part to play in much of his work — in the sampling of certain universes, in forecasting and in determining market size.

In his daily routine the industrial market researcher is required to tabulate figures and so becomes familiar with averages, percentages and distribution — the basics of data presentation. This appendix attempts a middle road in which it is assumed the researcher has already grasped the rudiments of statistical theory but is not interested in, nor ever likely to need, the most sophisticated statistical techniques. It is an introduction, no more, to three subjects which most industrial market researchers face at some time in their careers:

- [ ] *Sampling theory*, necessary for large interview programmes where the universe (or a stratum of that universe) is made up of companies of a similar size.
- [ ] *Establishing the relationship between two variables*, useful in forecasting and determining market size.
- [ ] *Time series analysis*, another forecasting technique useful where there is an established trend and regular fluctuations from it.

Sampling

Selecting the sample size
In large populations or universes the cost of interviewing every respondent is prohibitive. By selecting just a small proportion of the total it is possible

to describe the companies that have not been interviewed and to state the extent to which the description reflects reality. This is known as probability sampling, so called because the probability of errors in a result derived from a given sample size can be calculated. The theory is governed by two statistical laws:

1. THE LAW OF STATISTICAL REGULARITY

If a large number of companies are selected from a particular universe, they will represent the universe in all characteristics. The larger the sample, the greater the likelihood of the sample being representative of the total population. It is, however, important that the sample is picked randomly — that is, every company has an equal chance of selection — and that the sample is large enough to overcome irregularities which could occur through the inclusion of those with abnormal characteristics. The larger the sample, the more accurate the results. In most industrial samples selected from a large universe, 50 companies would be considered a minimum and 200 is a more respectable minimum sample size.

Of course, if the population includes a number of disproportionately large companies, as is so often the case in industrial markets, this method of sampling would be inappropriate as the inclusion or exclusion of any large companies would distort the result.

2. THE LAW OF INERTIA OF LARGE NUMBERS

This is the corollary of the law of statistical regularity. It states that large groups of data show a higher degree of stability than small ones. Although in a sample the size of some companies will be larger than average and some will be smaller than average, there will be a tendency for these discrepancies to cancel each other out. The larger the sample size, the greater will be the accuracy as the differences are cancelled.

Calculating sample error

Even if a sample is drawn correctly, only by a fluke will it have exactly the same characteristics as the total sample. However, this area of uncertainty can be estimated by computing the standard error for the sample mean. The size of the standard error, when applied to the technique of sampling for a proportion depends on:

(a) the magnitude of the proportion
(b) the sample size.

Thus, for a given sample size, the larger the proportion the higher the standard error and the greater the area of uncertainty. Similarly, for a given proportion, the larger the sample size the smaller the standard error and the smaller the area of uncertainty.

APPENDIX 1 STATISTICAL METHODS

Researchers find the standard error of the proportion one of the most useful measures of accuracy. For example, out of a sample of 200 electricians, 32 per cent (64) said that they were likely to buy a new type of cable. The standard error of this proportion can be calculated from the following formula:

Standard error of a proportion (SE) = $\sqrt{\dfrac{pq}{n}}$

where:

p = population proportion expressed as a decimal fraction and not as a percentage

q = 1 − p

n = sample size

hence: sample proportion = $\dfrac{64}{200}$ = 0.32

Applying the formula:

$$SE = \sqrt{\frac{0.32 \times (1 - 0.32)}{200}} = \sqrt{\frac{0.32 \times .68}{200}} = 0.033$$

This indicates that the area of uncertainty about the sample proportion of 0.32 is ± 0.033, and it can be shown that one can be 68 per cent confident that the true population proportion will lie within these limits, viz between 0.287 and 0.353.

In practice, it is conventional to apply a more stringent test, viz, the 95 per cent confidence limit. This is the area bounded by the sample mean ± two standard errors.

Therefore, at the 95 per cent confidence level, the estimate of the population proportion of companies likely to buy the cable:

= sample proportion ± 2 x SE

= 0.32 ± 2 x 0.033

= 0.254 and 0.386

= between 25 and 39 per cent.

Of course, sample proportions may be inaccurate for other reasons such as:

☐ errors in recording answers
☐ respondent vagueness
☐ bias in interviewing
☐ errors in analysis
☐ substituting a company because one already chosen cannot or will not help
☐ errors in interpretation
☐ incomplete sample frame.

Estimating the reliability of results obtained from samples

Very often the researcher knows what level of accuracy he requires from the results. For example, at the time the study is being considered he may establish with the sponsor that accuracy of ± 5 percentage points (at 95 per cent confidence limits) is acceptable for the commercial decisions that will be made. In other words, if 25 per cent of a sample gave a certain answer, one could be sure that the true result was between 20 and 30 per cent.

At this stage, since we are working at the 95 per cent confidence limits, we depart from the use of the term SE and substitute the term E for error; and E = 2 x SE.

The researcher can work backwards to determine the size of the sample that should be used. It must, however, be understood that error varies according to the proportion giving a certain answer. If 50 per cent of a sample give an answer, the error is much greater than if only 3 per cent give an answer. Error is, therefore, dependent on the proportion. This means that the researcher must choose an error for the purposes of calculating his sample size, knowing full well the chances of the actual answer coinciding with this figure are quite remote. He may, however, be able to make a reasonable guess. Let's say that he expects 25 per cent will give a certain response to an important question, and he is prepared to accept an error of ± 5 per cent (at 95 per cent confidence limits), then the sample size can be derived as follows:

$$n = \frac{4pq}{E^2}$$

where:

n = the sample size
p = the proportion of the sample with the attribute we are trying to measure
q = the proportion of the sample not having the attribute we are trying to measure (ie, q = 1 - p)
E = the desired level of accuracy expressed as a decimal fraction.

In the example given, the calculation would be:

$$n = \frac{4 \times 0.25 \times 0.75}{.05^2}$$

$$= \frac{0.75}{0.0025}$$

n = 300

If the researcher is prepared to accept a close approximation rather than a precise figure, he can select his sample size using the chart on page 207.

Stratified (or quota) sampling

It is usually possible to recognize groups of companies (strata) with characteristics more uniform than the wider industrial universe of which they are a part. Companies manufacturing chemicals differ from those involved in mechanical engineering which in turn are very different from banks and financial institutions. By sampling strata, the researcher reduces the wide sample variability which would occur within the whole universe. Within each stratum a random sample can be selected.

The most widely used methods of stratifying markets is by industrial groupings − Standard Industrial Classification (SIC) in the UK and Nomenclature Générale des Activités Economiques dans les Communautés Européennes (NACE) in Europe.

In order to use a stratified sample it is necessary to know what groups comprise the total population and in what proportions.

For example, a company selling electro-pneumatic hammers may wish to know how many companies own or rent hammers in the construction industry. From various directories and construction industry statistics it can be shown that in the UK there are 46,000 builders, 10,000 electricians, 10,000 plumbers and 5,000 heating and ventilating engineers. These are known to be the major end-user markets for hammers. The technique of stratified sampling involves the following steps:

1. Decide on the total sample size (say 1000).
2. Divide this into sub-samples in proportion to the number of builders, electricians, plumbers, and heating and ventilating engineers. These form the quotas for interview.
3. Select companies at random within each stratum to arrive at the appropriate quota or sub-sample (650 builders, 140 electricians, 140 plumbers, 70 heating and ventilating engineers).
4. Add the sub-sample results together to obtain the figures for the overall sample.

An alternative approach is to have quotas of equal size, and weight them at a later stage to achieve an overall result. This has the advantage of providing analysis cells of a similar size, thus facilitating comparisons of data with a uniform base and accuracy. This can be important when comparing attitudinal data collected from each group of respondents. The steps in arriving at the overall sample result from quotas of equal size are:

(a) Decide on the total sample size (say 1000).
(b) Divide this into sub-samples of builders, electricians, plumbers, and heating and ventilating engineers − all of the same size (ie, 250 each).
(c) Select companies within each sub-sample until 250 have been interviewed.

(d) Weight each sub-sample by a factor based on the proportion that sub-sample is of the total (ie, 0.65 for builders, 0.14 for electricians, 0.14 for plumbers, 0.07 for heating and ventilating engineers).

(e) Add the weighted sub-samples together to obtain the figures for the overall sample.

Choosing the companies to interview

Random does not mean haphazard sampling. It refers to a precise approach in which each company has an equal chance of being selected. The most popular method used for choosing companies is to give each company a number and then select a number from a table of random numbers or a computer programmed to generate random numbers.

If a list of companies is in alphabetical order, it is generally acceptable (though not necessarily in the pure statistical sense) to select every nth one, the starting point being chosen at random. This approach is known as systematic or quasi-random sampling but must be treated cautiously as it could be biased if used where companies are listed in some non-alphabetical manner, for example by size or geography.

In stratified sampling, interviewers are sometimes allowed to choose their own companies to contact, the only instruction being to meet a pre-set quota (perhaps of industry class and size). This approach can be convenient and yield commercially acceptable findings but it is not random selection and results cannot be expressed in terms of their statistical accuracy.

Establishing the relationship between two variables

The coefficient of correlation

The fact that a relationship exists between two variables is usually obvious to the market researcher by plotting one variable against the other. Examples of variables which would be expected to have an inter-dependent relationship are:

- □ sales of portable compressors and the level of construction activity
- □ sales of spare parts and the age of trucks in the parc
- □ the age of a truck and its value
- □ the oil price and the reserves of oil
- □ sales of fork-lift trucks and the index of industrial production
- □ sales of a product and its price
- □ company sales and advertising expenditure.

The degree to which these variables are dependent on each other differs and can be expressed as a measure known as the coefficient of correlation. Correlation (ie, the relationship) can be positive, negative or zero and in the first instance can be tested in a scattergraph.

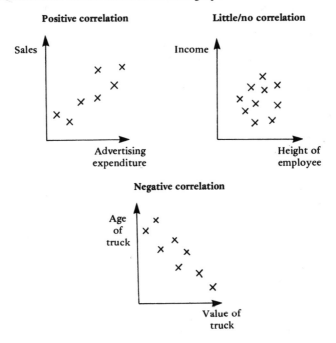

DIAGRAM 28
Scattergraph illustrations of correlation

The relationship may be one which is graphically demonstrated over time.

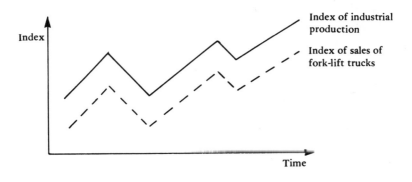

DIAGRAM 29
Correlation between two variables over time

331

The application of a proven relationship

When a relationship is shown to exist between two variables it is important to know which affects which. Spare parts sales are dependent on the age of trucks; sales of some products are dependent on their price. Spare parts and product sales are *dependent* variables while trucks and price are *independent* variables.

Knowledge that a relationship exists between two sets of data can be used by the researcher to predict a market size. Of course, he requires data on the independent variable and there is always a fear that this itself could be unreliable. Sometimes, however, there is a lagged relationship between dependent and independent variables which allows a more accurate prediction. The number of planning applications passed by a local authority will, for example, be associated with the level of sales of building materials in that locality; but the latter would lag behind the former by a period of six to twelve months.

Regression lines

When each pair of values for a dependent and independent variable are plotted on a graph, the closer the approximation of the points to a straight line, the higher the correlation. When all points lie exactly on a straight line or if they are plotted over time and show perfect sympathy in their fluctuations, then the correlation is at its highest.

The trend line in a scattergraph can be drawn by eye but its position will only be an approximation. A line of best fit can be drawn mathematically and is called a *regression line*. The purpose in calculating a regression line is to remove judgement and, therefore, human error from the fitting of the trend line. With an accurate trend line a more reliable estimate can be made of one variable from another. For example, a researcher could calculate the best estimate of an advertising appropriation to achieve a certain sales target or he could predict the sales of a product with a broad base of demand (eg, fork-lift trucks) from a published forecast of the index of industrial production.

The equation which describes a straight line in any graph is:

$$y = a + bx$$

where: y = the dependent variable
x = the independent variable
a and b = constants which are calculated from the following formulae:

$$b = \frac{\Sigma xy - \bar{x}\Sigma y}{\Sigma x^2 - \bar{x}\Sigma x}$$

$$a = \bar{y} - b\bar{x}$$

in which y and x are the dependent and independent variables as before and

$\bar{x}$ = average of the x values

$\bar{y}$ = average of the y values

The following example illustrates the application of the formulae using sales of photocopiers by a company and its advertising appropriation over a five-year period. The data is presented in table 24 overleaf.

Substituting the derived totals and averages in the equations we get:

$$b = \frac{317 - 52\,(5.6)}{15050 - 52\,(260)}$$

$$= \frac{317 - 291.20}{15050 - 13520}$$

$$= \frac{25.8}{1530}$$

$$b = \underline{0.0169} \quad \text{and}$$

$$a = 1.12 - 0.0169\,(52)$$

$$a = 1.12 - 0.8788$$

$$a = \underline{0.2412}$$

The regression line of y on x is therefore:

$$y = a + bx$$

$$y = 0.2412 + 0.0169x$$

Thus, the formula can be used to insert values of x (ie, advertising expenditure) to determine y (sales of photocopiers) for any future marketing campaign.

The marketing director may wish to know what sales target would be a reasonable expectation by doubling his last year's advertising appropriation to $130,000.

$$y = 0.2412 + 0.0169 \times 130$$

$$y = 0.2412 + 2.197$$

$$y = 2.438.$$

Therefore the best estimate of sales with an advertising appropriation of $130,000 is $2.4 million.

TABLE 24
Company sales of photocopiers and associated advertising expenditure

Year	Sales* ($m)	Advertising Expenditure ($000s)	Computed values		
	y	x	xy	x^2	y^2
1980	0.6	20	12	400	0.36
1981	1.0	50	50	2500	1.00
1982	1.2	55	66	3025	1.44
1983	1.4	70	98	4900	1.96
1984	1.4	65	91	4225	1.96
Totals	Σy 5.6	Σ x 260	Σ xy317	Σx^2 15050	Σy^2 6.72
Averages	$\bar{y}$ 1.12	$\bar{x}$ 52			

* All sales figures are adjusted to 1984 prices.

Calculating the correlation coefficient

The coefficient of correlation or r is a measure which helps the market researcher assess how close a relationship is between two variables. The closer the measure is to ± 1.0, the greater the level of sympathy between two variables. Anything in excess of 0.6 suggests a reasonable degree of sympathy. However, a value of 0.8 for r does not mean that a relationship is twice as close as a set of data producing a coefficient of 0.4. In fact 0.8 is much closer.

The formula for calculating the coefficient of correlation is expressed as follows:

$$r = \frac{n\Sigma xy - (\Sigma x)(\Sigma y)}{\sqrt{[n\Sigma x^2 - (\Sigma x)^2][n\Sigma y^2 - (\Sigma y)^2]}}$$

All the terms, with the exception of n, are explained in the previous table.

n = Number of pairs of values.

From the example on regression the value of each term can be derived.

n = 5
Σxy = 317
Σx = 260
Σy = 5.6
Σx^2 = 15050
Σy^2 = 6.72

334

Therefore, r =
$$\frac{5(317) - (260)\,(5.6)}{\sqrt{[5(15050) - (260)^2]\,[5(6.72) - (5.6)^2]}}$$

$$= \frac{1585 - 1456}{\sqrt{[75250 - 67600]\,[33.6 - 31.36]}}$$

$$= \frac{129}{\sqrt{7650 \times 2.24}}$$

$$= \frac{129}{130.905}$$

r = <u>0.985</u>

Time series

The application of time series analysis

Market researchers are constantly examining data recorded in periods which could be weekly, monthly, quarterly, annually or whatever. This numerical data is generally referred to as *time series*.

By plotting the data graphically the researcher may identify trends and cycles and by eye these can be projected to produce a forecast. Because the result would be subject to errors of judgement, the trend or cycle is fitted mathematically. Diagram 30 shows a time series of a company's sales over time.

An examination of this graph suggests two important features which help in the understanding of future events.

1. *A trend.* This is the long-term movement in sales which is steadily upwards year by year despite periodic fluctuations.
2. *Seasonal variations.* These are easy to recognize and show a generally poor second and third quarter and a good first and fourth quarter. Furthermore, there are some fluctuations in the curve which show no pattern at all. Superimposed on the overall trend there could be cyclical changes but these are difficult to recognize and anticipate.

Calculating moving averages

The industrial market researcher is most concerned with those two elements which can be anticipated, namely trend and seasonal variations. These can be calculated by the method of *moving averages*.

The method is best explained by means of an example. The data used to graph diagram 30 is shown in the sales column of figures in table 25.

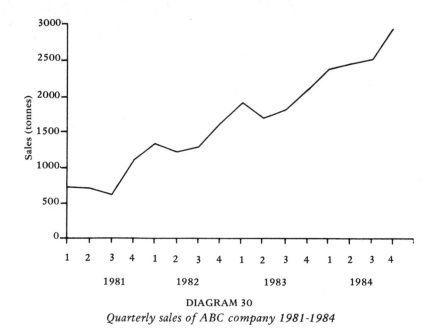

DIAGRAM 30
Quarterly sales of ABC company 1981-1984

The procedure for calculating the moving averages, trend and fluctuations, is in five steps:

1. Ensure that the sales data do not include the effect of inflation and that all periods are compatible.
2. Select a number of consecutive periods (in table 25, four quarters) and add them to arrive at an annual total. It should be noted that the choice of number of periods depends on the periodicity of fluctuations. This is usually evident from the peaks and troughs on graphed data. If the number of values chosen is 4, then the first four figures are added (quarters 1 to 4 in 1981), then the next four figures (quarter 2 in 1981 inclusive to quarter 1 in 1982).
3. Add each consecutive pair of moving annual totals to arrive at a centred total.
4. Divide the centred total by 8 to determine the trend.
5. The difference between the actual values (column 1) and the trend (column 2) gives the fluctuations from the trend for each quarter.

Calculating seasonal variations
The trend line can now be plotted graphically and extrapolated to obtain

APPENDIX 1 STATISTICAL METHODS

TABLE 25
Calculation of moving averages for ABC company 1981-1984
(all figures in tonnes)

Year	Qtr	Sales	Moving annual total	Centered total	Trend	Fluctuations from the trend
1981	1	741			not available	not available
	2	721			not available	not available
	3	623	3187	7017	877	− 254
	4	1102	3830	8182	1023	+ 79
1982	1	1384	4352	9337	1167	+ 217
	2	1243	4985	10491	1311	− 68
	3	1256	5506	11569	1446	− 190
	4	1623	6063	12657	1582	+ 41
1983	1	1941	6594	13756	1719	+ 222
	2	1774	7162	14829	1854	− 80
	3	1824	7667	15810	1976	− 152
	4	2128	8143	16959	2120	+ 8
1984	1	2417	8816	18313	2289	+ 128
	2	2447	9497	19745	2468	− 21
	3	2505	10248			
	4	2879				

TABLE 26
Establishing the seasonal variation

Year	Quarter 1	2	3	4
1981			− 254	+ 79
1982	+ 217	− 68	− 190	+ 41
1983	+ 222	− 80	− 152	+ 8
1984	+ 128	− 21		
Total	+ 567	− 169	− 596	+ 128
Average (÷ 3)	+ 189	− 56	− 199	+ 43
Adjustment for seasonality*	+ 6	+ 6	+ 6	+ 6
Seasonal variation	+ 195	− 50	− 193	+ 49

*Adjustment for seasonality derived by taking the averages and:

+ 189
− 56
− 199
+ 43

4 ⟌ − 23

= − 5.75, say 6

337

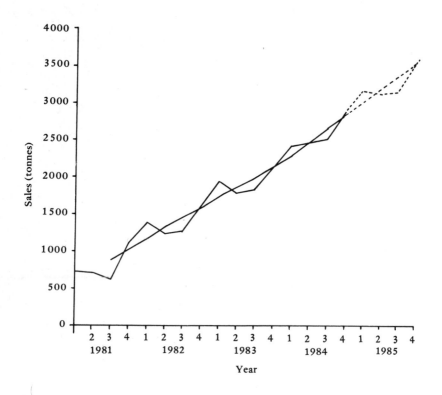

DIAGRAM 31
Quarterly sales and trends of ABC company 1981-1985

a base line forecast. However, a more accurate forecast needs to take account of the seasonal fluctuations. A prediction of these variations can be derived by

1. averaging the fluctuations from the trend for like quarters
2. finding their average
3. subtracting or adding this figure to adjust the seasonal variation (see table 26).

The trend line can be projected by adding 179 tonnes (the latest trend increase computed by subtracting 2289 from 2468) to each previous trend figure, ie quarter 3 trend = 2468 + 179 = 2647; quarter 4 trend = 2647 + 179 = 2826 etc).

By plotting the seasonal variations either side of the trend line, a forecast can be achieved for forthcoming periods (see diagram 31).

This approach is suitable for short-term forecasts of, say, four quarters where the seasonality is fairly regular. It cannot cope with wild fluctuations of data nor does it take sufficient account of any strong, recent trend since this type of effect is dampened by averaging with other figures.

Calculating compound growth

When dealing with time series the researcher usually needs to refer to the growth over the period. Calculating the annual compound growth rate requires the application of the following formula:

$$r = \left(n\sqrt{\frac{v2}{v1}} \right) - 1$$

where:

r = the annual (compound) growth rate
v1 = the earliest value of the variable
v2 = the value of the variable after n years
n = the number of years between v1 and v2
1 = unity

So, where annual compound growth rate is required for the UK market for a product which was worth:

1979: 369   ıit
1984: 563   ıit·

$$r = 5\sqrt{\frac{56?}{369}} - 1$$

$$r = 5\sqrt{1.5257} - 1$$

Using a scientific calculator or logarithms the fifth root of

$$1.5257 \text{ is } \log \frac{0.18348}{5} = \log 0.03670$$

This is equal to anti log 1.0882

$$r = 1.0882 - 1$$

$$r = 0.0882$$

$$\therefore r = 8.8\% \text{ per annum}$$

Index